Disaster Mental Health Case Studies

Disaster Mental Health Case Studies is a riveting collection of case studies by master clinicians that reveal how disaster mental health interventions must be tailored to meet the needs of survivors. Each unique case study is structured to give the reader an introduction to the community affected pre-disaster; a glimpse into the thought processes of the disaster mental health responders pre- and post-disaster; and a reflective selection of lessons learned as a result of the experiences. The 17 case studies offer the reader:

- Guidance on how to develop an empathic approach to disaster mental health response;
- Exposure to a diverse sample of disaster contexts, including naturally-occurring disasters, human-caused disasters, and disasters which occurred in an international setting;
- An understanding of the strategic approaches needed for disaster mental health service response, as well as an appreciation of the need for self-care when responding;
- A grounded and accessible writing style, bookended by chapters from the editors which thematically link and analyze the case studies.

Offering a rare and compelling view into the challenges, tragedies, pain, frustrations, and grief at the heart of disaster mental health work, this must-have collection is tailored to appeal to students of mental health and counselling, psychology, and social work; and working mental health professionals who would like to learn directly from experienced responders.

James Halpern, PhD, is Professor Emeritus and Founding Director of the Institute for Disaster Mental Health at the State University of New York at New Paltz. He is co-author of *Disaster Mental Health Interventions: Core Principles and Practices* and *Disaster Mental Health: Theory and Practice.*

Amy Nitza, PhD, is the Director of the Institute for Disaster Mental Health at the State University of New York at New Paltz.

Karla Vermeulen, PhD, is the Deputy Director of the Institute for Disaster Mental Health and an Associate Professor at the State University of New York at New Paltz. She is co-author of *Disaster Mental Health Interventions: Core Principles and Practices.*

"This much-needed volume will help all disaster workers and emergency responders, whether they are trainees or seasoned professionals, to better understand and navigate the real-world processes of disaster mental health response. It offers a unique description of the helping experiences, personal feelings, and reflections on lessons learned of individuals deployed in a comprehensive range of 17 natural and human-caused disasters, both domestic and international. This book is an invaluable training tool and deserves a place in the library of every emergency helper."

—*Josef I. Ruzek, PhD, former director, National Center for PTSD Dissemination and Training Division, adjunct professor, Department of Psychiatry and Behavioral Sciences, Stanford University*

"The editors of this book are leading experts in the field of disaster response. They have assembled a series of compelling case studies on the human effects of various kinds of disasters. It is remarkable that they have included so many of the major disasters the world has seen in the past thirty years; with these case studies, readers can be reminded of what may have been forgotten and what can be learned from these experiences. *Disaster Mental Health Case Studies* is a great service to those who study disaster, as it takes a vast literature and in one place presents the recent history of disaster."

—*Richard G. Tedeschi, PhD, coauthor of* Posttraumatic Growth: Theory, Research, and Applications

"The experience of reading *Disaster Mental Health Case Studies* is like peering into each contributor's personal journal while also getting useful instruction on what works and what doesn't in providing disaster mental health services. The diverse array of case studies shared in this well-organized, easy-to-follow compilation move the reader through a journey of understanding the impacts of disasters on individuals, families, and communities (and on ourselves) that's on a human, accessible level, which will make disaster mental health providers all the more effective in supporting survivors and responders."

—*Christian Burgess, MSW, director, Disaster Distress Helpline for Vibrant Emotional Health*

Disaster Mental Health Case Studies

Lessons Learned from Counseling in Chaos

Edited by
James Halpern, Amy Nitza, and
Karla Vermeulen

Routledge
Taylor & Francis Group
NEW YORK AND LONDON

First published 2019
by Routledge
52 Vanderbilt Avenue, New York, NY 10017

and by Routledge
2 Park Square, Milton Park, Abingdon, Oxon OX14 4RN

Routledge is an imprint of the Taylor & Francis Group, an informa business

Library of Congress Cataloging-in-Publication Data
A catalog record for this title has been requested

ISBN: 978-1-138-55918-9 (hbk)
ISBN: 978-1-138-55919-6 (pbk)
ISBN: 978-1-351-25226-3 (ebk)

Typeset in Times New Roman
by Taylor & Francis Books

This book is dedicated to the first responders, disaster mental health helpers, and spiritual care providers around the world who put their health and lives at risk in attempting to ease the pain of disaster survivors.

Contents

About the Editors

James Halpern is Professor Emeritus of Psychology and Counseling and Founding Director of the Institute for Disaster Mental Health at the State University of New York at New Paltz. He is the co-author of *Disaster Mental Health Interventions: Core Principles and Practices* (Routledge) and *Disaster Mental Health: Theory and Practice* (Thompson). He has received federal grants from United States Agency for International Development (for work in the Middle East), Centers for Disease Control, National Institute for Mental Health, and the Substance Abuse and Mental Health Services Administration as well as grants from New York State agencies (Department of Health, Office of Mental Health, Office of Homeland Security and Emergency Services, and Office of Victim Services) to develop and provide training and education in Disaster Mental Health. He has consulted for the United Nations on Assisting Victims of Terror and developed training modules for the United Nations Emergency Preparedness and Support Teams. He has also provided direct service to disaster survivors and served in a leadership role at both large-scale national and local disasters.

Amy Nitza is the Director of the Institute for Disaster Mental Health at the State University of New York at New Paltz. She specializes in mental health training and disaster response in international contexts. As a Fulbright Scholar at the University of Botswana, she studied the use of group counseling interventions in HIV/AIDS prevention among adolescents. In the Kingdom of Bhutan, she worked at the National Referral Hospital, providing direct services and training for staff. She has overseen multiple disaster mental health projects at the state, national, and international levels, and has received several grants for this work, including from New York State agencies and the New York State Health Foundation. She is Past President and Fellow of the Association for Specialists in Group Work, and Treasurer of the Society for Group Psychology and Group Psychotherapy (Division 49) of the American Psychological Association. She holds a Doctorate in Counseling Psychology from Indiana University.

Karla Vermeulen is the Deputy Director of the Institute for Disaster Mental Health and an Associate Professor in the Psychology Department of the State University of New York at New Paltz, where she teaches undergraduate and graduate courses on disaster mental health and grief counseling, and directs the Advanced Certificate in Trauma and Disaster Mental Health program. She holds a Doctorate in Applied Developmental Psychology from Fordham University, and a Certificate in Mental Health in Complex Emergencies from the Center for International Humanitarian Cooperation. In addition to teaching and research, she has coordinated the development and production of training curricula for the New York State Department of Health and Office of Mental Health, the American Red Cross, the United Nations, United States Agency for International Development West Bank/Gaza, and other organizations. She is co-author of the textbook, *Disaster Mental Health Interventions: Core Principles and Practices*, published in 2017 by Routledge.

Contributors

Basma Abdelaziz, is an award-winning writer, sculptor, and psychiatrist. She holds a master's degree in Neuropsychiatry and a Diploma of Sociology. A long-standing vocal critic of government oppression in Egypt, she worked for the Al-Nadeem Centre in psychological management and rehabilitation of victims of torture and violence for more than 10 years. She is the author of several works of non-fiction, including "Memory of Oppression" which is a psycho-political study of the torture system in Egypt. In 2016 she was named one of Foreign Policy's Global Thinkers for her debut novel, *The Queue*, which was nominated in 2017 in the long list for the Best Translated Book Award. She lives in Cairo.

Richard Bigelow, LCSW, LPC, Disaster Mental Health Supervisor, American Red Cross, is a Licensed Clinical Social Worker and a Licensed Professional Counselor in the state of Texas. He earned his bachelor's degree in Social Work from Colorado State University Pueblo in 1972 and his master's degree in Social Work from Our Lady of the Lake University in San Antonio, Texas in 1975. He served as a Board Approved Supervisor for LCSW and LPC candidates for many years. He received numerous local, state, and national awards and recognitions during his 29-year career in direct clinical practice and psychiatric hospital administration. He is a past president of the American Association of Children's Residential Centers and the National Association of Psychiatric Treatment Centers for Children. Since 2005 he has worked as Disaster Mental Health Supervisor volunteer for the American Red Cross. He is also trained as a Crisis Response Team Member by the Texas Department of Public Safety.

Stephen Brooker, RN, Dip.M.H, BSc, MA, St John of God Richmond Hospital, is a trained RN who has worked in several resource-rich and resource-limited countries running both medical and mental health services. Currently running a not-for-profit mental health facility in Sydney, Australia, Steve focuses on developing health services with skilled, motivated staff who have the needs of patients/clients at the core of their professional practice, reaching out to communities and partnership organizations to build and sustain excellence in clinical settings.

Wayne F. Dailey, PhD, Department of Psychiatry, Yale University School of Medicine, and Disaster Mental Health Chief, American Red Cross, has worked for decades in public sector behavioral health clinical care, policy development, research, and management. Following the 9/11 terrorist attacks he helped organize and lead the Connecticut Disaster Behavioral Health Response Network, which served as a model for many other states. Currently he serves as Disaster Mental Health Chief with the American Red Cross and is Associate Clinical Professor, Department of Psychiatry, Yale University School of Medicine. Dr. Dailey has worked in many mass casualty events, including Hurricanes Isaac, Sandy, Harvey, and Irma, wildfires, floods, tornados, the Boston Marathon bombing, and mass casualty shootings at Sandy Hook Elementary School in Connecticut, and at the Sutherland Springs Baptist Church and Santa Fe High School in Texas.

Erika Felix, PhD, is an Associate Professor in the Department of Counseling, Clinical, and School Psychology at the University of California, Santa Barbara, and a licensed psychologist. She received her BA in psychology from the University of Southern California and her Ph.D. in clinical-community psychology from DePaul University. After completing a postdoctoral research fellowship at UCSB, she continued as a professional researcher for several years before joining the faculty in 2014. Dr. Felix's research spans three related areas: (1) promoting adaptive recovery for youth following disaster, terrorism, or other collectively-experienced traumas, (2) youth victimization and its consequences, and (3) research and evaluation to improve community-based services. Her research has been funded by the National Institute of Mental Health, National Institute of Child Health & Human Development, National Science Foundation, private foundations, and local community organizations. Dr. Felix serves on the Board of the International Society of Traumatic Stress Studies and is a member of the American Psychological Association.

Tara S. Hughes, LCSW-R, International Institute of Buffalo, and Disaster Mental Health Volunteer, American Red Cross, is a Clinical Social Worker with 29 years of experience as a therapist, with a focus on working with children and adolescents who have trauma histories. She received her BA in Psychology from Boston College and her MSW from Boston University. She has volunteered with the American Red Cross in Disaster Mental Health (DMH) since 2002, after receiving training from both the Red Cross and the International Critical Incident Stress Foundation. She has responded to multiple natural and human-caused disasters with the Red Cross, including many where fatalities were a component of the incident. Tara served as DMH Manager at the Family Assistance Center after the crash of Colgan Flight 3407 in 2009, as DMH Lead at the Disaster Operations Center for the Haitian Earthquake in 2010, as DMH Chief after the Sandy Hook Elementary School shooting in 2012, the Boston Marathon Bombing in 2013, and the Navy Yard shooting in 2013, and as FAC Lead after the Pulse Nightclub shooting in 2016 and the Las Vegas shooting in 2017. She has also responded to large hurricanes, such as Katrina and Super Storm Sandy. She teaches as an Adjunct Professor at the University at Buffalo School of Social Work, and speaks across the country on topics that include trauma and disaster response.

Wismick Jean-Charles, PhD, Université Notre-Dame d'Haïti, is a priest of the Order of the Compagnie de Marie, and a visiting professor of research methodology and psychology at the Université Notre-Dame d'Haïti (UNDH). He holds a doctorate in Psychology from Fordham University in New York. He has done advanced studies in trauma at the International Trauma Studies Program at Columbia University and has received post-doctoral training on global mental health at the Harvard Program in Refugee Trauma (HPRT). He was the former Vice President for Academic Affairs at the Université Notre-Dame d'Haïti. He is a member of the team of the International Association of Applied Psychology (IAAP) accredited at the United Nations. Founder and Executive Director of the Center for Spirituality and Mental Health (CESSA), he is currently the Vicar General for his religious order in Rome.

Reine Lebel, M.Ed, Mental Health Officer, Médecins sans Frontières, is a counsellor and Gestalt therapist. She has volunteered with the Red Cross in Florida following Hurricane Andrew and in Malawi. She has worked in disaster mental health with Care and with Médecins sans Frontières (MSF), developing wellness programs for humanitarians, and has had the privilege to participate in many emergency missions including deployments to refugee camps in Albania and Macedonia during the war in Kosovo. She has responded with MSF and other NGOs in high tension and war contexts including Kashmir, Iraq, Jordan, Democratic Republic of Congo, Afghanistan, Central African Republic, and other countries. She also has deployed in response to natural catastrophes in Gujarat, Indonesia, Haiti, and the Philippines, and in Ebola epidemics in the Democratic Republic of Congo and Guinea.

Gerald McCleery, PhD, Disaster Mental Health Volunteer, American Red Cross, is a retired New York state licensed psychologist with more than

45 years of clinical, program operations, and senior management experience in behavioral healthcare in the not-for-profit, for-profit, and government sectors. He has extensive mental health call center experience, operating both the NYC mental health crisis line and the NY state substance abuse call center. He operated the September 11 Fund, American Red Cross, and NYC September 11 mental health benefits programs, and subsequently the Red Cross Hurricane Katrina mental health benefit program. He retired from full-time employment in 2016 and currently does consulting work. He is a graduate of Duke and St. John's Universities.

Margaret McGee-Smith, RN, Disaster Mental Health Reservist, American Red Cross, spent her career as a psychiatric nurse, primarily with the Buffalo Psychiatric Center. She has worked with seriously and persistently mentally ill inpatients, as a Community Mental Health Nurse, and with substance abuse clients in community and residential settings. As an American Red Cross Disaster Mental Health volunteer and now DMH Chief, she has deployed to more than 70 disasters around the world.

William L. Martin, PhD, Disaster Mental Health Adviser, American Red Cross, is a Clinical Psychologist, retired from active practice, and a retired U.S. Navy Captain (Intelligence). Involved with the Red Cross since 2005, he is a DMH Chief engaged in volunteer activities including developing training materials and teaching. He was a principal in developing the Red Cross Disaster Mental Health Management course and has contributed to Disaster Mental Health Fundamentals and Psychological First Aid course development. He serves as the Disaster Mental Health Adviser for Mississippi and, as a DMH Chief in the Red Cross, has participated in and led numerous DMH disaster responses both national and local. He currently lives with his wife, Shirley, on the Mississippi Gulf Coast.

Steven N. Moskowitz, LMSW, New York State Office of Mental Health, is the Director of Disaster Response and Emergency Preparedness for the New York State Office of Mental Health. In addition to his own Disaster Mental Health experiences responding to numerous events, he oversees the maintenance and coordination of a state-wide force of trained DMH responders who can be deployed regionally or across New York State following disasters. He also oversaw the crisis counseling response to several large-scale events including Hurricane Irene and Super Storm Sandy. Prior to joining the DMH field, he worked as a therapist, community services agency administrator, and family mediator.

Joseph O. Prewitt Diaz, PhD, Disaster Mental Health Advisor, National Capital Region of the American Red Cross, is a practitioner-scholar who has designed, implemented, and written about community-based psychological support programs in the Caribbean, the Americas, and South Asia. He has authored or co-authored 18 books in Spanish and English on psychosocial support and over 140 refereed journal articles. His work was recognized by the American Psychological Association by being awarded the International Humanitarian Award. He served as ARC Senior Technical Advisor for Psychosocial Support from 2005 to 2007. He is currently the Disaster Mental Health Advisor for the National Capital Region of the American Red Cross. His previous books include *Disaster Recovery: Community-based Psychosocial Support in the Aftermath* (2018), and *Advances in Disaster Mental Health and Psychosocial Support* (2008).

J. Christie Rodgers, MSW, LICSW, Senior Associate for Disaster Mental Health at the American Red Cross National Headquarters, oversees the Red Cross Disaster Mental Health program. Christie has held this position since 2013 and has deployed to over ten national disasters in that time, including the 2017 Las Vegas mass shooting event. In addition to these deployments, Christie has supported nearly every major disaster response since 2013, including Hurricanes Matthew, Harvey, Irma, and Maria. Christie is a clinical social worker with expertise in trauma and attachment. Prior to joining the Red Cross, she provided therapy and crisis intervention services to families adopting children from Washington, DC's child welfare system. She has also worked with incarcerated women and their children as well as homeless and runaway teenagers. Christie earned her bachelor's degree in psychology from Duke University in Durham, NC and her MSW from Catholic University of America in Washington, DC.

Diane Ryan, LCSW, Federal Bureau of Investigation's Victim Services Division, is a Licensed Clinical Social Worker specializing in trauma, critical incident response, and disaster mental health. She is currently employed with the FBI's Victim Services Division. Prior to that, she was Director of Disaster Mental Health for the American Red Cross in Greater New York. Diane has served at local and national disasters including floods, hurricanes, tornadoes, mass casualty transportation incidents, and the World Trade Center attacks. She led the development of the mental health/spiritual care response protocol for the 2009 New York City Family Assistance Center plan and provided posttraumatic stress protocols to 9/11 responders for several years after the World Trade Center disaster. Diane has presented on disaster, trauma, and critical incident response nationally and internationally, and has published on the topics of disaster mental health response, roles in respite centers for emergency service workers, disaster staff support, and collaboration with spiritual care providers.

John R. Tassey, PhD, Health Psychology Clinic, Oklahoma City Veterans Affairs Medical Center, and Department of Psychiatry, College of Medicine, University of Oklahoma Health Sciences Center, is Medical Psychology Program Manager and Director of the Health Psychology Clinic at the Oklahoma City Veterans Affairs Medical Center. He is an Adjunct Professor in the Department of Applied Behavioral Studies at Oklahoma City University. Dr. Tassey is also volunteer faculty in the Department of Psychiatry and Behavioral Sciences at the University of Oklahoma Health Science Center. He was appointed chair of the APA Task Force on the Mental Health Response to the Oklahoma City Bombing and also deployed to the Washington, DC area following the attacks of September 11. He provided training to mental health and spiritual care providers in the Greater New York area following the attacks of 9/11. He has responded to many disasters as a Red Cross volunteer almost since the inception of the Disaster Mental Health function, and was the Red Cross National Mental Health Consultant from 1998 through 2007. He currently serves as the American Psychological Association Disaster Resource Network coordinator for Oklahoma.

Mary Tramontin, PsyD, U.S. Department of Defense, is a forensically trained, licensed clinical psychologist. Her longest professional affiliation is serving as an American Red Cross volunteer as part of both disaster mental health as well as service to the armed forces. Dr. Tramontin has worked for the United States federal government for over 22 years, chiefly in consultative roles focusing on personnel risk assessment and mitigation, and enhancing workforce wellness. All of her professional endeavors are informed by expertise in the evaluation, treatment, and management of traumatic stress. Building on these experiences, Dr. Tramontin has written several peer-reviewed publications and is the co-author of *Disaster Mental Health: Theory and Practice* (2007).

Acknowledgments

We would like to thank current and former colleagues from the State University of New York at New Paltz who provided support, advice, and guidance: Dr. Gerald Benjamin, Dr. Glenn Geher, Dr. Jonathan Raskin, Dr. Laura Barrett, and most especially SUNY New Paltz President Don Christian. We all greatly value the diligence and intelligence of our Institute for Disaster Mental Health colleague, Program and Operations Manager Rebecca Rodriguez. We also deeply appreciate the insights and guidance of the Institute for Disaster Mental Health Advisory Board Chair Greg Brunelle and the other board members.

We thank our families for their unwavering support as we all worked long hours to complete this book. For James: wife Gail, and grandkids, who inspire hope for the future. For Amy: husband Ted and kids Eden, Hope, and Trey. For Karla: husband Michael and all parents, in-laws, and nieces and nephews.

Above all, we thank our 17 authors who worked so hard to distill their complex and often distressing experiences into valuable case studies that can now be used to educate the next generation of disaster mental health responders. They're true heroes for extending themselves, not only during the events they describe here but in disaster after disaster, and we believe the world is a better place thanks to people like them.

Disclaimer

The views and opinions expressed in this book are those of the authors and do not reflect the official position or policy of any government or non-government agency, organization, or university. The examples used in the case studies are based on the authors' experiences with disaster survivors. However, they have been altered where needed to protect the privacy of these individuals.

Chapter 1

Introduction

James Halpern, Amy Nitza, and Karla Vermeulen

Disasters don't just rob people of homes, property, and sometimes lives; they create extreme stress and trauma. Emergency managers and first responders place the psychological needs of disaster survivors second to saving lives and providing temporary shelter, food, and water. However, addressing psychological needs following disaster is now more appreciated and planned for than at any time in the past. It's also better understood that restoring basic necessities does not just satisfy physical and practical needs, but psychological ones as well. There are fewer stigmas around requesting mental health support post-disaster. This is fortunate because in the United States and around the world, disasters are becoming more frequent and more intense. The U.S. has the most extreme weather in the world with tornado, hurricane, and wildfire seasons, along with the most gun violence, mass shootings, and mass killings in the developed world. Countries with less frequent natural disasters and less gun violence can nonetheless face daunting challenges when disaster strikes due to poverty, lack of response capacity, poor building construction, lack of medical supplies, and so on. These difficulties can extend survivors' suffering and delay their recovery, placing them at higher risk of developing extreme mental health reactions in response to the disaster.

A growing body of research has guided the practice of disaster mental health. We know that disasters that are big and bad and long will have significant mental health consequences in the short and long terms. They will cause both transient distress in the majority of survivors and long-term psychopathology in a minority of survivors (North & Pfefferbaum, 2013). Following disaster there will likely be an increase in grief and traumatic grief, alcohol and substance misuse, depression, anxiety, post-traumatic stress, and family conflict (Bonanno, Brewin, Kaniasty & La Greca, 2010). We also understand the risk and resilience factors that make some people more vulnerable to developing symptoms. For example, knowing that children are particularly at risk for lasting reactions allows planners and responders to better target assistance to them, their parents, and schools. We can also identify other vulnerable and at-risk populations, such as the frail elderly, people living in poverty, those who have been injured, and those with disabilities (Halpern & Vermeulen, 2017). But our understanding of what clinical tools to use with different individuals and populations is still in the early stages: Precisely because disasters, the people they impact, and survivors' needs and reactions are all so diverse, it's difficult to conduct standardized research that allows us to develop evidence-based interventions we can recommend for everyone. Additionally, disaster mental health (DMH) responders need to be flexible and adapt to each situation and each survivor they encounter, and historically there have been few opportunities to learn from each other's experiences through traditional academic publications.

The case study method used for this book is intended to provide detailed, rich qualitative information and insight to improve practice and to further research. Case studies are often used in exploratory research. They can help us generate new ideas that might be tested by other methods and can illustrate how theories and practice are applied in real life situations. For example, research has guided us in working with parents after a disaster. We know that we can support children by encouraging parents to maintain routines, like helping children to have regular bed and wake up times. But the research does not tell us how it feels to enter a community or family assistance center where there has been a school shooting or explosion and children are injured or dead. The research does not inform us about the challenges faced when trying to help clients who have been the victims of political violence or who are suffering from a virus that could kill anyone – including exposed DMH helpers. So, we have worked with practitioners involved in the DMH response to 17 domestic and international disasters to capture their lived experiences throughout the event, in hopes that readers will be able to incorporate the lessons learned into their own future responses.

This book is intended for students of mental health and school counseling, psychology, and social work – and for working practitioners who want to learn directly from their disaster response peers. By providing the reader with more in-depth case studies than are found in any comparable text, it could stand alone or be a companion to *Disaster Mental Health Interventions: Core Principles and Practices* (Halpern & Vermeulen, 2017), which describes the impact of disasters and how to support survivors.

This collection of case studies, written by seasoned clinicians, demonstrates how disaster mental health interventions can be tailored to meet the needs of clients impacted by different disasters, under very different circumstances. Each case offers lessons learned and guidance for practitioners who want to assist clients at what is arguably the most difficult time in their lives. In recounting their experiences at disasters, contributing authors give us a rare and compelling view into the challenges of doing this work. They not only describe the impact on disaster survivors, but also tell us how their involvement affected them personally. We hope their insights will help you work more effectively with survivors.

Before we look at the individual cases, we will review some of the basic disaster mental health practices that are likely to be a part of every response.

A Brief Overview of the Practice of Disaster Mental Health

There's a saying in this field that "if you've seen one disaster, you've seen one disaster," and the same point applies to disaster survivors. Every event is unique, as is everyone who has experienced that event.

The part regarding survivors is essential to remember as there can be a tendency, in the chaos and often overwhelming demands you may encounter after a major event, to assume that everyone who went through a particular disaster is going to experience identical reactions, and therefore they'll all benefit from the same interventions. Obviously but unfortunately (since it would make our jobs much easier!) this is not the case. Each person went into that event with different pre-existing resources, stressors, personality characteristics, and history of coping with adversity. This means they perceived the disaster differently while it was unfolding, even if they were literally in the same room when it happened. They also will have differences in their recovery resources, coping style, access to social support, and sense of self-efficacy that will influence how smoothly or bumpily they adjust to their disaster experience and losses. Therefore, DMH practice lesson number one is to remember to treat each survivor as an individual – as you doubtless would do during your usual mental health practice – and don't fall into that trap of generalizing expectations because of the collective nature of the traumatic experience.

And the same lesson applies to your own expectations going into a new response. As you gain experience in the field, you'll probably start to feel more confident in your ability to help survivors and cope with whatever the next disaster throws at you. That's natural and positive, but we encourage you to never assume that what worked last time will automatically suffice next time. We can't emphasize enough that each disaster and survivor group is different, so you'll need to work differently to help them. As you'll read in these case studies, some of the most experienced responders whose stories are included here are also the most humble, acknowledging that while they can certainly apply some lessons across events, they also have learned they need to go into a new response with an open mind and heart, ready to adapt to whatever they encounter.

With that need for flexibility established, there are some evidence-based, trauma-informed interventions that are recommended by the American Psychological Association and other professional groups as effective treatments for Post-traumatic Stress Disorder and other extreme reactions. It should be part of every DMH helper's on-site preparation to know what, if any, community resources are available for survivors who need referrals for these evidence-based longer-term treatments.

However, the primary focus of the disaster mental health response is not on addressing the minority of people who do develop these extreme reactions, but on the majority, if not the entire population, who experience "post-traumatic stress reactions." These can resemble PTSD symptoms but are generally short-lived and less extreme – which is not to say that they don't feel terrible for the people experiencing them at the time. These responses make sense given the traumatic event and subsequent losses these survivors are processing, and they can occur across multiple realms:

- Emotional.
- Behavioral.
- Physical.
- Cognitive.
- Spiritual.

The range of possible reactions within each of these realms is vast, and each individual survivor will experience their own unique combination of symptoms at any given time. While these varied reactions are common and reasonable in response to a particularly traumatic event, it's important for you to be aware that they're often shocking and overwhelming to those experiencing them. Survivors may fear that they'll never feel better, or that they're going crazy. Some people may feel weak for not being able cope better – or guilty about how well they are coping relative to those around them. It's particularly challenging when members of a couple or family are responding differently and can't understand or support each other's reactions.

As a result, an important DMH intervention is to provide psychoeducation about *why* survivors are feeling the way they're feeling. We want to normalize their reactions – but without describing them as "normal" since that can feel invalidating to people in the throes of this intense response. Instead, we suggest this approach when working with a distressed client:

- Describe their feelings as reactions that make sense given what they've been through.
- Explain that most people who experience these strong feelings after a disaster start to feel better once some time has passed and the situation starts to stabilize.
- Explain what they can do to access more mental health support if they don't start to feel better over time, and/or they would like to speak to a helper now.

That approach acknowledges and validates the person's current suffering while creating an expectation of recovery, and while providing resources to help in the event that additional assistance is indeed needed now or later.

Beyond that very basic, but often very helpful, provision of psychoeducation, most of the earliest DMH interventions are based on delivering Psychological First Aid (PFA), which you'll see mentioned in almost every one of these case studies. PFA focuses on providing immediate support for disaster survivors' interrelated practical and emotional needs, and restoring a sense of safety. The goals are to remove any barriers to recovery and to kickstart survivors' natural resilience. There are many different models of PFA, though all share the same core goals. All are short-term (you might have only one conversation with a survivor and never know how they fare in the future) and focus on returning the person to their pre-disaster functioning, not fixing every issue in their life.

Our PFA model (Halpern & Vermeulen, 2017) includes these elements:

- Being calm.
- Providing warmth.
- Showing genuineness.
- Attending to safety needs.
- Attending to physiological needs.
- Providing acknowledgment and recognition.
- Expressing empathy.
- Helping clients access social support.
- Helping clients avoid negative social support.
- Providing accurate and timely information.
- Providing psychoeducation and reinforcing positive coping.
- Empowering the survivors.
- Assisting survivors with traumatic grief.

We'll point out that when people with any kind of mental health background study PFA, their immediate response is often along the lines of, "well, of course those are things I would do with anyone in distress!" Indeed, the elements themselves are simple and seem like common sense. However, in the heat of a disaster response, common sense is often overwhelmed by the stress of trying to attend to dozens or even hundreds of survivors, so it's essential not only to study PFA but to practice it through roleplays or other exercises so you're able to implement each element as needed. You can and should take a PFA training with the American Red Cross or other organizations, or through various online programs, before you consider responding to a disaster.

Beyond PFA, DMH helpers often need to draw on other clinical skills to address the stress and uncertainty in the post-disaster community, including:

- Correcting distorted self-cognitions among survivors who are unfairly blaming themselves or others, or who have exaggerated perceptions of ongoing threats.
- Rumor control, as false information inevitably springs up to fill the vacuum of official news about the event.
- Mitigating conflict, as perceptions about unfair distribution of resources or the ongoing stress of living in a crowded shelter elicit anger and frustration.
- Assessment and screening to ensure that needs at the individual and community levels are recognized and, if possible, addressed.
- Referrals for long-term care for those who need a connection to a community-based mental health professional. Of course, this applies to cultures and communities where there is an existing mental health infrastructure and professionals who are available to provide treatment. Where this is not the case, introducing a sustainable approach to training paraprofessionals and building local capacity can be an important DMH role.

Remember that your role typically involves supporting colleagues and other responders as well as disaster survivors, so encouraging them to practice stress management and self-care is important, as is attending to your own needs in those areas in order to maintain your ability to help others.

We hope this very brief summary of the goals and practices of disaster mental health response makes it clear that the specialty requires an intense level of dedication and flexibility. More detailed descriptions of PFA and other early interventions in DMH can be found in *Disaster Mental Health Interventions: Core Principles and Practices* (Halpern & Vermeulen, 2017), and we encourage you to seek out as many training opportunities as possible through the Red Cross and other organizations to be sure you build up the range of skills you'll need to support survivors. As the case studies you're about to read demonstrate, the work is hard, but many practitioners describe their disaster mental health responses as among their most gratifying professional experiences.

A Guide to This Book

The book you're about to read consists of 17 case studies divided into three sections. They include a number of high-profile disasters that most readers are likely to be familiar with, as well as several others that may not be as well known:

Natural Disasters in the United States

- 2014 Mudslides in Oso, WA, by J. Christie Rodgers
- 2005 Hurricane Katrina in Louisiana, by Gerald McCleery
- 2013 Wildfire in Yarnell, AZ, by Margaret McGee-Smith
- 2016 Floods in Mississippi, by William L. Martin
- 2011 Tornado in Joplin, MO, by Richard Bigelow
- 2012 Super Storm Sandy in New York City, by Diane Ryan

Human-Caused Disasters in the United States

- 1995 Bombing of the Oklahoma City Federal Building, John R. Tassey
- 2001 World Trade Center Attack in New York City, by Mary Tramontin
- 2012 Sandy Hook School Shooting in Newtown, CT, by Wayne F. Dailey
- 2012 Shooting and Fire in Webster, NY, by Steven N. Moskowitz
- 2014 Mass Murder in Isla Vista, CA, by Erika Felix
- 2016 Pulse Night Club Shooting in Orlando, FL, by Tara S. Hughes

International Disasters

- 1998 Las Casitas Mudslides in Nicaragua, by Joseph O. Prewitt Diaz
- 2010 Earthquake in Haiti, by Wismick Jean-Charles
- 2013 Asylum Seeker Camp Riots on Nauru, by Stephen Brooker
- 2013 Massacre at Rabaa Square in Egypt, by Basma Abdelaziz
- 2014 Ebola Outbreak in Guinea, by Reine Lebel

These cases have been chosen to reflect different types of events in different geographic locations, and include natural and human-caused disasters of varying scope, intensity, and duration. They resulted in different reactions, challenges, and interventions; they also occurred in communities with diverse populations and disparate access to resources that necessitated a range of cultural and contextual considerations which the authors describe. The experiences of the DMH responders in this collection of events contribute to lessons learned of a remarkable breadth and depth.

At the same time, this list is a small and non-representative sample of the countless disasters that could have been included in each section. For every disaster that is described, there were numerous others that we wish could have been included. The selection of these specific events is not intended to elevate their significance over that of any others. Similarly, the authors whose experiences are shared here are in many cases one of a number of DMH responders who could have written about their roles in that disaster; in that way, each chapter reflects only one story of many. Each of the included authors is a mental health professional who was involved directly in the response in a DMH role. Many were responding to a disaster in their own community or region; others were deployed to the disaster site through an agency that was invited to respond, such as the American Red Cross or Médecins sans Frontières. The dynamics and challenges of responding to a disaster in one's own community versus being deployed to the site are very different; toward that end, the authors describe the community context in which they were responding, as well as their own thoughts and considerations as they prepared to enter and engage with that community as a DMH responder.

Each case study follows the same outline:

Author background: Authors from different mental health professions present their varied backgrounds, their motivations for becoming involved in disaster response work, and their levels of experience. Some describe themselves as entering the scene well prepared and trained while others saw themselves as less experienced, trying to adapt their clinical training to the chaos they encountered.

Pre-disaster community: Authors describe the community and culture they entered and how it shaped their expectations and approach to helping. Communities varied enormously in terms of resources, familiarity with disaster, and mental health services available. The authors discuss working with different types of populations and cultures, how they joined and worked with police, firefighters, clergy, oppressed political groups, the very poor, parents of young children, LGBTQ populations, and so on.

The characteristics of the event: Client and community reactions are shaped by the size, expectedness, duration, and cause of the event. Each chapter provides a description of a different kind of turmoil that you, the reader, might encounter should you be asked to deploy to a similar event.

Thoughts pre-disaster: Authors discuss their thoughts and preparations before going out to a response – their immediate reactions when they first got the call to help. Readers should note authors' apprehensions as well as their different self-care plans and levels of experience and confidence. Few report feeling fully prepared to respond, but all rose to the occasion using techniques that may be valuable for new helpers to adopt.

Response experience: Authors describe what they saw and heard – the impact of the event on survivors and the populations impacted, as well as the practical challenges they faced and the significant clinical actions and interventions they practiced. The reader might consider which interventions seemed most consistent with your own style. Do the case studies suggest you would benefit from additional training and practice?

Post-response adjustment: In this section authors describe the personal impact of the event and response, their reflections on the experience, and what they thought and did returning from assignment. Please note that engaging in disaster response should never be taken lightly. The authors all recognize the need for self-care in order to maintain wellness and competence to serve others.

Lessons learned: Authors summarize what they took away from their experience and what they view as useful to practitioners who may be involved in disaster response in general and/or responding to a similar type of disaster.

If you're new to the field, the case studies presented in this book are intended to prepare you for the experience of assisting clients in a chaotic situation where there may be few facts and much uncertainty. When an author describes an event, think about how *you* would prepare to respond if it were you receiving that call. There might be smoke, debris, news reports of casualties. You might be traveling far from home to support a group of strangers, or you might be balancing professional and personal demands if the disaster strikes your own community. When you enter a disaster scene, shelter, or family assistance center, you're entering "disaster world" – a world of confusion and trauma and need. We hope these case studies provide you with some exposure that will help you be more ready and more effective when it's your time to respond. If there is one thing that is certain in this field, it's that there will be no shortage of disasters in the future. By reading this book, you can absorb the wisdom of these 17 DMH practitioners and improve your capacity to help when needed.

We are grateful to each of the authors who shared their stories with us; we found their descriptions of the moments of human connection they achieved, as well as the moments of uncertainty that they faced, to be both informative and inspiring. We hope that you will learn as much from their experiences as we have.

References

Bonanno, G.A., Brewin, C.R., Kaniasty, K., & La Greca, A.M. (2010). Weighing the costs of disaster: Consequences, risks and resilience in individuals, families, and communities. *Psychological Science in the Public Interest*, 11, 1–49.

Halpern, J., & Vermeulen, K. (2017). *Disaster Mental Health Interventions: Core Principles and Practices*. New York: Routledge.

North, C.S., & Pfefferbaum, B. (2013). Mental health response to community disasters: A systemic review. *Journal of the American Medical Association*, 310, 507–518.

Section I

Natural Disasters in the United States

Chapter 2

Natural Disasters Section Introduction

Karla Vermeulen

When my fellow editors and I teach students and professional responders about how disasters' characteristics tend to correlate with survivors' typical psychological reactions, we talk about how people usually have an *easier* (though not an easy) time recovering from natural disasters compared with those who experience intentional acts of malevolence. Intuitively that should be no surprise: Unlike events where someone actively intended to cause harm, these weather- or geology-related disasters are usually seen as random acts of nature, completely uncontrollable, or as acts of God that often generate painful questioning for those who believe in an omnipotent deity. That certainly can be traumatic for those believers who are now robbed of their faith or are forced to question the benevolence of their God. Disaster mental health responders should be prepared to hear questions like "How could God have let this happen?" – unanswerable questions that may best be referred to a chaplain or spiritual care provider, but whose significance for the survivor should not be minimized.

Still, we generally see that survivors of natural events tend to have a less difficult time accepting what has occurred, largely because there is no one to blame, except God/karma/one's higher power or deity – or just the rotten luck of being in the wrong place when a particular natural disaster happened to strike their spot on the map. There usually aren't criminal investigations or trials that prolong survivors' exposure to the event, and natural disasters are less likely to be politicized or to become fodder for ongoing media punditry. Sometimes the impact of these disasters is limited to property damage with no human casualties or injuries. Dealing with a flooded basement or a tree through the roof might be stressful and expensive, but not necessarily traumatic. Those impacted can focus on recovering from their losses without a lot of the secondary stressors that often surround human-caused events, as the chapter introducing that section of the book will describe.

However, no one should ever claim that going through a natural disaster isn't difficult at best and potentially traumatic at worst. These events may cause people to lose their homes and all of the precious belongings those homes contained. Sometimes they lose their communities if they choose or are forced to relocate permanently. People can die in natural disasters, as can pets, and survivors may have feared that they or their loved ones were going to die, which is an experience no one forgets. Recovery periods can be long and exhausting, and there are never enough resources to go around.

We also see that even when betrayal, blame, and anger seemingly shouldn't be present in response to natural disasters, these emotions are frequently a part of survivors' range of reactions. And the effects of these feelings are powerful, even if they sometimes seem irrational to responders. Put yourself in the shoes of a survivor who has just lost their home to a natural disaster:

You could be blaming meteorologists, volcanologists, hurricane chasers, emergency managers, law enforcement, politicians, and everyone else who should have recognized this threat and protected their constituents – you – from it. Clearly, you think (accurately or not), *someone* should have done a better job of warning you, or of putting more effective protective measures into place.

You're probably angry at your local authorities for failing to push through a federal declaration of emergency that would bring more resources to your county, and you're definitely upset about the runaround you feel your insurance company is giving you.

You're mad at the media for being present with their intrusive questions and cameras, and then you're mad at the media for moving on to the next disaster and abandoning your community when there's still so much work that needs to be done to clean up.

You might blame your pets or livestock for not sending stronger signals about the approaching earthquake. Why didn't the horses/dogs/spiders make their premonitions clearer? That may sound silly, but people sometimes go through elaborate mental gymnastics in order to avoid being caught off guard again in the future.

Which brings us to the key point to be prepared for when trying to support survivors of natural disasters: It's very common for them to blame themselves – not for the event itself, usually, but for ignoring a warning or otherwise acting or failing to act in some way that could have prevented or mitigated the harm they experienced. You may hear people say things like:

- Maybe the horses/dogs/spiders did send a clear signal and I was too busy to recognize it! I won't make that mistake again.
- I should have protected my belongings better, put our valuables up high or in a safe deposit box, or bought a better home insurance policy.
- If only I had followed the evacuation warning, we wouldn't have been trapped when the flooding hit.

- I think God is punishing me for something I did before (or something someone in my family or community did before, depending on beliefs about karma or collective responsibility and retribution).

Sometimes this self-blame is appropriate. People can be careless and let an insurance policy lapse, and they frequently disregard warnings that might have spared them from exposure to harm. In such cases survivors have to find a way to forgive themselves for real mistakes that they made. Sometimes the self-blame is exaggerated, distorted, or based on an inaccurate belief. Either way, it's an attempt to control the situation – and to prevent it from ever happening again in the future. Rational or not, the message to oneself is that "I made a mistake this time, but that won't happen again." And this can lead to more productive behavior in the future like improved compliance with the next warning, but it often comes at a cost of guilt and self-blame that can increase distress for survivors of these events.

And of course, it's impossible to seize control of our fates fully, and that lack of control and the resulting sense of helplessness is often the most troubling emotional reaction you'll encounter in survivors of natural disasters. While some weather events are predictable, many natural disasters are largely unexpected, or they seem so remote and unlikely that we can shrug them off and carry on living where we want to – in a flood plain on the coast or by a river, in the vast swath of the US referred to as Tornado Alley, even on the side of an active volcano. And then when the volcano erupts, or the fourth "hundred-year flood" occurs in a decade, or the tornado's path cuts through one's town, survivors feel powerless and sometimes question whether they want to stay in a place that no longer feels safe.

The takeaway point here for readers is that from the mental health perspective, we often frame natural disasters as not *quite* as terrible for survivors relative to events resulting from human-caused behaviors. While that is generally (though certainly not universally) true, we also need to remember that less terrible is still terrible enough, as the accounts you're about to read make clear.

The six case studies in this section describe two major hurricanes, a flood, a tornado, a mudslide, and a wildfire that not only burned thousands of acres and destroyed more than a hundred structures, but took the lives of 19 firefighters. These events hit major cities and small towns across the United States. All involved numerous fatalities as well as property damage that displaced residents, so some survivors were both homeless and bereaved. Several of the disasters damaged or destroyed important parts of community infrastructure including roads, schools, places of worship, and even hospitals. Some raised questions about whether certain neighborhoods should ever be rebuilt or if those locations were simply too hazardous to allow people to return to in the era of climate change.

The authors of these case studies are all experienced mental health professionals and most had extensive disaster response experience prior to the events they describe here, but one (Rodgers, in the next chapter you'll read) was doing her second major deployment, and we suspect many readers will identify with the trepidation she describes when heading into the scene. Most deployed to distant regions to provide support, and they describe the challenges of entering an unfamiliar community and trying to connect with residents and local responders who might mistrust outsiders. They also all describe their mixed feelings about reaching the end of their deployments and returning to the normalcy of home, knowing there were still so many unmet needs at the site. On the other hand, one of our authors (Ryan, Chapter 8) was working in her own community through the complex recovery from Super Storm Sandy and describes the exhaustion of participating in a response that lasted for months. New DMH responders would do well to consider your pacing as you head into a response: Are you looking at a sprint or a marathon?

The authors worked in diverse settings, often moving from site to site and doing outreach in impacted communities. This brought many of them close to scenes of devastation and exposed them to difficult sights, sounds, and smells. One responder (McCleery, Chapter 4) provided support via telephone from a 211 call center after Hurricane Katrina, experiencing a surreal contrast between the intense emotions he was exposed to while fielding questions from people desperately seeking food, shelter, medical care, and information about missing loved ones, while working from a safe and relatively comfortable space distant from the physical damage. Most describe working long days, sometimes followed by sleepless nights in a staff shelter or sharing a motel room with a chatty – or snoring – roommate. All emphasize the importance of actually practicing good self-care, including accessing social support on-scene and from home.

As the case studies in this section show, natural disasters can literally shake the foundation beneath survivors' feet, or wash away their entire community. These are the most common kinds of events DMH responders are likely to be deployed to, in their own communities or in other areas. They're an important training ground for what might seem like more intense reactions in a human-caused event, but as the diverse experiences and important lessons learned by the authors of our chapters in this section show, responding to these events is the core of disaster mental health response. You can't do better than starting with learning from their experiences.

Chapter 3

2014 Mudslides in Oso, WA

J. Christie Rodgers

I am a clinical social worker with experience working both in a non-profit management setting and as a clinician providing trauma and attachment-based therapy to foster children and their families. While looking for a change from my clinical role, I was lucky enough to be hired as the Senior Associate for Disaster Mental Health at the American Red Cross National Headquarters in Washington, DC. This is the only paid position at the American Red Cross focused full-time on Disaster Mental Health and it turned out to be the perfect combination of my interests and skills.

When I took this position in August 2013, I was new to disaster work and to the American Red Cross, which led to a very steep learning curve. To gain experience quickly, I joined the local Disaster Mental Health team in Washington, DC and my manager and I looked for opportunities for me to deploy to national-scale disaster responses. At the time of the Oso mudslide, I had only responded to a handful of local house fires and one national-scale flooding response. The mudslide provided an opportunity for me to gain experience responding to a large mass casualty incident, so despite my management position at national headquarters I was deployed to the response in the role of a "boots-on-the-ground" Disaster Mental Health worker.

The Pre-Disaster Community

Four small neighboring communities in Snohomish County, WA were impacted by the mudslide: Arlington, Darrington, Oso, and the Sauk-Suiattle Indian Reservation. While relatively close in proximity, each of these communities has its own distinct boundaries, culture, and challenges. They are all connected by State Route 530, a two-lane highway that was washed out by the mudslide, leaving Darrington and the Sauk-Suiattle tribe disconnected from Oso and Arlington for months. Clusters of homes and neighborhoods are also found along Route 530 between these towns.

Arlington, 18 miles east of the mudslide, is the largest of these towns with a population of 17,926, according to 2010 census data. Over the past

20 years, Arlington has grown tremendously in population, becoming a suburb of the cities of Marysville, Everett, and Seattle. The town of Darrington, 12 miles west of the mudslide, had a population of 1,347 in 2010, while the town of Oso is four miles east of the mudslide with a population of 180 people. The Sauk-Suiattle Reservation is five miles north of Darrington and has approximately 200 members.

Like many of my fellow responders, I was an outsider to the communities impacted by the Oso mudslide and therefore I had limited knowledge of what these communities were like before the incident. During my deployment, I learned quickly that each of these communities, especially Darrington, Oso, and the Sauk-Suiattle tribe, were significantly economically depressed and also had somewhat of an isolationist culture. I learned later that approximately 21 percent of Darrington's population lives below the poverty line and over 65 percent of the students at Darrington public schools are eligible for free or reduced-price lunches. Given the high rates of poverty in Darrington, it is not surprising that drug and alcohol abuse are also significant problems, particularly methamphetamine use. Unfortunately, mental health and substance abuse resources are also very limited in this area.

Darrington's main industry depends on logging, with the largest employer in the area being the local wood mill. I learned during my deployment that prior to the incident there had been concerns about mudslides occurring in the area because of the potential impacts of logging on surrounding mountains. After the incident, there were differing opinions within the community as to whether logging was the root cause of the incident or not.

The Disaster

On Saturday, March 22, 2014, at 10:37 a.m., a mudslide occurred four miles east of the town of Oso, WA, wiping out an unincorporated neighborhood known as Steelhead Haven. The debris field from the slide covered approximately one square mile and was reportedly one mile deep in some places. Residents did not have any warning in advance of the mudslide and therefore were not able to evacuate. Forty-three people, including seven children, were killed in the mudslide, and 49 homes and other structures were destroyed. Most of the children who died attended Darrington public schools. The majority of people who lived in Steelhead Haven were killed, leaving very few people displaced by the event. The slide also dammed the North Fork of the Stillaguamish River, leading to severe flooding upstream and displacement of the small number of residents who lived in surrounding homes.

First responders from both sides of the mudslide were deployed immediately to the scene and, by the end of the day, eight people were rescued from the debris, all of whom survived their injuries. Local residents who lived nearby also assisted with search and rescue immediately after the incident.

Once the incident site was secured, volunteers were directed to sign up at local fire departments to assist with recovery efforts. In the weeks and months following the incident, hundreds of volunteers from Snohomish and neighboring counties were utilized in this capacity. Workers and volunteers continued searching until remains from the final victim were identified and confirmed on July 22, four months after the mudslide occurred.

The slide also severely damaged and cut off a portion of State Route 530, the main road to the town of Darrington. As a result, it added over an hour to what was previously a 30-minute commute from Darrington to Arlington. This led to financial and logistical challenges for Darrington residents immediately after the incident, many of whom worked in Arlington. An alternate road for local traffic was opened approximately a week after the mudslide.

My Thoughts Pre-Response

The day of the mudslide, I was participating in a two-day National Transportation Safety Board training about an hour away from my home in Washington, DC. When we learned of the event, my manager made a few phone calls to advocate for me to be deployed for more experience. While at the training the next morning I was approved for deployment and booked a flight for later that afternoon. A co-worker drove me to my house, waited in the car while I packed as quickly as possible, and drove me to the airport.

On a personal note, things in my life were complicated at the time. I was married to my previous husband and our relationship was not in a good place. Leaving with short notice for 10 days and without the opportunity to say goodbye to my husband in person made an already difficult situation even more challenging. I was concerned about deploying at a particularly tense time in our relationship, but I was also relieved to be able to focus on something else and to help other people.

I was nervous about whether I was prepared to do the job and about how other Disaster Mental Health responders would receive me. I had only been in my job for about seven months and had not had the chance to meet many volunteers yet. Would they like me? Would they know how little disaster experience I had? How would my supervisor on the disaster response feel about supervising the new national headquarters Disaster Mental Health employee? While these thoughts were all running through my head, I was also looking forward my second deployment and the opportunity to help those impacted by the disaster.

My Response Experience

I was assigned to work in Darrington with about 50 other Red Cross responders, 10 of whom were Disaster Mental Health (DMH) volunteers.

With the road washed out, it took about two hours to drive from Darrington to Arlington (where other Red Crossers were assigned) so those assigned to work in Darrington slept there as well. And because the few hotel rooms in Darrington were taken by media crews, we stayed in a church hall converted into a staff shelter. We were each given our own cot and a chair to lay our things on. Without much privacy and the challenge of tuning out multiple snorers at once, it was difficult to get adequate rest, which undoubtedly added to the stress levels we all experienced.

Once I made it to Darrington, I was assigned to do outreach to the people living outside town, between Darrington and the mudslide. I was paired with John, another Red Cross DMH volunteer, and we were instructed to go door-to-door in the neighborhoods along Route 530 checking on people and offering Red Cross services. In addition to offering Disaster Mental Health and Disaster Health Services ourselves, we could encourage people to go to the community center in Darrington where they could get donated food boxes and gas cards to help with increased commuting costs.

We met Linda at one of the first houses we visited. She was married to the owner of a local company that had access to heavy machinery. As a result, her husband and his crew were helping with search and rescue/body recovery at the incident site. We stood in her driveway while she shared her experiences over the past four days. We learned that Linda and her husband had over 20 people staying at their house since the day of the mudslide, in spare beds, couches, and cots set up in every corner. Some of the guests were her husband's employees who wanted to be closer to the incident site so they could maximize the daylight hours to help with search and rescue. Others were friends and neighbors whose homes flooded when the river was washed out by the mudslide. Linda was making sure everyone was fed and had what they needed, and as a result she had not left her property for the past four days.

She told us that her husband's crew gathered at her house after sunset every night to drink together and share their experiences from that day. They were working alongside federal search and rescue teams, using their own equipment to move trees, cars, and parts of houses to find the bodies of those who were buried in the mudslide. Linda knew it was important for her husband and his employees to be able to spend time together at night and process their experiences. But she was also concerned that they were drinking more than usual, not sleeping enough, and that some were struggling emotionally but not willing to admit it or take a break from the work.

As Linda shared all of this, my first concern was her stress level. I used Psychological First Aid to support her and to encourage her to take care of herself while she was caring for so many others. She shared that getting a manicure would be a significant stress reliever, but she didn't think she could take the time. We talked about what would make it easier for her to be able to get a manicure and whether any of her friends might be willing to join her. While I could not make Linda prioritize self-care, I did my best to help her identify other small things she could do for herself during this intense time. I saw Linda a number of times over the following week and continued to check in on her stress level. A few days after our first meeting she was excited to tell me that she had finally left the property and she had freshly manicured nails to prove it.

My other major concern was Linda's husband and his crew. Linda was friendly with a number of the wives and girlfriends of her husband's employees and they shared similar concerns about their significant others. Linda made it clear that these were tough, hard-working men who were not likely to admit if they were struggling emotionally. Thankfully Linda was open to brainstorming ways we could support them. We decided that a major priority was to get SAMHSA's 24/7 Disaster Distress Helpline number in each of the crew members' hands. That way they could reach a counselor anonymously any time of the day or night. We came up with three ways to get the number in front of them. First, we taped it to the outside of the fridge where the beer was kept in Linda's garage so they would see it every time they got a drink. Second, I gave Linda small wallet-sized cards printed with coping tips and the Disaster Distress Helpline number and she gave them to the wives, girlfriends, and families of each of the men. Finally, we put the wallet-sized cards in discreet places in Linda's house and garage so the men could take the cards without anyone seeing them. Linda also added the cards to a bag of donated gear that were being distributed to each crew member.

Over the course of the next few days, John and I visited Linda several times to check in with her and to find out how her husband and his team were doing. During one visit, Linda invited us to stay into the evening so we could meet her husband and his crew. She would introduce us to the group as they arrived and they could decide if they wanted to talk to us or not. We were grateful that Linda trusted us enough to include us in such an intimate gathering.

When the first group arrived, Linda introduced me to her husband and I spoke to him for a while about his experience at the incident site. He pointed out a couple of crew members he was keeping an eye on because they were young or they had multiple "finds" that day. It was clear to me that these men and their families were doing the best they could to support and watch out for each other while facing unthinkable circumstances.

Because the Red Cross Disaster Mental Health team assigned to Darrington was small, we had the opportunity to bond and hear about the work that other team members were doing. We met every evening to discuss our experiences that day and get our assignments for the next day. In addition to the outreach John and I did, our DMH team provided services at multiple local churches, the break room of the local logging mill, the Sauk-Suiattle Indian Reservation, and the community center where people gathered every day for lunch and nightly for community meetings.

After five or six days of supporting Linda and others through outreach, I was asked to go to the incident site with another DMH responder, Anne, and two mass care workers who were providing coffee, water, and snacks to the first responders focused on body recovery. This was the first time Disaster Mental Health had been requested at the incident site and it was a great opportunity for us to better understand the full scope of the disaster.

We drove down Route 530 in a Red Cross Emergency Response Vehicle (ERV) and were waved through by the police officers manning the road closure. A quarter mile down the road we encountered the decontamination station that was administered by the Army Reserves. Every person, search dog, and vehicle that went to the incident site was required to be decontaminated on the way out.

When we reached the point where the ERV could not safely drive further, Anne and I continued on foot to the respite area where first responders and their search dogs could take breaks. It was a cold and rainy day and tents had been set up with heaters inside them to allow responders and their dogs to get warm. We delivered coffee and snacks and introduced ourselves to the small groups in each tent. The mood was quiet and somber and Anne and I each quickly concluded that this was not the time or place to strike up conversations. These responders were in the midst of doing a very difficult and demanding job and they were focused on the task at hand.

On our way out of the last tent we ran into one of the Darrington firefighters we had met a few days earlier. He offered to show us the incident site, so we followed him through a muddy patch of trees. Within 10 yards we were standing on the edge of a mile-wide expanse of churned up mud, logs, houses, cars, etc. We learned it was a mile deep in some places and that remains of 30 people were still buried beneath. There were excavating grids made of stakes and string laid out in sections to help the search teams stay organized. We could see roofs of cars and a mangled tricycle. In the distance large machines moved trees and other oversized items out of the way. I made a mental note to myself that the machine operators might be the crew members of Linda's husband. On the other side of the mud-covered area was a mountain without a face. Where a thick forest had been a week before, there was now a brown crater that merged with the surrounding muddy landscape like a glacier's tongue. While we stood there taking in this overwhelming scene, wafts of a pungent, distinct smell stung our noses. We looked at our guide and he quietly confirmed our suspicion, that we were smelling decomposing bodies.

Visiting the incident site had a significant impact on me emotionally. While our small group drove the ERV back to Darrington that afternoon, I knew that I needed to talk with someone about it. Because of my role as an employee and the new leader of the Red Cross Disaster Mental Health program, I wanted to avoid reaching out to a DMH responder for support if possible, although typically I would encourage any disaster worker to seek time with a Disaster Mental Health responder. After thinking through my options, I decided to ask the Red Cross Disaster Spiritual Care responder assigned to Darrington and she agreed to meet with me later that evening. She listened while I described my experience and cried from the intensity and sadness of it all. I slept deeply that night, and thanks to the time I spent getting my feelings off my chest, I was able to show up to work the next morning.

Another important aspect of self-care while on a disaster deployment is staying connected to home. My husband and I had agreed to talk on the phone every day that I was away. However, the three-hour time difference between the east and west coast proved to be more of a challenge than we anticipated. The days we were able to speak at a reasonable time for both of us, our conversations felt more difficult to me than supportive. The work I was doing seemed so much more important in the grand scheme of things than the small day-to-day things my husband could share. But at the same time, it felt trivial to try to explain the experiences I was having. How could he relate to them? In retrospect, I found that I had very little energy to put toward our relationship while in the midst of the life and death circumstances of a mass casualty disaster. However, I did fit in a few morning runs while I was in Darrington since running is an important part of my normal self-care routine. Given the emotional weight of this response in particular, it was essential for me to make time to clear my head and release my stress.

I was deployed to the mudslide response for two weeks, and while I was emotionally and physically exhausted by the end, I also struggled with leaving the operation. A community vigil was scheduled for the evening after I left and I was disappointed that I couldn't be there for it. Although I was only there a short time, I felt connected to the community and invested in the long-term wellbeing of individual community members. I knew that my role was short-term but it was difficult to separate myself emotionally, knowing that I could not be in touch with any of them after I left. I was comforted by the knowledge that my fellow DMH responders would likely be there for another couple of weeks and that the communities impacted by this tragic event were incredibly resilient and self-sufficient.

My Post-Response Adjustment

I left Washington state on Saturday with the intention of having Sunday to relax before attending a mandatory multi-day staff meeting starting Monday. Unfortunately, my connecting flight was cancelled, leaving me stranded overnight in the airport. When I finally got home on Sunday afternoon, I was completely exhausted. I did what I could to rest and recuperate that evening and showed up to work on Monday morning for the start of the meeting.

Walking into the conference room that morning, I felt overwhelmed. My experience felt enormous, heavy, and life-changing, but my co-workers knew none of it. When they asked me how my deployment was, they were looking for a 15-second response, which felt disingenuous to me. I did my best to craft an answer but was relieved when the meeting started and I didn't have to talk anymore. During our first break, my manager approached me, said she could tell I needed time to recuperate from my deployment, and told me that I was excused from the meeting. I was extremely relieved and was able to take the next three days off.

I was taking a weekly improv comedy class at the time and the next session was a few nights after I returned from deployment. I decided to go, thinking that it would be helpful. Our teacher introduced a free-association game to the class. When it was our turn, we were to say the phrase that the person before us said and then the first word or phrase that popped into our head. The person before me said "Washington" and the first thing I thought of were the words "dead bodies." As I said it, I was overwhelmed with emotion and started crying. The teacher noticed and stopped the game. Thankfully I had known these classmates for over a month and I felt comfortable sharing a little about my deployment with them. They listened and supported me as best they could. That night I learned the lesson to not jump back into regular life activities too quickly after deployment.

Lessons Learned

- Interactions you have as a Disaster Mental Health responder will not all feel significant. Not everyone will want to talk with you. And those who do may not be having particularly dramatic experiences. That is okay. It's still important for you to be there, supporting survivors and responders as best you can.
- Starting conversations with strangers or "milling around" can feel awkward at first. You will find your rhythm and what feels comfortable for you. Find ways to help in a tangible way (moving supplies, handing out water) while making yourself available for conversations with survivors and responders.
- You will not be in touch with survivors for long. Advocating for opportunities to improve an individual, family, or larger group's experiences, including connecting them with longer-term resources, can result in benefits that go far beyond what you alone can provide. Keep an eye out for opportunities as well as concerns/issues that should be elevated through your supervisor.
- I have found that normalizing what people have experienced and providing psychoeducation about typical stress responses are invaluable tools for a Disaster Mental Health responder. It's not uncommon for

people to be afraid or ashamed of the feelings they are having simply because they have never felt them before.

- Be grateful for people's willingness to share their experiences with you, likely without knowing you for more than a few minutes. They may be going through the worst day or week of their lives and it is a humbling privilege to be part of it.
- Don't let the perfect be the enemy of the good. Disaster responses are chaotic by nature and will never unfold the way textbooks describe. Typically, leaders will not have the precise number of resources they would like to have (human, material, etc.) to facilitate the ideal or "perfect" response. Do not let that stop you from using what you have in the best way you know how to serve disaster survivors and fellow responders.
- Know yourself. Be familiar with the specific signs that your mind and body give when you're reaching your maximum stress level, fatigue level, or when you simply need to make a change. Maybe your eyelid starts twitching when you're about to get sick or you get short-tempered when you've heard one too many heart-wrenching stories. Pay attention and acknowledge when your signs appear.
- Once you know your signs, know what helps you. Maybe you need a full or half day off, or you need to call home, exercise, or spend time alone. Once your body and mind start showing the signs that you need to do something, do not ignore them. Figure out what feels restorative for you and make time for it.

Chapter 4

2005 Hurricane Katrina in Louisiana

Gerald McCleery

I am a psychologist who in 2005 was the CEO of Link2Health Solutions, a subsidiary of the Mental Health Association of NYC, where I also served as Deputy Director. In those capacities, I was administering a variety of call center related programs such as LifeNet and the National Suicide Prevention Lifeline. I was also doing 211 and 311 board work. These call center numbers are used throughout the US as access numbers for essential community services. In terms of disaster mental health experience, after the attacks of 9/11, I operated the September 11th Fund and later the American Red Cross 9/11 Mental Health Benefit Programs.

Katrina hit on Monday, August 29, 2005. Based on a variety of circumstances, the United Way 211 center in Monroe, LA became the state-wide "go to" Katrina call center and information resource. During the first week my organization received a call from a United Way representative asking if we could send a volunteer to help the 211 call center in Monroe, which was already staggering under the pressure of the crisis. I offered to help as soon as I could get there. Two days later I flew to Little Rock, then drove to Louisiana to begin what, in hindsight, I consider to be among the most difficult and yet most rewarding weeks of my entire professional life.

The Pre-Disaster Community

The effects of Hurricane Katrina were felt in many areas on the Gulf Coast, including Mississippi, Alabama, and Louisiana, but the most profound impact was in New Orleans. Much of the flooding and many of the nearly 2,000 deaths in the region were the result of significant breaches and catastrophic failure of the levee system, disproportionately affecting high poverty areas of the city such as the Lower Ninth Ward.

New Orleans in 2005 had significant levels of poverty, and a predominantly African American population. An evacuation order was issued before Katrina, and while many people did evacuate, as many as 20 percent of the people either chose not to evacuate, or were unable to because they did not have the means to do so. The New Orleans Superdome was designated as a place that people could shelter who could not evacuate the city, but it subsequently became very clear that this site was not prepared logistically to safely shelter the many people who ultimately required immediate help and support.

The Disaster

At that time, Katrina was reported to be one of the largest and strongest hurricanes ever recorded to make landfall in the US. It hit on the morning of August 29 and proved to be an overwhelming disaster event for the people of New Orleans, with effects that continued to be felt long after the actual storm. These catastrophic effects were the result of both the physical impact of the storm itself, combined with notable system response failures. In the City of New Orleans, the storm surge caused approximately 23 breaches in canal levees and floodwalls. The final death toll reported by the Louisiana Department of Health was 1,464 people.

The catastrophic flooding effects occurred both acutely and over time. A number of weeks after the disaster I was able to visit the Lower Ninth Ward and I saw that the entire infrastructure in sections of the community was either severely damaged or was entirely gone – homes, schools, churches, community centers, and more had simply been demolished or washed away during the storm. Much of the remaining housing was uninhabitable.

Some people who had been unable to evacuate the city found emergency shelter at the Superdome, but the demand exceeded capacity there. Ultimately, many people who remained trapped at the Superdome were evacuated to emergency facilities in Houston, TX and elsewhere. The floodwaters did not immediately recede, and significant numbers of people had to be rescued by boat and by helicopter from their homes and from other locations where they had gathered. It was not until several days after the storm that an organized National Guard response began to restore some semblance of visible order and control.

My Thoughts Pre-Response

My organization received a call from the United Way within a few days of Hurricane Katrina asking if we could possibly contribute volunteers to help support the 211 call center in Monroe, Louisiana, which had become a key information resource for the state. Based on my own call center operations experience in New York including my familiarity with 211 operations, and based on the urgency they described, I made an on-the-spot commitment to go to Louisiana to help out.

Somewhat naively, I didn't immediately question whether I would be able to be helpful. How to get to Louisiana was the immediate question since travel to the New Orleans airport itself was not possible. I decided to fly to Little Rock, Arkansas, rent a car, and drive south approximately 175 miles to Monroe where the United Way had arranged temporary housing accommodations with local volunteers. Monroe itself is just under 300 miles from New Orleans and although it was impacted by the hurricane, it experienced nothing close to the effects that were felt in New Orleans.

I arrived at the United Way office late on the fifth day post-Katrina. My first impressions were memorable even to the present day. They had managed to clear out a conference room area where they had set up what looked like approximately 40 call station desks, most of which were unmanned. There were wires everywhere. There were many sheets of newsprint pasted somewhat haphazardly on the wall at the front of the room with information about local resources. One of the staff who greeted me explained that most of the people there at that moment were not in fact United Way staff, but rather were local volunteers. The actual staff had apparently worked around the clock in the first days after the storm and needed relief. I have a vivid memory of thinking to myself "these are not experienced call center people – rather they are local community people, such as mothers with teenage children in tow, trying to be helpful in any way that they can be." The first waves of real concern started to wash over me as I thought to myself "no one is really in charge here at the moment." This situation gradually improved during the week I was there, with improved orientation for new volunteers as they arrived onsite.

My Response Experience

My actual work began the next morning. My recollection is that by around 8 a.m. there were 20 to 25 volunteers of all types at work in the makeshift call center. The phones seemed to be ringing non-stop and continued to do so until the evening at this 24/7 operation. Within a minute of finishing one call the phone would ring again. I quickly learned that only a handful of the volunteers there had any mental health experience, and so those of us with such experience were grouped together in the rear of the room. We handled our share of the regular calls that were coming in, and the other responders were told that they could and should transfer "mental health calls" to this group. Whether or not such calls should be transferred was left to the discretion of the volunteer call-takers.

Several factors seemed to be driving the nature of the calls we received at that time, including:

- The extent of the profound storm devastation in the community. People had experienced life and death circumstances, widespread flooding continued for days, and entire communities such as the Lower Ninth Ward were virtually destroyed.

- Many regular systems (for example, health clinics and schools) were inoperable.
- Law enforcement systems were themselves overwhelmed.
- Information was very fragmentary and fluid.

The types of calls and callers varied tremendously. There were local calls requesting rescue and evacuation. There were basic calls seeking information about the possibility of accessing fresh food and water. There were many anxious non-local calls requesting information about missing persons; these were very difficult to process because at least for the first few days there was no type of central registry established to connect people in search of information about missing family members. There were calls from people in shelters who simply wanted to talk to someone about the trauma they had experienced. I remember receiving a call from a truck driver with a truckload of donated coffins, thinking they would be useful, but with no idea where they should be delivered. I received a call from a woman whose home was surrounded by water. Her husband relied on oxygen tanks that were now empty, and she called asking if there was anything we could do to help. A referral to the overwhelmed police was all we could offer. I was working from a safe and secure location, with a place to sleep and food to eat. I found taking repeated calls from people who were not in the same circumstances to be profoundly difficult. I recall thinking that while I could not resolve many of the circumstances of the callers I spoke with, what I could do was listen and communicate that I had some understanding of what they were experiencing. I also communicated that they could call back as often or for as long they needed to, and that someone would be available to speak with them. I did get a sense that for many people, our willingness to listen compassionately did offer some comfort in very difficult circumstances.

Around my third day there, the center director asked me if I would consider setting up some type of support group for the volunteer staff, and I agreed to do so. I set up a once-a-day, late afternoon group support meeting open to any staff or volunteers who cared to join. Around 8 to 10 staff attended each session. I did not have any particular protocol in hand to guide this work, rather, this was on-the-spot improvisation. Essentially, I recall offering everyone who attended the opportunity to share the experiences they had been having. Those experiences varied considerably. For example, at least a couple of the volunteers were people whose own homes and property had been severely damaged or destroyed by the storm. I found it extraordinary that they had volunteered to help others while coping with their own disaster response issues. My recollection is that virtually everyone felt somewhat overwhelmed by the experience. There was very little we could do to fix many of the problems that people were experiencing, or to lessen the pain they felt. And the relentless call volume was stressful in and of itself. We talked about and practiced the power of supportive listening. I remember the first session ending with a rather spontaneous "group hug" and feeling buoyed by the essential caring and goodness of a group of strangers thrust together under very difficult circumstances. I believe that this volunteer support group was somewhat helpful. I also believe that compassion fatigue had the effect of limiting the tenure of some of the volunteers. It helped that during my tenure, some new volunteers arrived almost daily at the call center to refresh the pool.

Two very difficult calls stand out in my memory. The first was from a single mother with two young children who was also looking after her own mother, who was apparently suffering from bipolar disorder and who at that moment was beginning to show manic symptoms. The bipolar woman's health care system provider was inaccessible. The woman called me very concerned about the safety of her children with one desperate question: "What should I do?" Having worked for a number of years in a state hospital admissions unit, I had a fair amount of direct experience dealing with people with uncontrolled mania. I decided that it was important to speak with the bipolar woman myself and I asked that she be put on the phone. I took the fact that she agreed to talk with me as a somewhat positive indication. Her speech was a bit pressured, but it was possible to have a fairly rational conversation. Based on the conversation I made a remote determination that she did retain some level of self-control and did not have any aggressive intentions to her daughter or to the children. I asked for and received a commitment from her to that effect. I spoke again to the woman who had called and suggested keeping some separation between her children and her mother to the extent that was possible, to continue to try to reach the health care provider, and to call back immediately if the situation deteriorated. I did not hear from her again.

The second call that stands out was one of the last ones I took during my week there, and one of the ones I found most troubling. The man whose call I took explained that he was calling me from a shelter, since his own home had been destroyed. He relayed to me that before and during the hurricane his wife (who had a terminal illness) was at a local nursing care facility. She had died during or immediately after the storm. Knowing that she was near death, he told me that for weeks he had been collecting things like hair and nail clippings so that he could have "pieces of her" even after she died. I found that odd but strangely poignant. He told me that all of this was washed away when his home was destroyed by the storm and that he found that devastating. I spent a considerable amount of time on the phone with him, mostly just listening to his story and attempting to offer some basic emotional support. He communicated that he was very appreciative that I had simply taken the time to listen.

This call had a profound impact on me. I remember getting up, walking outside, sitting on the curb, and crying uncontrollably. In that moment I decided that I had given all that I could. I went back to my room that night and drove back to Little Rock the next morning.

I had disaster response work experience several years earlier, running the September 11th Fund and American Red Cross Mental Health Benefit programs after the attacks of 9/11. At different points during my week in Louisiana, I recall thinking that this disaster was considerably different in a number of respects. Apart from the fact that a terrorist attack is different from a natural disaster, Katrina seemed like a rolling, progressively unfolding tragedy whose effects would not be fully understood for a long time. The loss of entire communities and infrastructure would take more time to fully understand. The chaos that followed after Katrina seemed somehow different than what happened after September 11th. And the resources that were being brought to bear in the Katrina response, while substantial, did not begin to match the levels of support that had been mobilized after September 11th. Some of the September 11th recovery responses were clearer and more specifically defined, in my opinion. For example, rebuilding the World Trade Center seemed like an inevitability in one form or another. Rebuilding the Lower Ninth Ward communities in New Orleans was less of a certainty. The health care system and resources in New Orleans were more permanently affected than comparable systems in New York City had been.

My own self-care practices that week were not especially well planned or effective. I remember feeling utterly exhausted at the end of each very long day, wanting nothing more than to sleep. The family that volunteered a place for me to stay while I was there was extremely gracious and supportive. I did keep in touch with my own family and my work back in New York, arranging for some additional volunteers from among my staff. I also remember that sharing information about the dire circumstances in Louisiana somehow relieved some of the stress. In hindsight, I think it would have been prudent to take more frequent breaks while I was manning the telephones.

My Post-Response Adjustment

I had an assortment of feelings as I headed home the next morning. First and foremost, I was grateful to be leaving behind the acute pressure of this disaster phone work. Doing this work was much more stressful than I imagined it was going to be. The devastation in New Orleans and surrounding areas was extensive and life-altering. Very little, if anything, was working after the storm. Even basic information was unreliable and difficult to come by or trust. Basic staples such as food and water were difficult to find for many people. So many people were suffering so much, and it seemed likely that this would continue for a considerable time (which it did). So, in addition to feeling grateful about being able to head home, I felt very sad that no amount of magic would be able to reverse or fix what people were enduring. There were no quick or easy remedies. This felt very overwhelming.

I think that the final component of my feelings was some sense of pride that I had at least tried to make a contribution. And I had shared that experience with a group of very wonderful, giving people, many of whom had endured their own storm-related difficulties. Although I know that I could not answer every question I received when the phones rang, nor could I fix every problem, I did also know from the responses I got that people sincerely appreciated a caring, supportive voice when they called, and a willingness to listen compassionately to what they were experiencing.

Lessons Learned

This was more than 12 years ago. I have since retired after more than 45 years of work in a variety of mental health settings and capacities. As I think back on that week in Louisiana, I have realized that this was one of the most difficult and challenging weeks of my entire professional life. It was a jolting reminder of the reality that sometimes, through no fault of their own, some really bad things can happen to really good people.

Another lesson I learned is that while 211 or 311 information and referral (I & R) systems are a valuable component of our human services systems, they are not designed to function as disaster mental health response systems. For example, even without a great deal of specialized training, 211 or 311 call center operators can provide up-to-date information about the location of emergency shelter, food, or clothing resources. Those same call center operators likely find it more difficult to respond adequately to the emotional needs of callers who have experienced disaster or terrorism related trauma. Large-scale disasters require a variety of system responses, and ideally there should be some level of pre-planning to mobilize coordinated I & R and DMH supports.

To someone deploying to a situation like this for the first time, I have several pieces of advice including:

- Know that this can be extremely stressful work. Plan on limiting your exposure to manageable periods of time.
- Perfection is usually impossible to achieve. Take comfort that you will be making a meaningful, humane contribution in support of people who have likely suffered considerable trauma.
- Share your experience with colleagues as you do the work. You can find strength and support from colleagues undergoing the same experience.
- Reflect afterwards on what you did and how it may have affected you. Share those experiences so that others can benefit from your perspective.
- Doing this work by phone, rather than face-to-face, comes with its own challenges. First, over the phone there are no visual cues to guide

the work, or to see how something you have said or asked has affected the caller (either positively or negatively). Also, you may only have one opportunity to get the support intervention right – it can be challenging for a caller to reach the same phone support staff member in a call center environment if additional or other follow up contact is desired.

- The primary point of contact following many disasters like Katrina or the World Trade Center attack, or a life-threatening pandemic, is over the phone. If you are asked to provide mental health support at a call center, understand that although you will not be at the physical center of the disaster, you will be in the middle of the action and doing very important crisis counseling.
- Many calls are requests for practical information (e.g., what roads are open, where is the nearest shelter, where to get food and water, where is the closest open pharmacy or health clinic). Although you may not have much information especially in the early stages, it is important that you get and disseminate as much of this accurate information as possible. In the early stages of disaster this is often the most important mental health intervention.

Chapter 5

2013 Wildfire in Yarnell, AZ

Margaret McGee-Smith

I'm a Registered Nurse with over 40 years of psychiatric nursing experience, mostly with the Buffalo Psychiatric Center. I spent 15 years on inpatient units caring for the seriously and persistently mentally ill, and 17 years in out-patient services as a Community Mental Health Nurse, providing onsite mental health assessments and counseling at a county jail. After retiring, I worked with substance abuse clients in community and residential settings.

I've always had a strong desire to help others. That, in combination with my poor impulse control, is what brought me to disaster mental health (DMH) work. In 1999, a co-worker asked if I would like to volunteer with the American Red Cross (ARC) DMH program. They were looking for volunteers to go to Puerto Rico to assist victims of Hurricane Floyd. Without prior knowledge regarding the ARC or how I might help anyone in a disaster, I immediately said yes. My first assignment was not a good experience. I ended up in North Carolina rather than Puerto Rico as I expected, I had no idea what I was doing, and unfortunately didn't get much support from other workers as the DMH activity was new to the Red Cross. Still, I knew that this was meaningful work and despite my negative introduction I was steadfast in my urge to continue. Since then I've served on over 70 disasters. I have grown in my ability to assist those who are affected as well as supporting fellow disaster response volunteers. I've developed leadership skills through on-the-job experience and training, and I presently serve as a Disaster Mental Health Chief. Most importantly I've developed friendships with volunteers from around the world.

The Pre-Disaster Community

Prescott is a city in Yavapai County, located in the Bradshaw Mountains of central Arizona at an elevation of 5,400 feet. According to the 2010 census, the population was 39,843. Almost half of the 15,000 households were made up of married couples with children. A majority of Prescott's residents were White, followed by Native Americans, African Americans, Asians, and Hispanic or Latino. The city was founded in 1864 and is home to the oldest rodeo in the country; to this day it maintains its western feel. It's the kind of place where everyone knows each other and has longed billed itself as "Everybody's Hometown."

The Prescott Fire Department, founded in 1885, is the oldest in Arizona. Prescott has a long history of fires. The most notable was in 1900 when a great fire destroyed most of the buildings in the Red Light district, including the Hotel Burke, opened in 1891 and previously advertised as "the only absolutely fire proof building" in the city. Until the Yarnell fire, no lives had ever been lost.

The Granite Mountain Hotshots were an elite group within the Prescott fire department. They were founded in 2002 as a fuel mitigation crew, and by 2008 had risen to the level of a Hotshot crew. The Hotshot title is given to crews of 20 men who meet high physical standards and have the ability to undertake dangerous and stressful assignments. They're trained in suppressing wildfires and are assigned to work in the hottest part of fires. They're also trained in search and rescue in addition to disaster response. All of the Granite Mountain crew members were well known in the community and lived in or around the Prescott area.

The Disaster

Yarnell, a small community of approximately 700 residents, is located 33 miles south of Prescott, on Highway 89. As you enter Yarnell there is a sign that states: "Where a desert breeze meets the mountain air." Its economy is based on ranching, mining, and services to travelers and retirees. Like much of the Southwest, Yarnell was experiencing a severe drought that, in combination with extreme heat, added to the potential for wildfires.

On June 28, 2013, at 5:36 p.m., lightning ignited a wildfire on government lands near Yarnell. Initially the fire was determined to be about one-half acre in size. On June 29, local crews engaged in firefighting operations, but the fire seemed insignificant and resources were even being sent back home. However, as the day wore on the fire began to grow rapidly. On the morning of June 30, the Granite Mountain Hotshots began their assignment on the Yarnell Hill Fire which had now expanded to 300 to 500 acres. The fire was advancing on the Glen Ilah subdivision in Yarnell, and strong winds with gusts up to 41 miles per hour were creating erratic fire behavior. At approximately 4:40 p.m. on June 30, the Granite Mountain Hotshot crew made its last radio broadcast about their situation: "Our escape route has been cut off. We are preparing a deployment site. I will give you a call when we are under the shelters." Nineteen of the 20 Hotshot crew members perished, making this the third deadliest U.S. wildfire since 1991. In addition to the 19 lives lost, there was a total evacuation of Yarnell and partial evacuation of Peeples Valley. The fire grew to over 8,300 acres, and at least 600 people were under mandatory evacuation orders; 127 buildings in Yarnell and two in Peeples Valley were destroyed. The fire was not fully contained until July 10.

My Thoughts Pre-Response

Disasters are never convenient, even when you indicate that you would like to deploy. When I was called, it was early summer in Western New York, my garden was in bloom (but needing work) and I was loving the weather.

I had listed myself as available to deploy on the Exchange, a tool we use to let the Red Cross know if we are available for an assignment, so when I received the call to go to Arizona as the Disaster Mental Health Lead for the Yarnell Hill Fire, I was not surprised. I was told that 19 firefighters had died, and the fire was not contained, so I would be working both an ongoing and multi-casualty disaster.

It's easy for me to get anxious when responding to a multi-casualty disaster, especially given that I would be acting as the Disaster Mental Health Lead. I did my best to stay calm and focus on what I needed to do to be ready to leave. I pulled out my "to-go bag" with all my essentials. I took time to pack the right clothes, both for the high temperatures outdoors and appropriate clothing to visit families or attend a memorial service.

While on the plane, I planned to thumb through my manager's handbook and then catch a nap since I knew I'd lose a few hours with the time change. As we say in the Red Cross, "Eat when you can, sleep when you can, sit when you can."

My Response Experience

On arrival in Phoenix, I immediately went to the rental car counter and picked up the car that was reserved for me. While at the airport I looked for other Red Cross volunteers who might need a ride to headquarters; we always try to share rides to reduce cost. I didn't see anyone with Red Cross paraphernalia milling about, so I headed to Prescott. I was glad I was alone so I could use the time driving the 99 miles to think what my first move would be when I arrived.

The headquarters was located in an unused retail store the size of a Kmart. The building was quite large and it seemed like there was more room than needed – but that changed quickly as different activities set up their work sites. I immediately reported to the Disaster Operation Lead who provided "situational awareness," meaning an overview of what was currently known about the event. He reported that a total evacuation of Yarnell and a partial evacuation of Peeples Valley had been ordered and the Red Cross was supporting two shelters, one at a college in Prescott, and the other at a high school in Maricopa County.

At least 600 people were impacted by the mandatory evacuation. The job director then introduced me to a local DMH staff member who had been working since the beginning of the disaster. I asked her who the Disaster Mental Health State Lead was and she stated, "that must be me, I am from the largest chapter in Arizona." I knew she wasn't the State Lead, but she had been working the Disaster Relief Operation (DRO) from the beginning and seemed eager to help. I asked that she remain at headquarters as my assistant. My goal was to mentor her and to provide her the opportunity to learn on the job. Mentoring is essential for capacity building and retention of Red Cross volunteers, and it's also extremely helpful to have someone local who is familiar with the geographical area and understands the impact the disaster had on the community.

In an overview of the services that Disaster Mental Health had been providing, she reported that local DMH, along with Health Services and Mass Care, had been staffing the shelters and supporting the families who were evacuated or had experienced the loss or damage of their home. She also stated that DMH had been present at Fire House #7 when the bodies of the Granite Mountain firemen had been returned to Prescott. Red Cross volunteers provided childcare and a canteen, but were not working with the families of the deceased at the fire station. The Red Cross typically offers condolence calls (now known as Integrated Care Teams) where Disaster Mental Health, Health Services, and Spiritual Care or Family Services meet with families of the deceased to provide emotional support and financial assistance when needed. In this case, the Health Services Lead advised me that we would not be making condolence calls. The fire department had already established teams made up of a police officer, a chaplain, and a trauma specialist and sent them in teams of three to each of the victims' families' homes. When I heard this, I was disappointed that we were not included in the teams, but not surprised. I've learned from previous multi-casualty disasters to be prepared to work in highly political environments where local responders may be protective of their "territory." In addition to the political environment, I also thought working with firefighter families might be challenging, as there is a unique bond between the families and the firefighters. This special relationship may prevent families from opening ranks and allowing others into their lives.

Even though we were unable to assist directly with the bereaved families, we were tasked with providing a "compassionate presence" at the memorial service for the firemen. The memorial service was going to be a large event, which included Vice President Biden as well as the one remaining fireman as speakers. Not only had we been asked to be present inside the auditorium but were also going to be stationed outside of the auditorium to provide additional support to members of the community who were unable to go inside the event.

The logistics involved with assigning Mental Health staff to the auditorium and various community outposts was a bit overwhelming. The task was given to me with limited time and direction to get completed. I had to assign DMH volunteers to the various posts, and noticed quickly that there were more sites than the roughly three dozen volunteers we had at the time. Additionally, there was a map posted on the wall with X's indicating sites where staff should be assigned; however, this map was stuck to the wall and couldn't be moved. What started as quite a daunting and overwhelming task ended up being completed within an hour with the help of another team member and her ideas on how to assign staff. As always, I was impressed with the willingness of volunteers to jump in and do whatever is needed to get the job done, and reminded that you never work alone in the Red Cross.

As we were setting up the assignments, I received a call from two Prescott mental health agencies, Northern Arizona Regional Behavioral Health Agency and the Crisis Response Network, Inc. offering to assist the Red Cross with the memorial service. This support was well received by the Disaster Operations Lead and came just at the right time for the DMH team. Both agencies closed for the day so they could work with the Red Cross. We paired up the staff from the local mental health providers with at least one DMH volunteer, enhancing our staff by 52 additional members and establishing an effective and collegial working relationship. The experience was positive for both the DMH team and local agencies, which led to the local agencies requesting further Red Cross training in Disaster Mental Health, something they had not had time to receive before the memorial. Compassionate presence at these kinds of events consists of just that, being present and ready to serve if needed. Our assignment at the memorial service was to offer tissues, water, and a handout that provided coping tips. I remember one young man who took a bottle of water from me but refused the tissues. I happened to stand next to him as the last alarm bell was rung for each of the firemen and tears were rolling down his face. He looked at me and I handed him the tissues. We never spoke, but I was there if needed.

In addition to mental health, a spiritual care volunteer was present and supported the operation, which was yet another reminder that in the Red Cross you never work alone. This gentleman truly made an impact on me and left me with many thoughts that I still carry with me. Prior to attending the memorial service, he assisted DMH staff in developing a handout with mental help tips that volunteers could give in addition to water and tissues to those attending the service. He also developed a list of what DMH volunteers might expect to occur at the memorial. The purpose of the list was to reduce the unknown and to prevent volunteers from being caught emotionally off guard, enabling them to better support those attending the memorial. He mentioned numerous expectations, but three that continue to stand out in my mind were the moving music of bagpipes, the ringing of the last alarm bell for each fireman lost, and most importantly his final guidance, which was "when you start to feel overwhelmed, remember, their pain is not your pain." I said this to myself many times that day, and many times since, when supporting others impacted by disasters.

DMH helpers not only attend to the well-being of disaster victims, but we're also responsible for looking after the well-being of volunteers. It is not often that our group is volunteering in a situation where we're responding to a multi-casualty loss and an ongoing disaster at the same time. Just as our spiritual care volunteer supported the Disaster Mental Health team with his list, he also suggested that we provide a private area where all staff could have an opportunity to take time to think about the firemen and the people they are trying to help. Since we were in a former retail space, I found a dressing room for the disabled which was just the right size for this space. He suggested that we print pictures and biographies of each of the 19 firemen that were lost, plus the one surviving fireman, and hang them on the walls; that we set up a small table with a white tablecloth and 19 flameless candles as well as another picture of the survivor; and that we place a green plant in the room. He stressed it had to be living, not plastic, which was symbolic of life. Lastly, he recommended that we include a book that the staff could sign with their names and where they were from.

Putting the room together was quite a team process for Disaster Mental Health. The room, including the activity of putting it together, was instrumental in helping the staff process their feelings about the loss of so many young lives. The plan was to give the book to the Prescott Fire Department at the end of the operation, letting them know how many people from so many different places cared about Prescott. At the end of the operation the spiritual care volunteer came to me and thanked me for all my help. I replied, "but you are the one with all ideas," and he responded, "but you made it happen," He was right – I made it happen, but none of it would have happened without his ideas. We were a great team and I will never forget what a privilege it was to work with him.

During each disaster I have volunteered for, I usually have at least one learning opportunity and this operation was no different. There was an elderly gentleman, a local retired psychologist, who offered to volunteer for the memorial service. A staff member working at the desk interviewed him, but after realizing he was no longer licensed, applied the standard rules regarding unlicensed mental health providers and turned him away. Instead of going with my heart and trying to figure out a way to utilize this potential volunteer, I trusted the rules and the decision of my staff member and didn't press further. At the end of the day I thought, "What harm would someone providing a compassionate presence at a memorial service really do?" I was aware of the impact that the Yarnell Hill Fire had on the community. Many in the area knew a member or family member of the Hotshot Team. It was in fact a community tragedy and it was important for all members of the community to take an active part in any recovery activity. I know that it's important to abide by Disaster Mental Health standards, but at the same time it's important to be compassionate to those who want to help and think more broadly when finding ways to utilize spontaneous volunteers. (I should note that the ARC rules on eligibility for DMH changed in 2016. Retired mental health professionals are now eligible if they held a license and maintained it in good standing upon retirement, and had no disciplinary action recorded by the issuing board.)

Even though condolence calls were not being made, DMH volunteers were extremely busy supporting evacuated residents and other community members. There were 34 disaster mental health volunteers assigned to the disaster operation, mostly licensed mental health counselors followed by social workers, psychologists, psychiatric nurses, and one psychiatrist (who did an expert job ironing the white tablecloth for the memorial room). In addition to assisting with the memorial service, they made home visits, provided coverage at designated service sites, and assisted at the shelters. Most importantly, they supported all Red Cross staff assigned to the operation.

Because this was both a natural and a mass casualty disaster, additional emotional support was provided for DMH as well as all volunteers. In addition to the memorial room, a support group was offered by DMH daily, where volunteers could share any issues that arose for them throughout that day. Spiritual care often provided a moment of reflection following our morning meeting, and on the day of the memorial service, members of the Yavapai Tribe performed a special native blessing for all the volunteers who wished to take part.

My Post-Response Adjustment

When I return home from a disaster, I try to re-establish my normal routine as quickly as possible. I start by calling friends to let them know I'm back, and try to remember how my TV remote works and the numbers of my favorite channels. I talk to my family about the experience and spend time with them. I know that my family misses me, but they're proud of my volunteer work and discuss my assignments with their friends and co-workers.

When I returned home from this disaster, I was relieved to step off the plane into 70-degree weather; Arizona heat is almost unbearable for this northeast gal. The first thing I did when I arrived home was to greet my husband, then the dog, and then I wrote my name in the dust on the living room table. My family asked about the disaster and what my role was, but they were mostly glad I was home and did not ask too many questions. Several neighbors offered thanks to me for going to the disaster which I graciously accepted.

Disasters can be all-consuming. We work long hours, spend our days and nights together, talk about all of the challenges we've faced, eat our meals together, and even spend our days off together. It's easy to forget that we have another life at home. What I find most often when I come home from any disaster assignment is that everyone has moved on while I am just beginning to process what has happened. I feel I am emotionally weeks behind everyone else and it can take me some time to catch up. Many people will ask me about the disaster, but most want a very superficial explanation. At some point, a DMH volunteer will call me to check in and see how I am doing and re-cap my experience. One of the things I find most helpful when I get home is talking to others who have served on disasters. They ask probing questions and tend to be good listeners. As I mentioned, disasters are never convenient, and even though it takes a few days to get back to "normal," I can't think of a more meaningful way to be a positive force in this world.

Lessons Learned

- It's okay not to know it all – things change quickly in the Red Cross and you may have missed the last memo. Just ask.
- As I stated earlier, it's important to rest when you can rest, eat when you can eat, and sit when you can sit. When I hear volunteers say that they're not hungry when food is being served, I strongly advise them to take advantage of the meal. Things can change quickly on a disaster and you may find yourself wishing for an MRE (Meals Ready to Eat). The same goes for resting and sitting: Do it when you can.
- It's especially important to avoid being tired. Most of my judgment errors have occurred when I was tired. I don't mean just a lack of sleep, but a lack of down time. Many volunteers resist taking a day off. This often leads to bad judgment calls or increased irritation with co-workers and clients. Whenever I've been abrupt or agitated with a volunteer it was a direct result of exhaustion.
- Don't come to work sick. This results in your co-workers becoming ill, but worst of all you can spread your illness to disaster clients whose immune systems are already depleted by the increased stress in their lives. Ridiculously simple advice, but I wish I could tell you how many volunteers come to work sick.
- When assigned to a multi-casualty disaster be sure to pack clothing appropriate for a memorial service. I've worked several assignments where I've had to ask the volunteer to either change clothes or purchase clothing appropriate for a home visit or memorial service.

- Be sensitive to the spontaneous local volunteer (now called Event Based Volunteer). Refer them to the appropriate Red Cross resources, and find ways that they may support their community. I still regret what occurred with the retired psychologist whose offer of help we did not accept and vowed that it would not occur again if I were able to prevent it.
- Remember that a "compassionate presence" may be all that is required of you. Be comfortable with that.

Chapter 6

2016 Floods in Mississippi

William L. Martin

I retired from a private clinical psychology practice in 2000 and was happily cruising with my wife on a sailboat until 2005 found us on the Mississippi Gulf Coast when Katrina came visiting. Four or five days later, while checking on my damaged boat, I came upon a group of Red Cross volunteers setting up an Emergency Aid Station and casually enquired, "could you use a clinical psychologist?"

Since then, I have been active in Red Cross Disaster Mental Health (DMH) training nationally and locally. I have done numerous national deployments as a "foot soldier," but more typically work in leadership roles within DMH. In the Red Cross, I felt there was an opportunity for me to utilize my clinical skills and the management and leadership experiences I had acquired through my military career. As the Red Cross DMH Adviser for Mississippi, I was regularly called upon to respond to and lead mental health services in disasters in the state.

On becoming an Event Based Volunteer, I sat down and jotted notes on what I remembered about immediate mental health support in crisis, much of this based on my experience as a Marine combat veteran and a Navy officer. The old action words of military psychology were helpful: ***Immediacy*** (get there as quickly as possible), ***proximity*** (go to where the trauma occurred), and ***expectations*** (see survivors as impacted, but not helpless and impaired) continue to guide my interventions.

The Pre-Disaster Community

Mississippi has unfortunately experienced a high frequency of natural disasters. Tornadoes are common. Flooding is recurrent, and the coastal area is vulnerable to tropical storms and hurricanes. From the north, through the Delta and on the coast, residents have been impacted multiple times. Mississippi is geographically diverse with only a few cities of moderate size; most of its population is dispersed in more rural, smaller towns.

It typically ranks among the most impoverished of states, with predictable limitations on infrastructure and support to its residents.

The frequency of natural disasters has provided opportunities to learn how to respond. The influx of Federal mitigation funds, especially since Katrina, has led to more resources but preparedness and training are challenged by a high turnover among disaster responders. This has been a negative factor in the state and for the Red Cross.

Mississippians are personally resilient and adaptive, but even in non-disaster settings the resources are always limited, while the need is always infinite. Significant socio-economic, cultural, and racial differences are pronounced in both rural and urban areas. There are clusters of embedded poverty distributed geographically. Small communities, many unincorporated, are defined by schools and churches. Religious leaders are a significant factor in daily community life. "Us versus Them" issues can emerge along political or social/cultural lines.

Education in the state is a continuing challenge with the associated limitations for economic development. Health care resources, physical and mental, are clustered around larger communities and are less available in more rural areas. The state does have an effective network of regional Community Mental Health Centers, although their resources are challenged even during non-disaster periods.

The Disaster

In early March 2016, heavy rainfall began to impact the Mississippi Delta over a week and both gradual and flash flooding began spreading into numerous communities and rural neighborhoods. Many areas had limited warning as the flooding began after dark. Flooded roads and vehicles complicated evacuations and response. Flooding became more pronounced in the northwestern Delta and into the southeastern area with 15 counties becoming significantly affected. Many of the areas had clusters of individuals who were especially vulnerable because of chronic health needs, disability, low socio-economic status, and limited resources for self-care and transportation.

Shelters were initially opened in each affected county; many were managed by churches and community groups and supported by the Red Cross. As is typical, not all were populated by survivors as Mississippians tend to rely on self, family, and friends, but all required support. Mobile feeding and fixed feeding sites (typically collocated with shelters) were established over time. The extensive flooding, continuing rain, and movement of high water through numerous watersheds led to the need for extended evacuations and prolonged need for alternate housing, which was already a critical need in most impacted communities.

My Thoughts Pre-Response

I was notified by the Assistant Director for Operations for the Red Cross response that a state-wide Disaster Response Operation (DRO) was being initiated and I was selected as the Disaster Mental Health Chief for the operation. Being retired, and with my wife, Shirley, being home to take care of our Golden Retriever, Buck, I was available.

The first challenge is always situational awareness. From previous response experiences I knew to expect the early chaos, the scramble of trying to identify local resources and prioritize initial responses, all complicated by the limited intelligence available. The frantic rush to gain situational awareness and conceptually organize a response plan, the intense operational tempo early in a DRO, and the struggle to communicate and coordinate with others across the state, is always a personal and a professional challenge.

Decisions have to be made and it is critical to remember that these decisions must be made with incomplete information. Uncertainty about those early decisions is both frightening and invigorating. One must remember that disaster response is a series of actions, each taken in the "here and now" and each an effort to make things a little better rather than a little worse. This is the process of disaster response whether seen from the perspective of the disaster director, the mental health responder, or the survivor. I felt anxiously confident I could have a positive effect over time, both through tactical decisions I made and through personal encounters with leadership, workers, and survivors.

My Response Experience

At the macro level, a disaster response is defined by the organizational infrastructure of the responding organization. There are many moving parts and these are not well-lubricated, hence there is heat, a grinding friction, if all are not moving toward a common purpose. Leadership and management are critical. The concept of operations chosen and the personalities involved greatly influence the experience of the mental health practitioner. The experiences and skills of the responders are also instrumental in defining the impact and outcome of each individual's interventions.

The first tasks, even for the practitioner, are always conceptual and involve appreciating the nature and scope of the disaster and those impacted while deciding what DMH service delivery plan would be most effective. The initial concept for operations from DRO leadership established a central, bare-bones headquarters staff operating out of Jackson in central Mississippi, with operations to be directed and supervised from North and South Districts located about five hours apart.

While the Department of Human Services in Mississippi has primary responsibility for shelters, the Red Cross supports and/or staffs these shelters and provides material resources. I reached out to our Community Mental Health Center partners across the state, knowing from experience that our state DMH volunteers would be largely unable to respond because of work commitments or for personal reasons. I asked that these partners provide, as they have in the past, as much presence at the shelters as possible during the critical early days while we were awaiting the arrival of Red Cross DMH workers. As it turned out, shelter populations were small and transient. Those impacted either found other accommodations or chose to stay in their flood-impacted homes in challenging circumstances. Only one shelter remained open over time and that closed by day 15.

As DMH workers arrived, they would provide itinerating and on-call support to shelters in addition to outreach responsibilities. It was essential that DMH workers be mobile and flexible as to their roles, and also essential they reach out to where survivors were located across the dispersed geographic areas. That meant physically basing and housing the workers in dispersed locations to avoid wasteful time spent traveling. I knew that would create challenges for management, supervision, and support.

In Mississippi Red Cross, we prioritize early outreach to affected areas using mobile outreach teams that typically operate from temporary outdoor sites referred to as Points of Presence (PoPs). As the project lead coordinating these PoPs, I made a request to bring in sufficient DMH volunteers from around the country to resource this plan. The intent was to staff the central headquarters minimally, so I was asked to locate myself in the South District. This facilitated working with the South District Director in coordinating initial efforts toward deploying PoPs, but it complicated my communications with the North District. As the North and South District DMH managers arrived, I oriented each to the disaster and shared the service delivery plan and initial priorities, urging them to work with their District Directors in coordinating PoP efforts as soon as resources were on the ground. It is always frustrating to not be able to personally meet and orient each of the DMH workers as they arrive, but that is a reality of geographically dispersed, district-based operations.

Once the PoP plan was agreed upon by leadership, quick training was conducted for workers. Working with community leadership, sites were selected and multiple teams hit the field. Neighborhood by neighborhood we were going to the client, establishing that critical human engagement and delivering material support as well. As a casework plan had by then been approved and Red Cross Casework was eager to get started, we expanded the PoP model, organizing what we called Mini-Community Recovery Centers where caseworkers actively opened client cases and then assisted clients in acquiring needed materials. DMH would be a central feature at these sites, acting as site leads and to "meet and greet" clients, manage crowd/traffic flow, and manage client expectations. Clients were to be given the opportunity, but never pressured, to tell their story. DMH would provide a compassionate presence, make that critical "human to human" connection, and engage, as needed, in critical assessments and interventions.

The intervention model I use and teach through our orientation process emphasizes an awareness that response and recovery from disaster is a process that occurs over time and the goal is to always encourage clients/ survivors to assume personal responsibility and control, where possible, over their own recovery. Giving clients the opportunity to make decisions, to take positive action steps, is both subtle (i.e., "Would you like one bottle of water or two?") and obvious (i.e., "We have shelters available if you feel your home is now unsafe or unhealthy").

The intervention starts with DMH approaching the client, introducing him or herself by name and role, asking for informed consent (i.e., "Can we talk for a few minutes?"), and offering an opportunity for the client to tell their story. As we use active listening skills, we are essentially triaging the "Three R's" of Red Cross DMH protocol: Reactions, Risks, and Resiliency. We observe and note reactions (i.e., that set of stress-induced responses to disaster) in order to identify those responses – cognitive, behavioral, or physiological – that are complicating or interfering with recovery. These problematic reactions become the focus for the set of typically simple coping skills (i.e., anxiety management, thought stopping, and behavioral actions) that DMH teaches and actively coaches, as we intervene to stabilize or mitigate. Through what amounts to cognitive restructuring, we try to normalize the reactions (i.e., "These are understandable reactions … it is the disaster that is abnormal") and direct optimal steps toward recovery.

A major part of this direct intervention is to model an awareness that all coping occurs in the "here and now." It is as much an attitude as a skill. We must recognize that for the practitioner or client caught up in the mass of the disaster, all that has happened, or all that must be done over time, is simply overwhelming. It is only in the immediate present that we can take the steps to make things a little better rather than a little worse. Repeating that simple process time after time moves us all down the road of recovery.

The DRO evolved and the service delivery plan and priorities changed late in the second week, as casework outreached to as yet unreached individuals and recovery (versus response) efforts became the central focus. DMH operations moved into more of a support role, responding to "hot shots" (i.e., immediate outreach in response to DMH referrals) and clearing cases where clients had been more routinely referred to DMH by other Red Cross workers. Some of this requires mobile teams doing outreach, but much is done via telephone contacts: checking for unmet needs, making referrals, or providing resource information.

The intense tempo of earlier operations, the 12–14-hour days, slows somewhat at this stage, but this "slower" pace is itself demanding. This is when Red Cross workers, including DMH, start thinking about going home, and start questioning themselves about the value of their engagement, feeling underemployed or dissatisfied with their accomplishments. This is when workers began to realize that they will leave to return home with so much still left to be done. This is when mental health leadership at the manager and supervisor level has to be very active in support of all workers. I have always felt that mental health leadership should be about 80 percent support and only 20 percent direction. Support includes making sure workers have situational awareness, providing the tools to take care of themselves and do their jobs, and helping workers understand and appreciate the value of their contribution so they may experience a sense of personal accomplishment. While this support is always necessary, it is even more important as things slow down.

Throughout this DRO, I was able to spend time at our outreach sites working directly with clients and colleagues. It was there, confronted with so many in distress, so many needs and wants, and so few answers and solutions, that I felt the most personal distress and opportunity. It is so easy to slip into that disaster-driven sense of being overwhelmed, lost in all that needs to be done, all those people in need, and to feel personally inadequate to the challenge. It seems so easy to say – yet so terribly hard to remember – to always go back to "what can I do, right now, with this client, to make things a little better rather that a little worse?" That effort to empower the client in their own recovery in fact empowers me to hang in there, to engage, to be personally committed, to feel more satisfied with the value my skills and effort bring to the challenge.

I know from previous experiences how critical it is to pace oneself; to know when to take a break and when the work day is over. The daily routine is grinding, typically 12–14-hour days and the telephone is always on. I am usually up before dawn, catching up on email, working on situational awareness, setting priorities, working on mid-course corrections, planning my day. Operations start early with activity and team meetings for the day's detailed assignments, perhaps loading vehicles with disaster emergency supplies, and coordinating with other activities. There is a rush to get this done quickly and to get workers and oneself into the field. Through the day and evening there are always unforeseen situations that emerge, requiring problem-solving. It is always challenging to try to stay proactive, to plan ahead and not be reactive. It is during the reactive situations that we all feel the most intense stress.

In many ways, a DMH worker is never "off" work. Always sharing a motel room or staff shelter with other workers (a standard Red Cross practice) complicates time off if the roommate happens to want advice about a favorite but neurotic aunt, or just wants to chat into the later hours. Social time, perhaps sharing a meal, can be challenging in that a casual exchange with co-workers can quickly create a dual relationship conflict. Learning to set boundaries becomes very important in self-care. I find it helpful to take a break during the day, to take a walk around the parking lot and just get my head out of the weeds – to reflect on "Where am I?" and "What do I need to be working on now?"

I was back working out of the South District by day 15 and had a very experienced DMH Manager on the job in the North. Operations there would continue but the South District was wrapping up response operations and moving to recovery efforts. It was time to downsize. Leaving the job, I said my goodbyes to DMH workers, transitioned leadership to the DMH Manager in the North, did my final reports to leadership, and out-processed to return home.

My Post-Response Adjustment

It is always difficult to leave a DRO. The work is always unfinished. While every worker gets an evaluation before leaving, I always seem to leave wanting more feedback, more reassurance that my contribution has been worthwhile. I think we all feel that … but then that may just reflect some neediness on my part. I try to mentally review the operation and my decisions and actions, to remind myself of accomplishments, and not just focus on the continuing needs. Not having had more personal contact with all the DMH workers is always frustrating. Geography and time impose boundaries. In a practice carried over from my military career, I do my own personal debrief, writing a narrative answering: what happened, what went right, what went wrong, and why did it go wrong. This is my effort to grow professionally from lessons learned.

Walking out the door on that final day is difficult, even painful, for me. I always feel at a loss, going from the intense tempo of operations and engagement to … nothing. My wife is well acquainted with my moodiness on arriving home. There is the excitement of getting home, the frenzy of being greeted by my Golden Retriever, Buck. Then the brief story of "how was it?" before I dump the accumulated laundry and collapse into my chair, 90-pound lap dog in place, and start catching up on the weeks of sleep deprivation. Over the next several days of lawn mowing, long walks, and reflection, I gradually move back into a "normal" routine. But the intrusive memories of things that went well, and those things that didn't go so well, things I wish I had done differently – they persist.

Lessons Learned

Every DRO is different but there are some fundamentals that endure and unfortunately must be learned and relearned through the hard school of personal experience.

- Plan … don't react.
- Build consensus where possible, use direction where not.
- Ultimately, it is about engagement and relationships with others, clients and staff. That is the value and impact … and that can get lost in the rush to just do something.
- It is important to have a "battle buddy" with whom one can just relax. I was fortunate on this DRO to have a close friend and respected DMH colleague available. We have worked together and supported one another before, and we made an effort to protect a time block in the evening for us to have dinner together. That became valuable decompression time for both of us.
- I always need to remember that when I am helping the client to better manage those normal but disruptive reactions to a disaster, to cognitively engage or re-engage in their own recovery, to reconnect with their pre-disaster life supports and to know how important all that is, then I am being instrumental in their struggle. That's the value added.
- I need to deliberately remember it is not up to me to "rescue" this client. I am part of a team, and the client, the survivor, is also a team member, and that team is working toward resourcing recovery. That process, with all its starts and stops, is only accomplished one step at a time.
- I try to remember … we don't solve problems, we empower individuals to be responsible for themselves, for what they can do for their recovery, and all of that is in the "here and now." When we, responders and survivors, feel overwhelmed, we need to get back to that here and now.

Chapter 7

2011 Tornado in Joplin, MO

Richard Bigelow

In 2001, I retired from a blended career in direct practice of Clinical Social Work and Hospital Administration, after working in public and private psychiatric facilities for 29 years. Amid hobbies of fishing and travel, I decided to work as a volunteer. I created and worked in various programs through my church in La Feria, Texas.

When Hurricane Katrina hit the Gulf Coast in 2005, I signed up and was immediately sent to work as an American Red Cross DMH volunteer at the huge shelter operation at the Astrodome in Houston, TX and have continued to work with my local chapter. Until recently I was the only licensed DMH volunteer on call to the casework staff 24/7. I'm also trained as a caseworker and I enjoy responding to local disasters (usually house fires).

Generally, I try to deploy outside of my region once a year. I've deployed 11 times in 13 years. I'm a DMH supervisor and have served as a manager. However, when I deploy I try to go out as a service assistant (an entry level position) because it puts me on the front lines with clients and keeps me from the necessary, but tedious, administrative duties.

The Pre-Disaster Community

The city of Joplin is located in the southwest corner of the state of Missouri. According to the 2010 Census there were 50,150 people (90 percent White, 2.6 percent African American, 2.5 percent Hispanic; median age 34.7 and median income $35,000). Joplin serves as a center for shopping, education, and health care for a large rural area including southeast Kansas, northeast Oklahoma, and northwest Arkansas. Green, heavily forested hills surround the city, while many large chain stores and restaurants surround the old downtown. It's home to Missouri Southern State University and seven other small colleges. The city boasts a rich pioneer history dating back to 1840, and has the look and feel of most of the other Midwestern towns I have visited.

Joplin sits in what is commonly called Tornado Alley, the central strip of the U.S. that's most subject to frequent tornadoes. This storm was the third to strike the city since 1971. Emergency plans were in place and they had a warning system. Civil defense sirens were sounded 20 minutes before it hit, but many did not hear them and others ignored them because of past false alarms. No one was really prepared for a storm of this magnitude.

The Disaster

On Sunday, May 22, 2011 at approximately 5 p.m., an EF-5 (the highest damage category possible) multiple vortex tornado hit the southern end of Joplin, traveling east to west for 21 miles. It was nearly a mile across at its widest point. Winds were estimated at 250 m.p.h.

This was the seventh deadliest tornado in US history, leaving 158 dead and 1,150 injured. It is also considered the costliest, causing $2.8 billion in damage. Seven thousand houses were destroyed along with many businesses. Hundreds of cars and trucks were tossed and mangled beyond recognition. One nursing home was destroyed and all 21 residents were killed. A large hospital took a direct hit, but remained standing; the six patients who died there were on ventilators when power was cut off and the emergency generator failed. The hospital later had to be torn down.

Joplin High School was totally destroyed, but no one was in the building as graduation ceremonies had just concluded at the university stadium three miles north. Many local government infrastructure buildings were destroyed, including police, fire, and mental health facilities, so Joplin officials had to rely on emergency crews and vehicles from neighboring communities for assistance. Hundreds of huge hardwood trees were pulled out of the ground with their root systems attached, leaving large craters. Other trees were twisted off at the trunk, leaving jagged spires sticking up. The path of the tornado, dubbed "the footprint," was inaccessible for several days because of all the debris. Many severely injured people told of having to walk for nearly a mile to get help.

My Thoughts Pre-Response

I don't remember having any misgivings pre-deployment. This was not my first rodeo and I was fairly confident in my skills. The need was great, I was asked to go, and I had the available time. I had previously deployed to disasters where I worked with survivors who had lost loved ones and didn't have any trouble dealing with my own emotions at the time, so I expected that to be the case here as well.

Going in, I knew something about the scope of the devastation. One ARC criterion for making a mental health referral is that the survivor "knows someone who was killed." This included nearly everyone in Joplin, where ARC eventually logged 6,800 mental health contacts. Normal deployments are for two weeks. I signed up for three. In hindsight the third week was a mistake. The impact that the destruction and carnage had on me was greater than I imagined. I had to work hard to stay on top of my own mental health.

My Response Experience

I arrived in Joplin and started working on Sunday, May 29, one week after the tornado. The news of the day was that they had just found the body of a boy who had been missing all week. Driving home with his father after his graduation ceremony, he had called home to say they were trying to outrun the storm and to request the family open the garage door for their arrival. They did not make it. Their SUV was picked up and thrown into a ditch. The boy had been sucked through the open sunroof while the father tried to hold on to him. The boy's body had finally been found in a nearby pond covered with debris. Hearing this story upon arrival, the horror of Joplin became real to me.

I signed in at ARC Headquarters, located on the north side of town where there was no visible damage. Driving south towards the "footprint" there was increasingly visible damage. At first, I just saw a lot of downed tree limbs and missing shingles. Closer to the footprint there were houses still standing, but with major damage. It was still green and lush with lots of trees. Then I crossed a distinct line where there were no longer any trees or green grass, and the grey ground looked as if it had been tilled. Ugly, twisted stumps and piles of debris were everywhere. I was in the footprint for the first time. It was surreal, like being on the set of an apocalyptic movie. I can't really explain the flood of emotions that hit me, but I will never forget them.

Before describing some of the more memorable interactions I had with clients and ARC staff, I'll describe my general approach to DMH. In nearly all of my contacts I boldly wade in (see the Lessons Learned section for more about how I've learned to do this), armed with well-practiced listening and assessment skills, and provide basic psychological first aid. With most of my clients in any disaster, I:

1 Give them permission to feel their feelings.
2 Provide an opening for them to tell their stories.
3 Have them prioritize and tackle one task at a time.
4 Encourage them to take care of themselves first.
5 Encourage them to help someone else.

In Joplin I'd estimate that this strategy was effective in 90 percent of my cases. The other 10 percent either needed immediate connection to local mental health resources or I believed that they would need to connect later in their recovery. It's important to know how to make those connections on the very first day. Fortunately, Joplin was backed up by state-wide resources and regional mental health coverage was good (not always the case).

My first week assignment was a rotation of my two favorite jobs, Community Outreach and Sheltering. ARC sets up Community Distribution Centers, distributing water, hygiene items, gloves, cleaning supplies, tools, etc. A colleague and I loaded up our car with ice chests full of cold water and supplies and drove around the affected neighborhoods, stopping to talk with people wherever we found them.

I remember one stop where several neighbors were helping an elderly lady who lived alone get the water damaged furniture out of the house and make necessary repairs to a large part of a missing roof. I helped a guy move a damaged carpet to the dumpster. I asked him if he was related to the lady. He told me he had just met her, but he wanted to help her get her roof repaired before the next rainstorm. He told me he had patched his own roof with a blue tarp, but saw the greater need to get her roof repaired. I have seen this kind of neighbor helping neighbor many times at every disaster, and it's always very satisfying to see people whose own recovery is progressing so well that they're able to turn to helping others in need.

Later, I stopped by one of the outlying police stations and was invited to have lunch, and I entered into one of those interactions that make disaster response work so intense, and so rewarding. It's very common for people from out of town to show up with their own BBQ pit and just start feeding people. As a food hound I go out of the way to find them. That day there was a large group of Mennonite families working. This is a faith-based group that often arrives after disasters to try to help in whatever ways they can. The men were coverall-clad, had their own chain saws, and were making firewood out of the thousands of downed trees. The women were handing out homemade desserts (yes, they had rhubarb pie).

I noticed a group of law enforcement types gathered at one end of a large pavilion having lunch, so I waded in to eat with them. After some small talk, establishing where everybody was from, I learned of their mission: It turned out these guys were searching the woods with cadaver dogs, hunting for and bagging body parts. I just said, "I can't even imagine." It wasn't the time or place to probe them about any mental health needs, but just by being there and initiating a casual conversation, I indicated my availability. And, no surprise, one of them sort of hung back at the end and needed to tell his story. He was a young deputy sheriff with young children who was overwhelmed by the carnage. He told me that when they found "something" they had to try to determine if it was animal or human. We talked about many things, including the importance of self-care. He told me about his support system, including the fact that they had access to counselors through the department. Sometimes these guys are afraid that utilizing the department "shrink" will be seen as weakness in their macho world. He seemed to think it would be a good thing. I agreed with him.

These kinds of "tough guys" are at every disaster. I seek them out and just wade in. My red ARC vest gets me access. I usually don't tell them my job unless they ask. Sometimes after establishing rapport I will tell them I'm DMH and ask if they know someone I should talk to. I've received many referrals in this way. I give them my personal cellphone number and have never regretted it.

My second day assignment was at the shelter located on the University campus. I always check in with the director and the nurses' station, ask them for referrals, and give them my phone number. Then I wander around looking for people who are alone or who look sad or stressed out.

People in shelters typically arrange their cots to form little "communities" of families and friends. In one such community a young single mother seemed to be in charge. Staff had already warned me that she was angrily and loudly complaining about many things. Once again, I waded in. She told me her story. I told her that shelters often feel disorganized and chaotic, and invited her to come up with some ways to make it better. I enlisted her help in identifying people who might need to talk to someone. Later that day her youngest son was hitting people with a plastic sword. She took away the sword and gave it to me and said, "don't let him have it." The boy started attacking me and the only way I could stop him was to sit down in a chair and wrap him the way I have seen many special education teachers do. I told him I would let him go when he could control himself and not attack me. It took him about five minutes to calm down, then I let him go. He asked me about his sword and I told him that was up to his mother. The mother also settled down and organized a talent show later in the week. The boy and I became good friends and played ball a couple of times in the gym.

This kind of intervention is really not in any Red Cross training manual, but DMH volunteers need to be able to handle angry clients without internalizing it. In my experience, for about a third of the people who get really angry, it's because FEMA or the Red Cross has turned down their request for financial assistance. My job then is to calm the waters, while explaining why we won't be providing financial assistance yet still trying to protect the image of the Red Cross. Usually I can de-escalate the situation by just gluing my ass to a chair and listening empathically to their story. Sometimes I can't. I have been ordered out of a house or two, but I have not yet been threatened with violence.

During my second week I attended training for a new ARC program (Integrated Care Condolence Team). A four-member team (Mental Health, Nurse, Chaplain, and Caseworker) were assigned to make contact with the families of the deceased, offering services and $1,000 in burial-related expenses. Immediately after the training I was asked to join a team that was already working. The DMH worker had alienated the team and was being replaced. Apparently, the worker saw herself as an expert in grief counseling and was trying to teach basic Kubler-Ross to the team and the clients. She had been the record keeper for the team and had the information on the clients and the schedule. My first task was to get that information from her. It took about an hour to meet with her, hear her story and help her with her feelings of betrayal. She told me she was considering "just going home." I suggested that she sleep on it before deciding. I think she stayed and took another assignment. This kind of situation often arises for DMH helpers in our dual role supporting ARC staff as well as clients. It's also important to remember that we're never really off-duty while we're deployed. Even an after-hours beer in the hotel lounge can turn in to an intervention – one of the reasons why I don't give in to the temptation of a second beer....

During my time on the condolence team, I remember a session with a family who had lost a college-age daughter. We drove about an hour north to meet in the living room of the family farmhouse. As the large extended family told their story, showed us photos, and completed paper work, I noticed that their 13-year-old son sat silently in a chair, looking kind of lost. I told him that I had grown up in a farming community and asked him if he would be willing to show me their farm. We looked at and discussed the livestock, then as we sat on a fence rail, I asked him how he was doing with "all this." He told me about his sister and some of his special memories. He cried some and told me that he and his Dad were planning on taking the boat on a fishing trip, a favorite activity of his sister. I told him that sounded like a good plan. It was an example of the effectiveness of the ARC integrated team approach: While the other members stayed focused on the rest of the family, I was able to notice this boy's quiet distress, find a connection, and give him an opportunity to share some feelings he might have been bottling up. After that visit, the team stopped for lunch at a great catfish place on the way home, and I cleaned the pig shit off my boots. It may seem callous that we were able to change our focus so quickly to our next meal, but that kind of compartmentalization is necessary if you're not going to get overwhelmed by exposure to so many sad families. It doesn't mean you're not treating their pain respectfully.

In my third week I was asked to manage the six-member mental health team at the Community Center, a large two-story recreation complex set up with tables for all the agencies approved to provide information, goods, and services. We had our own table, but the job was to work the crowds inside and outside, giving directions and talking with anyone needing to talk. My job was scheduling, evaluating, and keeping our workers up to date on the latest information through twice-daily briefings. Factual, accurate, and timely information is a premium in the disjointed and ever-changing circumstances of a disaster response. Red Cross starts every day with a morning briefing at headquarters. With the advent of smartphones this daily report is accessible to all staff. Some administrators are better than others at keeping staff informed. All staff are reminded not to pass on rumors or speak for another agency. This is hard because we want to help and have trouble saying, "I don't know." (I remember midshift on my first deployment, someone asked me, "Do you know what time it is?" I thought, thank God, finally a question I can answer!)

I remember one incident where a young school counselor, just approved to work as a DMH worker, came to tell me about a woman she thought might be having a serious mental health crisis. I asked her if the woman was exhibiting any psychotic symptoms. She said "I don't know! Will you please just come with me?" I did. After a brief interview it was clear the client was bipolar, off her meds, and very manic. She was telling an animated story about her boyfriend who had been blown away and she was sure he was dead. Her sister was present and confirmed the story, and told me privately that the boyfriend had been abusive with her sister and "good riddance." The client told me she had not reported the missing boyfriend and gave me permission to help her make a report to the State Department of Public Safety. While making the report, I learned that disasters can be used as an opportunity for people who want to disappear. They also can open up pre-existing issues in a community, like conflicts between different racial or ethnic groups, which I also observed in this response. We always like to say that disasters bring out the best in people and usually that's the case, but not always. They also can exacerbate pre-existing mental health conditions as in this woman's case, so we connected the woman with the local mental health authority to follow up with her meds, and the next day I gave my team an impromptu workshop on conducting a basic mental status exam.

My favorite Joplin story came when I asked a middle-aged man at the Service Center about his story. He said he felt "very blessed" that he had been spared. He told me that he saw the storm coming and was trying to move his new BBQ grill into the garage. When he realized he was not going to make it he lay down in a small depression on the lawn. After the storm the neighbors were gathered outside. A four-year-old child, a neighbor, said, "Mr. Robert, I saw you out there and you had a giant butterfly on your back." I am generally pleased when I find people have some sense of spirituality. Their faith seems to help them with their recovery.

My Post-Response Adjustment

As I said earlier, I have responded to numerous disasters involving fatalities in the past and knew that I could handle working with survivors. The difference in Joplin was the size and scope of the devastation. I listened to stories about death nearly every day. Secondary trauma is very real, and, like all trauma, it stays with you forever. Every time I tell my Joplin story, I revisit some of the feelings that I had hearing the many stories people told me while I was there.

I always find one or more colleagues on the job to debrief with over a beer in the evenings. Red Cross requires workers to take one day off out of every seven. I spend it resting, relaxing, and reading something fun. I try to follow the same guidelines that I teach (eat, sleep, and exercise). I also find that 20 minutes of contemplative prayer each evening helps me.

As soon as I get home I try to schedule a day of fishing with my good buds. I am very fortunate to have a wife who is a retired psychiatric nurse and a sister who is a retired hospice nurse. I can and do share my stories with them while on the job and later at home. They understand that all they need do is listen.

Lessons Learned

- You can't fake empathy, but you must take care of your own emotional health. I'm sure clients can tell when you're not "feeling" them. Kids and older adults are especially perceptive. I've seen untrained staff try to hand out platitudes or issue false reassurances (probably wanting to feel better themselves), or try to focus on completing paperwork because they're not comfortable listening to a survivor's story. That's not serving the client.
- Boldly wade in. Most clients and staff will not seek you out. I look for opportunities (people sitting alone, gatherings of people, places of obvious conflict, designated smoking areas, etc.). You have to have the self-confidence to insert yourself into the mix because you're not going to be invited. Basic social skills and small talk work just fine as ways to generate that connection (How's it going? How you doin'? Are you OK? OK if I sit here? Damn it's hot; etc.). Once I create that opening, I can't think of a single client who didn't want to talk or at least have someone present with them. Because I know how important it is for them to tell their story, I may gently prompt, saying something like "Sometimes it helps to talk about it." If they're just not able at that moment I might give them referral contact information, or my cellphone number.
- Be aware of staff stress and politics. The only times I've been told to butt out is when someone else has asked me to speak to an angry staff member. Even then, they usually want someone to hear them about "how messed up things are." As DMH staff we can recommend time off to supervisors, job reassignment, etc. Sometimes the problem is the supervisor. These situations have to be handled individually and very carefully. It is my least favorite role.
- You can't fix anything although you will want to try. You need to be present and listen. Refer when you believe they need or will need help, but most people have within themselves what they need to heal. You can provide them with a road map, but then you have to have faith in

the process. It would be cool to see how they are doing in six months but that is not usually going to happen.

- Try to do the right thing with whatever is in front of you at the moment. Knowing what the "right thing" is with confidence comes with time and experience. I used to give my students this litmus test:

  1 Will it do any harm?
  2 Does it violate any of your professional ethics?
  3 Does it violate any of your agency's policies?
  4 Would you mind if your supervisor was watching?
  5 What does your gut say?
  6 Trust your gut.

Chapter 8

2012 Super Storm Sandy in New York City

Diane Ryan

I started volunteering with the Red Cross as a Disaster Mental Health (DMH) worker just after the TWA flight 800 disaster in 1996, when I saw a notice in the National Association of Social Workers newsletter that the organization was looking for volunteers. After many years in social work, I was very attracted to the concept of crisis work – to meet people where they're at when a disaster strikes, and to help them get through those initial stages of regaining their equilibrium and making decisions on their recovery. While I also have a psychotherapy practice, there's something about crisis work that I find very fulfilling; it's the art of being with someone so they're not alone and supporting them through their initial challenges.

I volunteered with the American Red Cross for 10 years, as a volunteer and then a leadership volunteer. Along the way I was employed in various other capacities, including in a children's hospital and then in a trauma and bereavement center providing support to responders and civilian victims post-9/11. I joined the staff of the American Red Cross as the Director of Mental Health in Greater New York in 2006.

As a volunteer and staff member I've responded to 9/11, floods and other weather events, explosions, tornados, building collapses, mass fatality bus, train, and aviation incidents, and too many fires to count. My role as Director of Mental Health for the ARC in Greater New York at the time Super Storm Sandy hit was to work alongside visiting mental health leadership to coordinate local and visiting personnel, liaison with mental health partner groups, ensure service delivery, and ensure that local and visiting disaster mental health workers were integrated into the response.

The Pre-Disaster Community

New York City is the largest and most densely populated city in the United States, with about 8.5 million residents packed into just over 300 square miles. It's also among the most culturally and linguistically diverse, with some 800 languages spoken. There are large populations of Asian

Americans (11.8 percent of the overall population) and people of Latino or Hispanic descent (27.5 percent of the city's population, primarily people of Puerto Rican or Dominican heritage). One-quarter of the city's residents are African American. Immigrants make up a significant portion of the population; more than a third were born outside of the U.S. Residents' incomes vary tremendously, especially in the borough of Manhattan, where the 2005 census found both the highest and lowest income tracts for the country, with an average household income of $188,697 in one neighborhood compared with an average of $9,320 in another. 18.5 percent of city residents live below the federal poverty line.

These specifics of demographics and population density magnified the impact of Super Storm Sandy and greatly complicated the recovery. While hurricanes are not unprecedented in the Northeast, the US had not previously experienced such a powerful storm directly hitting such a densely populated city. Like elsewhere, disasters in New York tend to have the most extreme effects on those with the fewest resources, and here there was a large population of working-class people before this devastating event. Additionally, because storms like this are unexpected and unpredictable, the full weight wasn't realized until afterwards. As a result, the demand for resources after the storm was very difficult to meet.

The Disaster

Sandy was a unique storm, as it was an end of season hurricane that ran into a cold front and then merged with a second storm. Sandy made landfall on October 29, 2012 at 7:30 p.m. just north of Atlantic City, New Jersey, after impacting Jamaica, Cuba, Haiti, and the Bahamas. Overall, she impacted an area the size of Europe and caused 146 deaths and over $71 billion in economic damage according to the National Hurricane Center.

Sandy's impact on the New York City region was devastating. The full moon at landfall, with high tides in the Atlantic Ocean and New York Harbor, caused unprecedented storm surges in a dense urban city that had hundreds of thousands of people living in flood-prone areas. The New York City transit system was shut down, hospitals and nursing homes were evacuated, thousands were evacuated in mid-town Manhattan for six days following a crane collapse, and a six-alarm fire in Breezy Point, Queens destroyed 111 homes. Close to 2 million people in the region were without power. Seventeen percent of the city's total land mass flooded. A gasoline shortage affected victims and humanitarian responders.

Those affected in the New York City area were predominately the working poor, the frail elderly who were unable to self-evacuate from high rise buildings, young children, the undocumented, those with language barriers, and individuals with functional needs. Mental health triage determined that those with the most need for disaster mental health support were those with homes not live-able in Queens, those with functional needs across the region, and those who experienced extreme panic or perceived threat to life.

My Thoughts Pre-Response

I remember that as I packed to come to ARC headquarters before public transportation shut down, I felt a sense of unreality about it all. Like a lot of people in the region, I was thinking that perhaps the storm would not be that bad and that there would be minimal impact to those affected. I was also hopeful that transportation would get back up quickly, and I would be able to work the storm as needed while being able to sleep at home. There was a lot of uncertainty at that point about whether it would make a direct hit on New York City. The most recent hurricane that had been predicted to hit the city, Hurricane Irene in 2011, mostly missed us and there had been other storms around the country that were near misses, and I think we were all hoping for that to happen here. I certainly wasn't expecting this to turn into a five-month-long response.

But as we watched the storm move closer, it became clear we were going to have some sort of serious impact. That process of watching the storm day by day, the models aligning, the tracking getting closer, getting the word that senior people from ARC national headquarters were coming in – little by little, all of that helps to prepare your mind that this could be something big, though there was still some hope that it would change its path. It became this kind of psychological mindset as it got closer and closer, and I recognized the need to become emotionally prepared. The logistical preparations had been going on for some time, but I remember finally accepting that this was likely going to be something very big and bad.

My Response Experience

There were many different and complex dynamics to this ARC response. Those of us working out of our headquarters in mid-town Manhattan packed our bags and arrived before the storm hit to turn our offices and cubicles into sleeping areas. Cots were provided, large newsprint sheets were taped to the glass windows for some sense of privacy, and motion sensor light switches needed to be immobilized so lights would not turn on each time someone rolled over in their cot.

There was tremendous concern as the storm approached; we began to receive situational reports and see the media coverage of the flooding and initial hospital evacuations from our Operations Center. As the full force of the storm approached, some of our staff were receiving phone calls from family reporting flooding and damage to their own homes. In extreme cases, some personnel were hearing that their loved ones did not feel safe at home but were not able to evacuate. As it was not possible for staff to leave the protection of the ARC building to check on their homes and families, all we could offer our colleagues was support and the option to be relieved of their shift. All opted to remain on duty and work through the long and difficult evening until word came in the morning that their families were okay.

I spent five nights sleeping in my office before, during, and after the storm. It was very strange to see colleagues walking the floor in their sleeping clothes and having casual conversations with supervisors as we waited in line for the showers. I remember one evening I was able to leave the building to get a bite to eat after the storm passed but before the transit system opened, and the feeling of surrealism as I returned to my office cot to go to sleep.

Ultimately, more than 17,000 American Red Cross (ARC) disaster responders arrived from all parts of the United States to serve between October 2012 and May 2013. The ARC served over 17 million meals/snacks and provided more than 81,000 shelter nights during that time. Our disaster mental health teams provided approximately 40,000 mental health contacts. Services were provided in shelters, hotels, at feeding trucks, via home visits, at community gatherings, and through neighborhood canvassing using ARC disaster mental interventions that are well documented and will not be described here.

There were many other significant staff stressors throughout the prolonged Sandy response. The arrival of so many visiting paid and volunteer staff from ARC offices across the country was moving and inspiring. However, it is not uncommon for there to be difficulties when others come in. Imagine a scenario where visitors come to your home for four or five months to be helpful: Some dilemmas around control and decision-making are inevitable and natural.

Additionally, many of the visiting staff came from suburban or rural areas and were not accustomed to New York City's volume of people, the tall buildings, our public transportation system, and the fact that we walk most places rather than drive. For many months, massive numbers of us would walk to and from the ARC building each day; the locals from the subway system and the out of town staff from their hotels. On many occasions I overheard fascinating observations and commentary on city life from those who were experiencing it for the first time. I remember the reactions of disbelief when we prepared those visiting staff for New Year's Eve by indicating that a million people could be arriving around the corner from headquarters to watch the ball drop, and if they did not want to be in the mix, they might want to return to their hotel and remain inside until the morning. Additionally, visiting staff arrived who had previously come to New York City to serve during the 9/11 response, and some re-experienced the stress and anxiety of that event.

There is a structure to ARC Operations during a disaster, but individual visiting leaders have different styles, and as people rotated in and out over those five months, there was a need to adjust to slightly different daily routines. There was a benefit in that as well, as I was exposed to many different styles of leadership and at the end of it all, was able to identify best practices in different areas for me and my regional team to incorporate moving forward. An additional challenge was building a long-term care program while in operational mode of an urban disaster that had no similar disaster to build from. Communication and coordination among human services agencies in a prolonged disaster is always challenging, and it took some time for agencies to identify each other and begin to assess resources and capabilities.

Additional unique characteristics of this disaster included the 2013 New York City Mayoral election which provided an intense political overlay to the city's response, and staff knowledge that the ARC was about to roll out a significant national reorganization meant there was some perception that personnel were being observed for merit in future positions.

The mental health staff who came from all areas of the country to serve with me during those long months were outstanding in skill level and I was very grateful for their sacrifice in leaving their homes and families to come to our aid. It was my intention to give back to them when their moment of need arrived, and I will always deeply regret that I was unable to deploy to them when disaster struck those good people before I left my tenure with the Red Cross.

The paid and volunteer staff of the ARC Greater New York is a group of very experienced responders, and many of us had been doing this work for decades. New York City averaged about nine disasters a day during that period of time and we had additionally served during 9/11, multiple mass casualty transportation disasters, and other extreme weather responses. There was something about Sandy that was different, that was harder. The challenges with prolonged mass care/feeding for such a large population over a significant geography were difficult and, at times, overwhelming. The number of families who were displaced and living in temporary housing for such a long time was hard to conceptualize. Our mental health team is extraordinarily skilled in providing trauma and grief support, but we struggled with how to provide interventions for those who were hungry, who had lost their jobs when they had to re-locate, and whose children had left their friends and schools. Our local disaster mental health volunteers were outstanding in their commitment to serve, despite juggling their own jobs and families, and some of whose own homes had been affected by the flooding.

Six weeks or so into the Sandy response, we heard the breaking news of the Sandy Hook Elementary School shooting in nearby Connecticut. Already fatigued and exposed to significant suffering, the news was devastating, and we needed to determine who would split from Sandy operations to serve in Newtown. Many of us had feelings of both wanting to serve and yet also to avoid something so horrific. I needed to take good measure of myself emotionally and physically before I decided that it would not be right for me to serve there as I could not be at my best – and the suffering was so great that it needed everyone who came to help to be at their best. It was the most difficult professional decision I had to make. I was able to help the cause by recommending other well-qualified mental health workers from my region to be assigned and then had the opportunity to support my friends/colleagues who did deploy by being a sounding board for them as needed while on assignment there.

In addition to sending personnel to support the Sandy Hook tragedy, during that prolonged period of the Sandy operation, the ARC Greater New York Region also responded to the usual nine or so disasters a day, including fatal fires and a ferry accident with more than 80 injuries.

Having learned from high rates of staff burnout and turnover in previous major events, the ARC has brought in a staff support program and a dedicated team to focus on personnel during a prolonged disaster. Those personnel had just under 3,000 significant staff mental health contacts during the five months of operations. Staff mental health interventions included making rounds, staging in food areas to promote conversation, creating and distributing "welcome bags" to arriving staff that contained comfort items, and scheduling stress-reducing mini-events to pull staff out of the work for a few minutes at a time. I was able to collaborate with a recognized, licensed massage therapy association to provide chair massage sessions to personnel scheduled at ARC headquarters. That was a tremendous support to staff and very popular. I asked our most senior leadership to schedule a chair massage at their first event to promote the concept that this was a good thing and that personnel should take a few moments away from the work now and then.

The 2012 winter holiday season presented difficulties for us. How could anyone take time off for the feast of Thanksgiving with our loved ones when so many people were concerned about feeding their families adequately? Instead, most of us worked on Thanksgiving. Senior disaster leadership arranged for a modest Thanksgiving meal for us that felt appropriate. There was a similar concern during the December holidays. ARC office celebrations were canceled across the region and senior leadership presented personnel with a small goodie bag with a thank-you note and some small tokens of appreciation. This was very well thought out by the administration and struck the right note.

My Post-Response Adjustment

This was a five-month hardship assignment that had the usual characteristics of long hours with limited time off, exhaustion, illness, and difficulty separating from the work. We had no idea of the length of the response and just kept going. After several months the impact on our loved ones became apparent as the news coverage subsided and much of the region looked as if it had returned to normal functioning. But there was still so much need and suffering that was not obvious. Although the post-9/11 work was also a prolonged response in our own community, everyone in the New York City area was affected by it and so understood the need for the ongoing operations. During Sandy, families and friends were unable to understand why our work pace remained so intense after months of the operation. They were accustomed to us deploying out of town for periods of time to serve at a disaster, but there was something about us being present yet unavailable for months that was so difficult for them. And we were likely too exhausted to explain it well. I recall a very difficult evening when I was too emotionally and physically fatigued to be helpful to a loved one who needed me and who did not understand why I could not be available, and it took some time for us both to move past that.

Mitigation for this in future events could include developing family support interventions to include information on effects of a prolonged response and how to cope. I recall seeing such documents from the ARC many years ago and perhaps it is time to re-examine that concept.

Lessons Learned

Overall, my experience working this disaster was a combination of adrenaline, exhaustion, and some frustration; but with moments of inspirational camaraderie, collegiality, and faith in the humanitarian response to tragic events. My lessons learned from the Sandy response include:

- Responders really need to have an accurate projection of the length of operations during a prolonged event so they can pace themselves appropriately, though that's not always possible and we may have to work to be comfortable with some ambiguity about the timeframe of the response. But in some ways, it was the open-ended nature of this response that was so stressful for all of us since it felt like we just had to keep going indefinitely. That was difficult for our families as well as for ourselves.
- Work hard to collaborate with others, understanding that large responses will bring in people with a wide variety of cultural backgrounds and disaster experiences. It can be difficult to keep adapting to a rotating cast of new volunteers and managers, but when the need is so great, everyone has a role they can play.
- Don't make assumptions about the decisions that are being made without understanding why. In a large-scale disaster it's easy to start questioning why things are being handled in a particular way, but there

are likely things you just don't know about that are informing those decisions. You need to trust leadership, who have the information on the bigger picture and the resources available, to make the right decisions.

- When the disaster occurs in your own community, there's a degree of personal impact and suffering that you'll feel, but you need to be able to put that aside in order to take care of others initially. But it's also important to be aware that you have to find some time, when the response is over and it's appropriate, to really reflect on the event and your experiences, and what it all means it to you. It's easy to try to avoid that and stay focused on helping others, but it's important to do. And a good way to do it is by talking and reflecting with your peers – with other responders who were involved in the operation and who may be more comfortable hearing about your pain and suffering than your friends and family might be.

Section II

Human-Caused Disasters in the United States

Chapter 9

Human-Caused Disasters Section Introduction

James Halpern

"Man is the cruelest animal."

– Friedrich Nietzsche

Disasters that are human-caused are more shocking, more horrifying, and typically result in more psychological impairment than those that are naturally caused. A human-caused disaster is often experienced as a profound betrayal. Disasters caused by terrorism or mass violence are most devastating. Many of our Western cultural narratives set people apart from the rest of nature. Extreme heat or cold, storm clouds, or colliding tectonic plates are not willfully choosing to kill or injure us. We live our lives expecting members of our own species to be thoughtful, careful, and certainly not malevolent, especially in life and death matters. Unfortunately this is not always the case, so human-caused disasters shake and sometimes shatter our assumptions about other people. This is especially so when there is immediate physical danger, and/or if there is the witnessing of death or serious injury to another. These two event factors are part of the criteria for the development of PTSD.

Of course, not all human-caused disasters are intentional acts of violence. It could be an accident (e.g., due to equipment failure), due to carelessness or neglect, or intentional malfeasance. A plane crash could have very different causes, and the cause can impact reactions. Consider three airline accidents that all took place in 2009. One was caused by a bird strike (the so-called "Miracle on the Hudson"), another was due to equipment failure (Air France Flight 447), and the third was a result of pilot fatigue (Colgan Air Flight 3407). After the Colgan Air disaster near Buffalo, NY, survivors struggled to understand how the airline could have put their loved ones in danger by overworking their pilots. Survivors are more likely to think that their loved ones died needlessly and blame negligent pilots, or greedy airline officials, or shoddy government regulators – or all three. If a plane is purposely taken down to accomplish a political goal, reactions can be even more severe. When humans perpetrate disasters by setting fires or committing mass murder, survivors are in a state of shock that is often followed with grief and loss and rage. Initially there is bewilderment, followed by a search to understand how this could have been prevented and who to blame for the failure of preventing the tragedy. Survivors of human-caused disasters have an additional burden – a search for justice. The chapters in this section describe events that have intense long-term consequences.

Human-caused disasters include events such as:

- Arson.
- Oil spills.
- Toxic spills.
- Transportation disasters (plane/bus/train crashes).
- Bridge collapses.
- Mass shootings/mass killings.
- Terrorist attacks.
- Bioterrorism.
- Power outages/blackouts.
- Violent public disturbance/civil disorder.

In this section, contributors describe their experience at a range of human-caused events. All six events were intentional and all of the authors/responders, with one exception (Pulse Nightclub shooting), lived close or reasonably close to the event. None of the events covered in this section could be considered "accidents." The Oklahoma City bombing, the attack on the World Trade Center, and the Pulse Nightclub shootings were all acts of terror; the first by a group of domestic right-wing extremists, the second by international Al-Qaida operatives, and the third by a lone gunman whose motives appear murky but who claimed he had an allegiance to ISIS. The perpetrators of the attacks in Webster, NY, Isla Vista, CA, and Newtown, CT, appear to have been mentally disturbed and their intentions remain murky, in part because they all died at the scene. The Isla Vista attacker killed men and women but was motivated by misogyny, a motive that has not received sufficient attention in examining the causes and prevention of mass violence.

Losses and the Myth of Closure

Some human-caused disasters can result in significant property damage, loss of income, and employment. In addition to the loss of lives and profound emotional trauma, the attack on the World Trade Center on 9/11 took a heavy economic toll on jobs, not only in the towers but throughout lower Manhattan. Downtown cab and limo drivers, restaurant and hotel workers, and manufacturing personnel were all impacted. One estimate suggested that New York City lost over 100,000 jobs as a result of the attack on the towers (Eaton, 2003). Livery cab drivers or restaurant workers who lost jobs after 9/11, along with their families, may have suffered significantly with little attention or concern from the community.

Income, homes, and jobs are recoverable but lives lost are gone forever. All of the human-caused events in this chapter resulted in loss of life that predicts significant psychological impairment. Families who lost loved ones are often described as strong and resilient, and many are – but they also continue to suffer their grievous losses. It's sometimes suggested that if a perpetrator is killed or executed, survivors will experience a sense of "closure." Should DMH workers reassure survivors that when a killer is caught, convicted, or executed, they will experience a sense of relief? Can survivors whose loved ones are murdered ever "put it behind them" and have the capacity to forgive? The short answer is no. This sort of closure characterized by phrases like "let bygones be bygones" or "forgive and forget" is a myth and does not reflect reality for many people in these circumstances. Through extensive interviews with family members after the Oklahoma City bombing, Madeira (2012) found survivors' reactions were filled with terror and anger. After it was established that perpetrators were guilty, after the convictions, and after the execution of one of the terrorists, there was no relief. Loved ones were not brought back to life and nothing was fixed. There was no closure. When Osama bin Laden was killed in 2011, 10 years after the 9/11 attacks, many family members and first responders cheered, but their lives did not go back to normal. Although case studies in this section focus on early interventions, DMH helpers should understand that survivors whose loved ones are killed will, at best, have long-term adjustments to make.

The Complexity of the Response

The response to all domestic disasters will include local and federal emergency management, traditional first responders, Red Cross, Salvation Army, and clergy. Disasters that are crimes bring an even more complex and sometimes chaotic response. For example, the attack on the World Trade Center was a mass transportation incident a crime, and a terrorist attack (not to mention a hazardous materials situation). As a transportation disaster, the National Transportation Safety Board (NTSB) should be in charge of the scene and the event. As a crime, all of local, state, and national law enforcement is involved. Local police, state sheriffs and troopers, and the Federal Bureau of Investigation are all on-scene. There may also be a military response with National Guard present. A disaster that is labeled a crime will also bring in local, state, and federal Office of Victim Services personnel who can provide a multitude of services to survivors, including short and long term-mental health support at no cost. The large number of agencies, government, and non-government organizations necessitates clear and thorough planning, studying responses to previous incidents, and carrying out exercises and drills that involve all responding agencies and mutual aid partners. Much of this planning, training, and exercises are carried out in accordance with the National Incident Management System (FEMA, 2004). Several authors of case studies in this section show us that although considerable effort has gone into creating clear plans for how a response is organized, things rarely work as planned.

Secondary Stress in Human-Caused Disaster

In human-caused disasters, the event is the primary stressor but there are always secondary events that compound the reactions. Often, the perpetrators of these disasters are killed or kill themselves at the end of the event. The perpetrators of five of the six attacks described in this section all died at the event. One possible outcome of this result is that survivors are left wondering about the motives of the killers. Sometimes the offender leaves behind emails, online posts, or journals that survivors inspect to get an understanding of the perpetrator's motives or personality as they struggle to understand how the unimaginable could have happened. The Isla Vista perpetrator left behind a very disturbing misogynistic "manifesto" that survivors, and (horribly) admirers, could read long after the event. Any kind of criminal investigation can lead to revelations about the killer that survivors examine and reflect on, causing them additional long-term stress. The Oklahoma City bombing and the attack on the World Trade Center resulted in criminal proceedings, trials, and legal claims that exposed survivors to reminders and stress.

Several authors of case studies in this section point out that another secondary stressor for survivors of human-caused disaster is exposure to extended media coverage. In the early aftermath of these events, the presence of the press shows families that they are not being ignored. However, journalists can be intrusive, calling survivors at all hours in search of an exclusive story. DMH can help survivors develop a strategy to deal with the press. Later in the response, there are lengthy print media articles, TV specials, and even movies about the events. Survivor families who do not want to be exposed to these distressing reminders can be startled in a movie theater when a trailer for the event is shown to the accompaniment of frightening music.

Another secondary stressor in these disasters is rehabilitation due to injury. Forty-nine people were killed in the Pulse Nightclub shooting and 53 were injured. Many of those injured were also grieving the loss of friends and loved ones. And bear in mind that these injuries can take weeks or months to overcome, and some never fully heal. The wounds are obviously painful in themselves, but they're also reminders of the loss of friends and loved ones.

Other secondary stressors are anniversaries and memorials for these events. Yearly memorials can often exacerbate distress and symptoms in survivors who predictably show "anniversary reactions." For an extended time after the event and on anniversaries, survivors can't help but see flowers, teddy bears, signs, and chalk memorials that a sympathetic public put on display on-site or around the event. DMH helpers can prepare survivors for the sights and sounds that accompany formal and informal memorials.

One final set of secondary stressors for survivors of human-caused disaster is that although the vast majority of citizens want to offer kindness and compassion, there may be a small, malevolent minority spreading misinformation, or claiming loudly that these events never occurred and that victims are frauds and liars. For example, almost immediately after the Sandy Hook school shooting, conspiracy theorists used social media to proclaim that the shootings were "fake news" intended to deprive gun owners of their Second Amendment rights. The public is generally so supportive and sympathetic that it's jarring for survivors and helpers alike to see and hear from these toxic and malevolent individuals. Helpers can be proactive by trying to protect survivors from this perniciousness, and by reminding survivors of the overwhelming kindness that exists for them. Still, even when the response falls short of outright denial that an event occurred, shootings and other attacks are often politicized by those who want to use them to advance an agenda, to scapegoat a particular religious or ethnic group, or to generally sow conflict, and that can greatly increase distress for all involved.

A Note on Self-care

The human-caused disasters described in this section are all mass casualty events, and contributing authors acknowledge the toll each response took on them and the need for self-care. The Oklahoma City bombing killed children in a day-care center; the Sandy Hook school shooting took the lives of young children and their educators; the Pulse nightclub shooting, the Isla Vista tragedy and the Webster shooting took the lives of young adults; and the attack on the World Trade Center took the lives of thousands and shattered our perception of safety. Responding to these kinds of events will take a toll on the responder. As you read these chapters, please take note of the different self-care strategies the authors used and consider what strategies you would use if and when you respond. Also, please note that only an experienced clinician with a self-care plan should take on such an assignment, so if you're interested getting involved in this kind of response, think about how you can start to acquire training and experience at less extreme disasters in order to prepare yourself for this most traumatic type of event.

References

Eaton, L. (2003). Job losses in New York City since 9–11 continue to grow. *The New York Times.* March 14. Retrieved from http://www.nytimes.com.

FEMA. (2004). *An Introduction to the National Incident Management System (NIMS) IS-700.B, Facilitator Guide*, June, 2018.

Madeira, J.L. (2012). *Killing McVeigh: The Death Penalty and the Myth of Closure.* New York: New York University Press.

Chapter 10

1995 Bombing of the Federal Building in Oklahoma City

John R. Tassey

I am a career clinical psychologist working at the VA Medical Center in Oklahoma City. I began there in late 1984 and never imagined I would still be there over 30 years later. I started a Health Psychology Clinic at the VA in 1989. I see patients in an outpatient setting and supervise research in smoking cessation, Hepatitis C health literacy, and chronic pain management. My career trajectory pre-April 19, 1995 was as a clinical researcher investigating health behavior.

After the Edmond, OK Post Office shooting in 1986 I became involved in training programs for mental health providers sponsored by the local American Red Cross (ARC) chapter. I saw disaster response as one aspect of community service and from 1987 to early 1995 I would show up when called, usually for no more than a day or two, to assist the shelter operations for floods, tornadoes, or single-family fires. I took the two-day Red Cross Disaster Mental Health class in 1992. In 1993 I agreed to be the Oklahoma Psychological Association's Disaster Response Coordinator and Red Cross local chapter Disaster Mental Health Chair. After April 19, 1995 these were no longer nominal titles and a series of events changed my career path.

The Pre-Disaster Community

Oklahoma City in 1995 was more diverse than its "White Buckle of the Bible Belt" reputation. Since before Columbus and certainly after the 1839 "Trail of Tears," Oklahoma has had a large American Indian population represented by 39 Federally recognized nations. While Christianity is the predominant religion, both Jewish and Muslim communities have existed since before Oklahoma statehood in 1907. Oklahoma City welcomed a large Vietnamese population in the mid-1970s after the US withdrawal from the Vietnam War, bringing an influx of the Buddhist tradition. Most major faith traditions were present in Oklahoma at the time of the bombing, and the interfaith response to this tragedy is present to this day.

Two events set the stage for our mental health response to the Federal Building bombing in 1995. In 1982 a school cafeteria water heater exploded during lunch, injuring 30 and killing five children and one teacher. Four years later, an employee at the Post Office in Edmond, OK, shot 20 co-workers, killing 14 of them. In 1994 the first American Psychological Association Oklahoma State Disaster Response Coordinator and Disaster Mental Health Chair for the ARC of Central Oklahoma turned his responsibilities over to me, stating "You might have to respond to a tornado or flood."

The Disaster

The Alfred P. Murrah Federal Building was built in 1977 in the heart of Oklahoma City (OKC). The building housed 14 federal agencies, including the Drug Enforcement Administration (DEA), Bureau of Alcohol, Tobacco, and Firearms (BATF), Secret Service, and U.S. Marshall's office, as well as recruiting offices for the Army and Marine Corps. Timothy McVeigh, one of the co-conspirators, admitted his criterion for potential attack sites was the presence of at least two of the three federal law enforcement agencies: BATF, FBI, or DEA. McVeigh also confessed to planning the attack on the anniversary of the 1993 Branch Davidian compound siege in Waco, TX and the 220th anniversary of the Battles of Lexington and Concord.

At 9:02 a.m. on April 19, 1995 a truck bomb exploded at the north side of the Murrah building. The blast destroyed over one-third of the nine-story building, and destroyed or damaged 324 other buildings within a 16-block radius, causing an estimated $652 million worth of damage. The explosion killed 168 people and injured over 680 others. Compounding this tremendous loss of life was the death of 19 children, 15 from a day care center located directly above the parked truck bomb. The adult fatalities also included three pregnant women.

The Murrah building was four blocks from the OKC Fire Department headquarters and six blocks from the Police Department. Their response was immediate. The local ARC chapter had an Emergency Response Vehicle (ERV) on scene within 30 minutes; DMH volunteers were there within 90 minutes. Perimeter security was established within the hour and isolation of the crime scene began that morning. The Murrah building was within a couple of miles of the major OKC medical centers; casualties were transported by ambulance, private vehicle, and on foot. Every medical center in the greater OKC metropolitan area initiated their disaster response protocols. By midnight of April 19, the last survivor was extracted.

My Thoughts Pre-Response

Most people living in Oklahoma at the time can describe where they were, what they were doing, and how they learned about the bombing. Many of my co-workers said they felt the blast; some said they heard it. I was at my desk and thought it was an April thunderstorm. We watched the television describe a gas line break at the federal courthouse, although the live pictures told us it was the federal building. My Red Cross pager directed me to report to the chapter and as I raced out the door my VA Chief told me to report back if I needed any assistance. When I arrived at the Red Cross chapter I learned that it was a bomb and not a gas line explosion. I arrived on scene in a shirt and tie and leather dress shoes – the clothes I would wear for the next 24 hours.

Our past Red Cross responses to local events required us to call a small group of mostly psychologists to assist with the relief efforts. I relied on those same people to help to establish our mental health response. At that time, I did not realize that the mental health response to the OKC Federal Building bombing would be immediately and continuously challenged by a large number of spontaneous volunteers attempting to access various venues – a complication described below.

My Response Experience

By the time we loaded up in the second Red Cross ERV and entered downtown OKC, no vehicles were allowed within two blocks of the scene. Our small DMH contingent went on foot to the Murrah building. The sidewalks were littered with glass. Perimeter security allowed us through but cautioned us to walk in the middle of the street to avoid glass falling from the office buildings. As we passed the Federal Reserve Building, I noticed the guards wearing military body armor and helmets and holding shotguns.

We arrived at the south side of the Murrah building and the structure looked intact. It wasn't until we circled around to the north side that the enormity of the destruction struck us. We found the initial site of the Oklahoma City Fire Department (OCFD) respite area and staged our mental health volunteers there. Seeing the OCFD Chaplain on the south mezzanine of the building, I went to announce our presence, get a closer look, and try to lend a more active hand with the rescue efforts. Survivors from the building were still filing out of one of the remaining stairwells. Firefighters not escorting survivors were carrying out armloads of weapons and ordinance, police and paramedics walked around with dirty, blood-stained shirts, and sheets cloaked small bodies underneath. All this activity was interrupted by the announcement that a second device had been found and the site was evacuated. We abandoned our ERV at the scene and retreated several blocks to the west.

Southwestern Bell Telephone's corporate headquarters was three blocks north of the Murrah building. That night they withdrew their employees and turned the building over to the OCFD to use as the Incident Command Center. This building was within the security perimeter and became the hub of all respite services for responders, OCFD and other mutual aid fire service personnel, local and federal law enforcement, and active duty, Oklahoma National Guard and Reserve airmen and soldiers. Several out-of-state Critical Incident Stress Management (CISM) teams arrived to support the rescue and recovery efforts.

By that afternoon, the Oklahoma State Medical Examiner (ME) designated a church three miles away as the "Death Notification Center." That evening, local funeral home directors and their staff were recruited under National Disaster Medical System Disaster Mortuary Teams (NDMS DMORT) to assist with collecting ante-mortem details to assist with the expected recovery and identification of remains. Two psychiatrists from the University of Oklahoma Health Sciences Center in Tulsa helped establish the mental health footprint there that evening. The next morning, I arrived as the designated Red Cross mental health representative. Around the crowded table at that first meeting were representatives from law enforcement, ME's office, and local and state politicians, including the governors' wife.

After that meeting, around 9 a.m., I received a call on a cellphone Red Cross had issued to me from the American Psychological Association Disaster Response Network asking if I needed any assistance from their office. I was looking out the window at hundreds of volunteers queuing up to help, many I recognized as fellow psychologists. I think I told her I did not know enough to know what I needed, but that we certainly had enough volunteers.

In fact, our OKC DMH volunteers were soon forced to organize the management of hundreds of mental health providers. This mission creep would come to include not only mental health providers of every profession, but also clergy and paraprofessional CISM teams. The management of spontaneous volunteers was facilitated by the declaration of a domestic terrorism crime scene. Perimeter security was very tight. All of the venues were protected by armed reserve deputies and Oklahoma National Guard and U.S. Air Force troops. Some venues, like the Operations Center, Death Notification, and Medical Examiner's Office were off limits to all but a handful of well-known and carefully selected mental health providers. Spontaneous mental health volunteers, after being screened by a hand-picked mental health team, were assigned in shifts to the Compassion Center (formerly the "Death Notification Center") to be a compassionate presence to the waiting families, support welfare inquiry telephone calls, or sort through the thousands of pieces of mail. "Just-in-time" training was provided by experienced Red Cross volunteers, sent from other states specifically due to their expertise in mass casualty incidents.

Most mental health volunteers showed up to serve the overall relief effort. They could be found making copies, carrying cases of water, sweeping floors and emptying trash cans, as well as in the more traditional DMH role. Many knew that access to the scene was a unique opportunity and honor, and they represented our professions proudly. I would be remiss if I did not mention that the selection and assignment process we implemented was not warmly accepted by all mental health providers seeking to volunteer. A few nationally prominent mental health professionals were outspoken about how we could not have had an "organized" mental health response since they were not involved. A few others labeled us as "elitists," not understanding that the PhDs and MDs in the "top spots" had a pre-existing and ongoing connection to Red Cross Disaster Services. I object to the characterization that we were not fair in our site assignments. We understood that our decisions could impact the long-term psychological recovery of the families and first responders. Our mental health screening team at the Compassion Center, had an axiom, "If anyone insisted on doing death notification they were definitely the wrong person for the job."

The Red Cross set up a phone bank in the church and staffed it with volunteers to establish a Disaster Welfare Inquiry (now called "Safe and Well") function. The first day at the Compassion Center we met every hour to get an update on the activities at the site, number of remains recovered, and the expected timeframe of the operation. We also established a very robust feedback system from the family members at the Compassion Center. Suggestion boxes were conspicuous in all locations where the families congregated. Every hour the suggestions were collected and ways to implement the comments were addressed; the culture of the place was "how do we say yes to these grieving families?" At least one mental health provider was assigned to each family. That provider was instructed to be a quiet, therapeutic presence and to report back any issues or problems they observed. I believe what we did was not as important as *why* we did it – we wanted the families, in their darkest hour, to know we cared enough to truly listen.

I noted above that OKC was more diverse than readers might expect; it is a shorter list to describe the Oklahoma populations that were open to mental health providers. First responders, non-dominant racial and ethnic group members, and the general blue-collar Oklahoma cohort (not mutually exclusive groups) were not on that list. The bombing of the Federal Building gave us a window of access to reach out, without stigma, to these groups. This access was facilitated by the almost universal "order," by those who could issue such orders, to their respective communities. It is well known that faith leaders are good mental health partners and this was certainly the case after the bombing. The Incident Command chain of command instituted mandatory CISM for first responders after every shift.

Surprisingly, small business owners, corporations, and local media also contacted the Red Cross to request mental health services for their impacted employees. Conversely, American Indian leaders reached out to the Red Cross Disaster Mental Health function, offering their centuries-old traditions of healing: smudging, sweat lodges and pow-wows.

Access and integration of the faith communities to the relief effort was assigned to the Disaster Mental Health function. While these were clearly spiritual and religious domains, mental health providers vouched for their inclusion/exclusion and vetted the "providers." Requests to include a particular religious event were made by family members, first responders, and faith leaders. The unspoken mandate was to seek a compromise so that we could honor each request, maintain the security and confidentiality of the setting, and limit any offense to the overall community. Within a few days of establishing the Compassion Center at the First Christian Church, an American Indian shaman offered to "smudge" the facility to "bring peace and repel evil forces." This gesture was warmly accepted by the family members and relief workers and set the tone for the ecumenical spirit of this site. Not all religious perspectives were allowed access. Messages conveying nihilism, racism, or conspiracy theories were turned away from the Compassion Center.

The Compassion Center evolved into a bustling multi-agency service center but the central, somber theme was that this was where individual families would be drawn from the larger community area into a private room to be told the worst news of their lives. Accompanying the ME representative would be a clergy member, and a carefully chosen mental health provider.

Self-care was scheduled into every venue and activity. OCFD required all personnel to report for "debriefing" at the end of every shift. In that era, a debriefing used the seven-step Jeffrey Mitchell Critical Incident Stress Debriefing (CISD) model of recalling and processing a critical incident. The National Guard and mutual aid units from across the State followed the OCFD lead. Every Red Cross volunteer, whether at the Chapter, at one of the respite sites, or at the Compassion Center, was required to debrief after every shift. Since the recruitment of mental health volunteers was not a problem we had plenty of volunteers to provide services for the duration of the rescue and recovery efforts. The protocol to capture everyone involved in the incident was heroic and well executed. Years later, when I would hear someone say they were involved in the OKC Bombing effort but never received a debriefing, I would think, they didn't know that they were in a debriefing, or they went to elaborate means to avoid it, or they just plain weren't there.

At that time, with the limited evidence available to us, we felt doing nothing would be worse than doing too much – but to our credit, we also knew the traditional CISD model would not be well tolerated in serial doses. The end-of-shift respite model that evolved during this incident came to look similar to the PFA practiced currently. Participation in end-of-shift debriefing was facilitated by a carrot-and-stick methodology. For first responders, the end-of-shift debriefing was the gateway for access to massage therapists, warm food, and release home. For the Red Cross volunteers, including the mental health volunteers, end-of-shift debriefings punched the ticket to be able to return to their assignment the next day. A SAMHSA (Substance Abuse and Mental Health Services Administration) Crisis Counseling grant was received for debriefing that was delivered to all OCFD and Oklahoma mutual aid services in the traditional CISM model after the conclusion of the incident.

The Disaster Mortuary Teams (DMORT) were staffed by NDMS personnel and included local funeral homes staff federalized to assist with the custody and cataloging of the remains. DMH met with a group of the DMORT members for an end-of-tour debriefing. Our conversation before this session centered around steeling ourselves for what we anticipated would be a very graphic and poignant discussion with a group of volunteers who had obviously been exposed to the worst this bombing could produce. One of the youngest members present described how it was an honor to be able to learn from the top forensic scientists in the US. One of the older members recalled his work in a funeral home during the Vietnam War. He emphasized how important it was for a family to have something to hold, and something to bury, no matter how small or incomplete. Not a person present complained about the long hours, the working conditions, or the task to be completed. Instead of being vicariously traumatized, all present were inspired by their dedication and humanity.

It was equally impressive to "debrief" a local affiliate television station. Our CISM team included a paramedic and a firefighter, a chaplain, and myself as the mental health advisor. We thought it would be just a handful of on-scene reporters and photographers. We commenced with a circle of about 50 station personnel, from the front office staff to the celebrity news anchors. We met in the broadcast studio since that offered the largest area to seat that many people, starting three hours before the evening broadcast. In typical Mitchell Model fashion we began with the "Fact Phase," asking where they were that morning. All had a story to tell about the bombing and their job, their family, their neighborhood – and each other. Just as impressive as their compassion and openness was their apparent disregard for the time. With literally only two minutes before the live broadcast, like a well-choreographed routine, they all got up, took their places and returned to their tasks. Needless to say, we never formally got to the other six phases. However, I think we started a conversation, provided some good self-care information, and created allies in the media.

In one of our too-many-to-keep-track-of meetings, the City Manager explained that he had a desk full of telephone messages that could be categorized in two piles: Musicians who wanted to throw a benefit concert, and mental health experts for hire who were available to advise us on what to do. Looking back, it's sometimes enlightening, but usually entertaining or down-right embarrassing, to review mental health practice guidelines for mass casualty incidents circa 1995. Fortunately, the Red Cross sent us their most experienced mental health volunteers. They worked out of the limelight to gently guide us and turn our good intentions and abundant manpower into a well-organized and effective mental health response. We were able to orchestrate several memorials, both publicly with the U.S. President and privately at the bomb site. We provided a constant and compassionate presence for families awaiting death notification. We designed and organized an end-of-shift debriefing that honored the mandate from the Incident Commander while providing a legitimate service to the participating first responders. We coordinated with the Mental Health Association of OKC to provide pro bono services to anyone impacted by the bombing, and Red Cross DMH set up a case management system to provide for the long-term needs of those impacted.

My Post-Response Adjustment

Since this incident happened in my community it is hard to pinpoint the moment of post-response adjustment. I feel better describing it as a post-response *accommodation*. It was four months later and 1,500 miles away from Oklahoma City when I got my first good night's sleep since the bombing. I returned to work at the VA after two weeks of working six days a week for Red Cross. I would still spend most evenings of the week and one day of the weekend at some bombing recovery-related meeting or event.

Since this event impacted everyone I knew, it was a regular part of our conversation. My children, aged 3 and 4 years, would tell people I worked for the Red Cross since that must have been what they heard as I was leaving and where I had been when I returned. The deaths of so many children the same age as my children simultaneously haunts me and empowers me to be a better father. My childhood friends, co-workers, and professional colleagues noticed the orthogonal trajectory my career took after April 19, 1995. My post-response accommodation compelled me to give back. The Red Cross volunteers that guided me through the mental health response to the OKC Bombing opened my eyes to all the available training and networking opportunities. I hope I am able to "pay it forward" for the countless hours of patience and advice expended on my behalf by several Red Cross staff and volunteers.

Lessons Learned

- Preparation should include not only training in skills, but also the establishment of relationships before an event occurs. Training should also address the big picture, not just the actual tasks one might need to perform. As an instructor, I know most mental health volunteers want to know what to do. *Where* we do what we do and *why* is more important to emphasize. Similarly, understanding how the Red Cross operates, and the overall response framework, helps me to navigate a disaster response with less frustration.

- Mental health providers responding to disasters can serve as the calmest voice in the room, guiding the response team towards productive decision-making. We sit in meetings with emergency response professionals charged with making real life and death decisions. Unchecked, that tempo of urgency soon can lead to a narrow focus, hurt feelings, and unnecessary setbacks. DMH's contribution is to slow down the conversation and facilitate more effective problem solving. We help to triage the problems to establish priorities and gather information to make the best decision. Being intentional in our decisiveness is different from indecisiveness. Managing the pace and being a role model for problem-solving in harrowing situations is not a novel skillset for mental health professionals. The lesson to learn is being assertive enough to advocate this pace to non-mental health responders.
- Remember that you are not alone in coordinating a response. The more quickly diverse ideas are entertained, the faster an optimal decision can be reached. Collaborative decisions and compromise create the best recovery environment. Autocratic decisions seem like a shortcut, but the consequences of an ill-conceived decision are magnified in a time-compressed scenario like a mass casualty incident. I operate in the disaster response environment the same as in my clinical practice: I rely on a wide network of specialist providers for consultation and referral. There is no need to guess or suppose when the right person to answer any question is within reach.
- Be open to learning new lessons. Almost nothing is as irritating as hearing "that's how we've always done it." Experience and training should be applied to solve new problems and not used to promulgate dogma. Over 25 years as a Red Cross volunteer and I'm still inspired by the Clara Barton quote, "It irritates me to be told how things have always been done. I defy the tyranny of precedent. I cannot afford the luxury of a closed mind."

Chapter 11

2001 World Trade Center Attack in New York City

Mary Tramontin

I began my clinical psychology career at the New York City Police Department (NYPD), though I soon transitioned to federal government service. On September 11, 2001, I worked as a forensic psychologist at a federal prison located across from NYPD Headquarters, five blocks from the World Trade Center (WTC). I also lived nearby in Brooklyn.

I discovered the compelling world of disaster response during graduate school in the early 1990s and volunteered in this field as a doctoral student. The American Psychological Association had signed an MOU with the American Red Cross (ARC) and recruited psychologists to train in and lead disaster mental health (DMH) activities. Growing up in the Bronx, I was often surrounded by people in need. My parents were Italian immigrants whose identities had been shaped by World War II. On an instinctive level, I appreciated the value of support during extraordinarily chaotic situations. I was captivated by the possibility of helping during disasters. After receiving my doctoral degree, I joined ARC's Greater New York Chapter (GNY). We responded to local fires, crane collapses, gas explosions, and mass casualty catastrophes like TWA Flight 800 and Swissair Flight 111.

The Pre-Disaster Community

The World Trade Center was located in Lower Manhattan. This dense, narrower part of New York City is graced with towering and grand corporate buildings interspersed with fewer, but equally stylish, residential structures. It is an affluent slice of the city, less than a mile across, and surrounded by water. In 2000, finance jobs made up more than half of the area's economy. This association with business, money, and profit – economic power and freedom – has been noted as a contributing factor to the selection of the 110-story twin towers as a terrorist target. Yet the 16-acre WTC complex had workers from all walks of life and diverse cultures. Underneath it were stores, eateries, and the subway.

From a disaster recovery perspective, New York City, and Lower Manhattan especially, are resource-rich: clothes, food, shelter, social support, medical and psychological services, money, and attention.

A resource also available to this community was first responder practice with a previous terrorist attack at the exact same site. The 1993 WTC bombing was the largest incident ever handled at the time by the New York City Fire Department (FDNY). Lessons learned resulted in extensive fire safety improvements and led some employers to enhance their emergency preparedness plans. This may have facilitated the almost uniformly orderly and cooperative evacuation process that took place in 2001. Anecdotally, many first responders believed that the WTC would be attacked again – that terrorists "would return for those buildings."

The Disaster

The morning of September 11, 2001 in New York City was lovely and warm, with a remarkably blue, placid sky. Flying low and loud down the length of Manhattan, a hijacked plane crashed into the North Tower between floors 93 and 99 at 8:46 a.m. While the world watched, questions as to whether this was accidental ended when a second hijacked plane dove into the South Tower between floors 77 and 85 at 9:03 a.m. From high, burning floors, people, some hand in hand, leapt to their deaths.

At 9:59 a.m., the South Tower collapsed, followed by the North Tower collapse at 10:28 a.m. And the World Trade Center attack was amplified by accompanying coordinated events: the assault on the Pentagon near Washington, DC, and the hijacking of United Airlines Flight 93, which ended in a crash in a Pennsylvania field.

This disaster was significant in the ways we traditionally measure impact, in terms of scope, duration, and intensity:

- Nearly 3,000 died. In addition to some 2,600 civilians, first responders suffered significant losses; 343 FDNY firefighters died. Law enforcement personnel who perished included 23 from the New York City Police Department, 37 from the Port Authority Police Department, and 3 from the New York State Courts.
- The recovery efforts at the site spanned nine months. The number of intact bodies was low, less than 300, and identification of remains still continues with improved DNA technology.
- The implosion of the Twin Towers spread dust, pulverized human remains, and debris, creating a chemically toxic environment for those involved in recovery efforts, as well as for area workers and residents. Fires emitting toxic smoke burned until the end of 2001. In the absence of any sufficiently clear or trustworthy guidance regarding the potential health impact, those at the site wondered but carried on.

- This terrorist attack represented an act of war, intensifying its meaning and distinguishing it from other disasters. Within 30 days, the United States military had bombed Afghanistan.

These unique elements coalesced to create a disaster whose impact persists. Some area residents were displaced, jobs were eliminated or relocated, roads were closed, and public transportation was disrupted. Those who remained would be intimate witnesses to the ongoing recovery efforts and daily remainders of that day, and subject to the degraded air quality. The death toll continues to rise as the NYC Medical Examiner's office adds people who died of illnesses caused by exposure to toxins from the site. The resultant asymmetrical "war on terror" is sustained and related acts of war occur locally, not only on distant battlefields.

My Thoughts Pre-Response

A DMH colleague and I were on call as the ARC GNY DMH leads. When the first plane crashed, we coordinated by phone. My colleague would drive to ARC headquarters. I would go to the scene. An on-site presence was standard operating procedure.

I mentally went into a practiced response mode – after all, this was an aviation incident, like many ARC GNY had responded to over the past decade. I possessed a skillset that our chapter had rehearsed and deployed many times, and I had a team and close "disaster buddies" to rely on. Our primary DMH lead was out of town so I felt an added level of responsibility, especially in the early hours of our response. This disaster was happening close to where I worked; my supervisors were supportive of my Red Cross activities, so I could manage both volunteer and work duties. I knew the area well, and planned to meet other ARC personnel at the site as we did routinely many other times.

My closest family and friends were not in the affected area, and I had checked in with them prior to heading to the disaster. My aim was to appraise the scene and report back as to needs. Proceeding to the site around 9:30 a.m., I felt supported, personally and professionally, and well equipped as a DMH volunteer.

My Response Experience

My Red Cross ID proved powerful, green-lighting me through NYPD barriers. Three blocks in the distance, fires burned from high in the buildings. Around my path on the ground, shoes, wallets, clothing, cellphones, and what may have been pieces of flesh were scattered across the sidewalks and the streets. These personal elements gave me pause. I did not linger, recalling the sage words of a police officer colleague. She had warned "not to look under the yellow blankets" at mass casualty events: best not to over-expose yourself to disturbing details.

On my way, I met other officials seeking to muster at the base of the Towers. The visceral sense of extreme danger was contained – until the collapse of the South Tower forced us to run. Seeking shelter in a nearby building, several of us huddled together. Smoke and debris rushed in, covering all in darkness and dust. My first thought was to chide myself for dying to deliver disaster mental health. Thick grey smoke and fine dust swirled in the air. Pay phones and cellphones stopped working. I had no way to connect with my ARC colleagues. I made my way back to my workplace and resumed ARC activities later.

By the end of that first week, we all were adjusting to the "new normal" of vigilance. We feared an additional attack even as we comforted those in concentric layers of impact around Ground Zero, including families who lost loved ones, displaced residents, those who had lost jobs, journalists, funeral directors, air traffic controllers, 911 dispatchers, airline personnel – and ourselves. Spontaneous volunteers as well as those coordinated under ARC's formal deployment system poured into Headquarters. We provided support, sometimes for months, at Ground Zero, worker respite centers, a Family Assistance Center, telephone hotlines, and at funerals and memorial services. My main focus was on Ground Zero and the respite centers, and organizing exit debriefings with our ARC Spiritual Care Workers when recovery efforts ended in May 2002. While capturing the complexity, intensity, and nuances of the response might require several chapters, I will focus on my DMH response experience at the respite centers.

The tremendous force of the towers' collapse left behind "the pile," a three-billion-pound mountain of damaged, pulverized, or incinerated marble, steel, glass, office furniture, paper, clothes, emergency service vehicles, plane parts – and people. At and near Ground Zero, the obvious, dark reality was that those who had perished enveloped us. The deceased would be hard to find and their bodies would not be intact. Yet they were in the air we inhaled, in the dust that covered lower Manhattan, in bone and tissue fragments, and embedded in the ground underfoot. This awareness permeated all efforts at Ground Zero.

While the mission was to shrink the mountain and clear the site, it had to be done with the utmost care. For firefighters and police, this was especially meaningful. The FDNY would leave none of their 343 fallen comrades behind. At any sighting of the missing in the rubble, construction would stop, and workers stepped down from their rigs. Clergy stationed on-site 24 hours a day were dispatched to offer a blessing before remains were transferred to a waiting ambulance for transport to the Medical Examiner's (ME's) office. With as much reverence as possible, the remains of firefighters and police members of service were carefully strapped in a stretcher and covered by an American flag. After the chaplain arrived for a blessing, uniformed personnel formed an honor guard to line the path leading away from the pit. These remains were escorted slowly into a waiting ambulance with flashing lights. All on site would stop still to pay respects. This makeshift yet dignified procession was repeated countless times, at all hours, day or night. It highlighted that these first responders, though most likely sensing the impossible odds that day, had laid down their lives to rescue others.

Through this process, a shifting community of recovery responders formed. Firefighters, police officers, construction and trade professionals, and sanitation workers industriously searched for remains, sorted and discarded debris, and worked on securing and restoring city infrastructure. Mass care workers from many humanitarian relief organizations prepared meals 24 hours, 7 days a week. Around the clock, volunteers were present to ensure that mental health and spiritual care needs were addressed.

Local respite centers were established for recovery workers to eat, take breaks, and even sleep. Two main ones were St. Paul's Chapel and the Salvation Army Respite Center, nicknamed the Big White Tent, the Bubble, or the Taj. Open around the clock, these safe havens embodied Psychological First Aid. They developed strict security boundaries, allowing entry only to recovery workers and volunteers. This protected those inside from the intrusion of the public and the media. From a mental health perspective, preserving recovery workers' privacy increased their sense of safety, allowing them to decompress more fully.

The respite centers offered much more than food, cots, and shelter. There were many surprising touches: meals from high-end restaurants; hand and foot warmers; Band-Aids; inspirational pamphlets; boots, socks, and gloves; heartfelt notes from children; colorful, encouraging homemade banners; cough drops, candy, and lip balm. Chiropractors, podiatrists, and massage therapists set up stations to tend to the needs of the body. Mental health, spiritual care volunteers, and animal-assisted support tended minds and souls.

The respite centers' powerful and palpable comfort and acceptance was in contrast to the intensity of the work site. Recovery workers could lower their guard there. Because the effort was protracted, they established routines for where to eat and rest. Not much was said the first few days and weeks. Everyone was in shock. But over time it became easier to talk – not only about sadness, frustrations, and fear but also about the food or the harpist or just the novelty of the experience.

Critical Incident Stress Debriefings (CISD) were conducted by many organizations, including ARC and NYPD. In 2001, debriefings were considered a best practice, especially in first responder circles. I appreciated what the model offered. These encounters opened paths to connect with those impacted early on post-trauma. Yet in the context of this disaster, with its huge scale, scope, and intensity, the core tenet of encouraging people to detail their experience felt counterintuitive. While we applied the practice, we modified the traditional model in our application. Food was always offered, and after introductions, psychoeducation, and discussion, many participants left. We debriefing leads stayed behind with those who wished to talk further. Few spoke of stress symptoms, but many were eager to mull over the event: "I see now that life is really short and I want to have children someday," or "I realized how much I loved my husband." These meandering, reflective conversations, often about meaning, would sometimes last for hours. We reverted to the essential counseling basic of "meeting our client where the client was," with gratitude for the responder organizations who were attempting to care for their own through such offerings.

This disaster's site-specific recovery requirements created a natural nexus between mental health, spiritual care, and animal-assisted support. Clergy were in demand. Their humble, quiet rituals grounded workers. As a result, we all learned to pause, and were less inclined to be hijacked by our automatic responses to the provocations around us. I often found myself pairing with our Spiritual Care workers, either to walk and talk or to compare observations. Chaplains were excellent role models in the "ministry of presence" – a way of "being" rather than "doing" or "telling" which focuses on inward preparation in order to be fully available to those who suffer.

Much of our work was with first responders. Each group had distinct cultural mores, rituals, language, and values so it was essential not to stereotype. Still, in general, first responders do not expect to feel helpless or horrified. They are action-oriented, courageous, want to help, put others' needs ahead of their own, push personal emotions and reactions out of their minds, and would rather give than ask for assistance. Therefore, in supporting first responders a main goal was to normalize common reactions. Pairing with a canine and their well-trained owner increased our effectiveness. Therapy dogs elicited hugs, petting, and affectionate responses. The dogs were unexpected, carried no stigma, and required no conversation – they brought spontaneous relief and a sense of normalcy.

The nine-month recovery effort was intense, busy, dirty, and rough. Like those in a war zone, recovery workers had a mission-first perspective. Symptoms, if any, would be delayed until the end. Stress and injury were to be avoided so as to not get off the line. We DMH workers essentially practiced combat stress relief. In this framework, another main goal was calming extended activation of the fight, flight, or freeze response. This can be seen as a form of aiding basic physiological processing – helping recovery workers to maintain their physiological equilibrium and avoid debilitating hyper-arousal. As in combat, such intense involvement posed the risk of throwing one's basic bodily processes out of whack. The more sensory overload with no reprieve, the more potential for problems.

We had naturally occurring, regular golden opportunities to facilitate emotional and cognitive processing. Sharing meals or taking coffee breaks at respite centers were lead-ins for connecting with workers, peers, organizational leads, and even visiting dignitaries. These small moments of connection could offer someone a chance to feel safe, accompanied, and normal.

Responders would often casually and spontaneously open up about distressing experiences. When this occurred, I would listen carefully, follow their lead, and avoid facile reassurances. I never wanted to risk those who were sharing their unfiltered impressions to feel under the microscope. Rather, I kept our conversations even-keeled, allowing these chats to go naturally where they would. There was a chance I might see the same worker again. And, after all, each had to return to duty soon after such short-lived encounters.

Seeing recovery workers on a consistent basis allowed us to form "therapeutic alliances." Using a collaborative, conversational style, we encouraged workers to tap into good coping strategies versus "we can't do anything about this." We listened for themes, and asked how parents, spouses, and children were faring.

Humor was welcomed. As a type of positive coping, it served to break the ice by offering temporary relief from the literal mud and mire of the pit and its heartbreak. I recall walking into the Big White Tent early one morning with another DMH worker at change of shift. Workers coming off or heading to the pile were sitting at tables eating breakfast. My colleague and I joined a group of firefighters she knew. Heads down, quietly eating, the mood was tense, somber, and low. Pushing through this atmosphere, my colleague began "busting their chops" about their obvious mood and depleted energy. Her quick quips grabbed their attention – they gave it right back to her. She normalized their reactions by knowing how to use their language, and appropriate humor, to connect with them. Soon we began bantering back and forth. They disclosed being discouraged after another cold, long night with few recoveries.

However, not all helpers were adept at applying humor or a light-hearted stance. Occasionally, DMH workers would show up with forced cheeriness and appear too bubbly or festive. The social context of respite centers, combined with recovery workers' bravado and graciousness, could be confusing to some, making it easy to misjudge. Humor was most effective when natural, offered flexibly, and when it was good-natured and kind in spirit and tone. Sarcastic, dark, and forced humor had a negative impact and could be harmful. I could not have pulled off the intervention my colleague had, but I was at ease with lighter irony, and appreciated spontaneous wit. Wasn't it Freud who wrote that humor is a higher order defense mechanism to cope with trauma and stress? To illustrate workers' use of humor, in addition to the time demands of the recovery efforts, there were over 400 funerals and memorials that would require a uniformed presence. Sitting one evening in St. Paul's Chapel in the early spring of 2002, several firefighters were reflecting on their experiences attending these services. They spoke in detail of how in the early days after 9/11, shock and grief were much more demonstrable, and that attendance was strong. Over time, even family members' reactions attenuated, and firefighters had to plan in-house who would be available to attend which event and plot logistics. This reflection led one firefighter to comment, "I feel as if I've become a professional mourner!"

Spiritual care disaster responders, affectionately called the "God Squad," played a special role requiring courage, presence of mind, and composure. Sixty chaplains from many faiths participated in the Morgue Chaplaincy. They had viewed death up close and personal under grueling circumstances. Similar to first responders, disaster chaplains are a distinct group: Self-selecting, brave, and resilient, they were well defended psychologically. They already had excellent strategies in place for what they had encountered. Our model in offering DMH support at the conclusion of the operation, therefore, was to meet each chaplain where they were on an individual basis. It seemed prudent to explore how they were doing physically, assess fatigue levels, ask if they had been able to remain in touch with loved ones and social supports, and have them consider whom they may reach out to if they so wished to process their experiences. We expressed our gratitude for their unique role and contribution while gently raising awareness about being receptive to whatever non-spiritual needs they may now have.

On May 30, 2002, the recovery operations at the WTC site formally concluded. Closing ceremonies included a solemn procession of personnel: NYPD and FDNY representatives, Port Authority police, Red Cross representatives, and others formed an honor guard as a truck removed the last girder from the pit.

Prior to the event, ARC DMH thoughtfully prepared for this transition. For many, Ground Zero had become a primary community: Those departing might face the expectable challenges of returning from a consuming and meaningful deployment. We were hoping to forestall reintegration problems. We offered times for workers to meet with DMH, though none attended. We also created handouts, "Some Thoughts about What to Expect as the WTC Recovery Work Ends." Our handouts included sections entitled "Normal Thoughts and Feelings," "Strategies for Handling Negative or Difficult Thoughts and Feelings," "What to Do if You are Overwhelmed," and a list of vetted resources. Our concluding paragraph read:

> You have just been involved in an extraordinary work. You have done all you could with determination and dedication. Your work has been a healing gift for us all. Now, after such an achievement, you are going back to life with a different purpose, different focus, different emotions, different people, a different pace. It takes time to figure out

how to move ahead without losing the importance of what you have just been through.

But it can be done.

My Post-Response Adjustment

This was the most powerful disaster I have experienced – it is an outlier in my disaster mental health career, and I was deeply touched by it for all the reasons highlighted. I was fortunate to have the disaster mental health community of practice in place from ARC GNY, including an established leadership team and known volunteers. Comrades from across the country joined us. Locals remained first in and last out and provided continuity of operations. Leaving routine, sustaining, heartfelt, and inspiring connections behind when the site closed saddened me. These relationships were my best form of self-preservation. I had someone I trusted at every turn. I reached out often and had long dinners with my disaster colleagues, one-on-one and in groups. We had a place to share our struggles, and to mine our collective experiences to inform future preparation and response. I did not know in advance how much I would turn to my disaster colleagues – but that is precisely why I highlight developing such social supports as part of your DMH career, especially in intense and protracted responses.

There are no prescriptive steps for immunizing us from disaster's reach when responding. Each event is unique. One's personal reactions will depend on a range of factors. I learned yet again the importance of being open to my feelings – and of continuing to allow disasters that are not directly personal to affect, shape, and transform me. When asked when this event was truly over for me, I appreciate that it has become a part of who I am.

Lessons Learned

Before

- Be mindful regarding your motivations for volunteering, and predetermine your level of commitment to respond. Awareness about these two aspects will help you self-regulate as well as balance disaster challenges. In large, intense, and protracted events, exercise caution about being swept up into the rush of response obligations.
- Develop a cadre of trusted disaster buddies. In the trenches of a very long, painful disaster, our interdependence was even more pronounced as we coalesced around our shared mission. Like first responders and chaplains, we are a distinct group, with shared values, rituals, language, and ideals.

During

- Not all disasters are physically dangerous for DMH responders, but some are. Extreme heat, cold, smoke, and toxic air are hazards that should not be overlooked. It's paramount to make your physical safety a priority. You may not always know this in advance. When in doubt, allow yourself the option of not responding.
- Large-scale, intense disasters induce a very high physiological arousal level. Since responding to the WTC Attack, I have learned to not underestimate the role of biology and the benefits of a calm presence and basic comfort. Words and verbal processing are not always essential, especially early on.
- Cultivate receptivity to the unique requirements of the disaster in front of you. Conforming to rigid procedures is not always necessary or even possible. As disasters become larger and more complex, routinized organizational roles and even disaster plans give way to improvisation. As mentioned earlier, our clinical approach was informed by what was going on around us. We joined forces with other allies and partners and worked closely with Spiritual Care and Animal-Assisted providers. We modified our interventions based on observed needs.

After

- Consider your disaster response as a deployment, no matter how short or long. Each disaster response requires you to leave the "normal" world behind to enter a dynamic, chaotic, and unpredictable environment. Disaster deployments test your mettle. When you re-deploy, or return home, there may be expectable transitional stress as you regain your footing. Post-response needs will vary. For example, you may simply be tired and require rest and recreation. Others may experience resurgence of old wounds and seek professional consultation. You may need to plan quality time with children, friends, parents, and other loved ones. Large events with many deaths often naturally engender existential questions and soul searching – and, perhaps, accompanying changes in one's identity.

Chapter 12

2012 Sandy Hook School Shooting in Newtown, CT

Wayne F. Dailey

I worked in leadership positions as a clinical psychologist at the Connecticut Department of Mental Health, a state agency with about 4,000 employees providing an extensive array of community-based services. I've served as Deputy Commissioner, Senior Policy Advisor, Director of Psychological Services, media spokesperson, and more. I was often in the media spotlight when bad things happened and the public wanted answers. Concurrently, I worked in private practice. I'm an Associate Clinical Professor in Psychiatry at Yale University and Senior Consultant for the Annapolis Coalition on the Behavioral Health Workforce.

Immediately after the 9/11 terrorist attacks I was asked to establish a statewide disaster mental health capability to address the emotional needs of Connecticut residents affected by terrorism and disasters. Although I've helped plan and implement many mental health programs, this was new territory for me. It didn't take me long to realize that among the best organized disaster mental health capabilities was the one operated by Red Cross, so I joined to learn how they did it. Since my retirement from Connecticut government in 2009, I've become very involved with Red Cross. I've served on many national deployments and a few international ones. When the Newtown shootings occurred, I was asked to initiate the mental health response.

The Pre-Disaster Community

Founded in 1705, Newtown is a picturesque, mostly white and affluent New England community of roughly 28,000. Nestling in the bucolic hills of western Connecticut, Sandy Hook is a village within the town where the scenic Pootatuck River flows gently under an old bridge, and where a few small shops and a breakfast cafe line the narrow road leading down to the bridge. The Sandy Hook volunteer fire department is about a mile to the east on a country road, a quarter mile away from the elementary school. The town's school system is well regarded, and from the disaster resource standpoint, considering its fire, police, medical, and social service assets, this community is better off than most.

With its quiet central green and historic churches, Newtown has a serene, hypnotic quality about it. In short, nothing extraordinary ever seemed to happen there. Perhaps this is why so many considered it to be a great place to raise a family: More than a quarter of the town's 9,000 households included children under the age of 18.

The Disaster

As the sun rose on the cold morning of December 14, 2012, just eleven days before Christmas, something unthinkable was about to happen. It began in the Newtown home of Nancy Lanza when her 20-year-old son, Adam, obsessed with guns and mass murders, shot and killed his mother as she slept in her bed. He then drove to the nearby Sandy Hook Elementary School where at about 9:35 a.m. he shot his way past a locked door into the school using an AR-15 style semi-automatic rifle. Within less than five minutes he had fired 156 rounds, including one final bullet from a handgun that he used to kill himself, just as police began to arrive. Most of the victims were shot multiple times at close range. The 20 murdered children were six and seven years of age. Six adults, women who worked as teachers and administrators at the school, were also killed. Two other school employees were wounded and were treated in a nearby hospital.

The scene for those still alive inside the school and for arriving first responders was horrifying. Many survivors had heard gunfire and screams. After the shooting stopped, school staff attempted to shield children from seeing the carnage by asking them to form a line, hold hands, and close their eyes as they were led outside the building. As initial forensic work was taking place inside the school, a temporary morgue was established under tents in a nearby field where bodies were taken for examination and identification.

As word of the shootings began to spread, frantic parents descended upon the school trying to locate their children. Most were reunited fairly quickly and rushed home, but as time passed many of those who could not find their loved ones gathered at the nearby firehouse, in the same building where public officials had established their incident command post. Soon, many state and local government officials arrived, including state and local police and the FBI. The state's governor was doing his best to provide updates to those present. As the day wore on, and with so many families still waiting for their children or for word about missing relatives who worked in the school, the tension in the firehouse became unbearable.

By mid-afternoon, after conferring with one of his senior staff, the governor came back into firehouse meeting room and told the gathered families that if they had not seen or heard from their loved one by now "… that was not going to happen." The room exploded with grief. People were told to return to their homes where they would be contacted as soon as more information was available.

My Thoughts Pre-Response

My morning on December 14 had an unremarkable start with a routine dental check-up. Following the appointment, the dentist gave me a complimentary toothbrush that I stuffed into my shirt pocket and headed off to Red Cross headquarters in Farmington, CT, to attend a pre-planned "after action" meeting to discuss our chapter's recent response to Hurricane Sandy. From the car radio I soon learned that two children had been shot at an elementary school in Newtown. As I drove toward headquarters, the number of reported casualties steadily increased, as did my driving speed and sense of alarm. I soon ran up the steps to the Red Cross building and saw our Operations Director running down a long corridor toward me. Out of breath, she asked if I could go immediately to the Red Cross field office in Bethel, CT, about five miles from Newtown, and initiate the mental health response for Red Cross until someone more senior arrived.

Without further instructions, I jumped into my vehicle and sped off toward Newtown. On the 30-minute drive, my mind raced through scattered thoughts. I have four grown children of my own and helped raise two of my younger siblings. So, my foremost concern was for the intense emotional pain of those present at the school and for the parents of victims. How many victims were there? The radio report kept changing. Were some children wounded, how many, how seriously? How many shooters? Had the shooting stopped? I don't recall thinking about myself or what I was getting into. I didn't feel fear, but I felt an intense sense of foreboding.

My Response Experience

When I arrived at the ARC Bethel office, I met briefly with the local Red Cross Disaster Services Director, who initially directed me to go to the Newtown Town Hall where several agencies were planning to set up a Family Reception Center for those affected by the tragedy. However, within a few hours a decision was made not to open the center, in part because distressed people looking for information about missing loved ones sped away from the town hall as soon as they learned that the most likely place to find such news was at the Sandy Hook firehouse.

After consulting with the Disaster Services Director, my Red Cross Disaster Mental Health colleague and I headed toward the firehouse. The old county road was choked with traffic, including what seemed like every TV mobile satellite truck from Washington, DC to Boston. By this time state police had closed two nearby exits to interstate I-84, making area roads nearly impassable. We parked our car and began walking the remaining mile to our destination.

Inside the firehouse incident command post we were greeted by a scene of controlled mayhem. The place was packed with first responders and government officials, and some family members of victims were present. The mood was grim. Though our presence and willingness to help was clearly evident, at this point there was little we could do or say to assist family members demonstrating an extreme degree of emotional shock. Our role was best served with few words, offering a compassionate presence as families sat in stunned silence. Our presence served as unspoken reassurance that we stood with them ready to help at any possible opportunity. Soon all of the families left for home after the governor announced that they would be contacted when more information was available. The remainder of the afternoon was occupied by coordination activities. We worked closely with the Connecticut Disaster Behavioral Health Response Network (CT-DBHRN). This was the group I had helped to establish following the 9/11 terrorist attacks and prior to my retirement from state government.

During the afternoon and evening, the number of volunteer mental health clinicians from Red Cross, DBHRN, and nearby Yale University continued to grow. At around 10:30 p.m., we were all called into a briefing led by state police. They explained to us that the medical examiner's office had completed the process of identifying those killed using photos of students and faculty from the school, physical descriptions, and descriptions of clothing worn that day. Incident command announced that the death notifications would be performed that night using three-person teams, including a state trooper, a clergy member, and a mental health clinician. The trooper would confirm the death while the clergy member and clinician would provide any spiritual and emotional support desired by the family. Although many of the clinicians had received prior training in the death notification process, this was the first time Connecticut had used three-person teams this way in a mass casualty incident. For several years prior to my retirement from state government, I had advocated for this team model in conducting death notifications in large-scale disasters with Connecticut emergency management and homeland security officials. However, I don't know how the decision was made to use it at Sandy Hook. In order to reassure the families regarding their personal safety, the state police assigned a state trooper to each family to closely watch over them and serve as a single point of contact during the coming weeks.

The teams were assembled by about 11:30 p.m., Friday night. At that point we loaded into 26 state police cruisers and drove to the homes of those of whose who had been killed. Each team had a folder with information about the victim, along with resource materials and benefits (including compensation for funeral costs), that were available for victims of crime through the FBI and the Connecticut Judicial Department. We were to leave these resources with the family with an offer to assist them with completing application forms when they were ready.

My team arrived at its destination just before midnight. The house was completely dark except for a single electric Christmas candle illuminating a window. The trooper knocked several times and we waited. Finally, a young couple in their pajamas opened the door. The trooper introduced himself as the mother fell sobbing. We were invited inside and after a brief introduction the trooper delivered the sad news.

The next three hours were among the most vivid and painful I've ever experienced. The couple asked many questions, expressed anxieties, fears, and intense feelings, and recalled tender and silly memories of their six-year-old child. There was no set formula for my interventions. Although I used elements of Psychological First Aid and crisis counseling, most of my response involved simple expressions of condolence, empathy, and support in the face of unimaginable heartbreak. There was one notable exception where I offered some very specific advice. I anticipated that the couple was likely to be barraged with calls from well-meaning family, friends, acquaintances, and the media. I therefore encouraged them to appoint someone they knew well and trusted to act as a buffer or screener between themselves and a potentially intrusive world. It turned out that many families found it helpful to have a best friend or family member take phone calls that could be returned when it felt right.

Throughout our visit the couple swayed in a seesaw of emotion from relative calm to open sobbing. An important challenge was to help the couple stay in the moment, recognizing that second guessing decisions made earlier in the day would not help; no matter how bitter the reality, we can't go back to change the past. The young mother stated that while agonizing, the formal notification of the death had at least relieved her anxiety that her child was suffering, in pain, or hiding somewhere in intense fear. The discussion finally reached a natural conclusion. The couple expressed deep appreciation and thanks for our visit. We returned to the command post where I participated in a quick operational debriefing.

Red Cross had booked a room at a nearby hotel where I arrived at about 3:30 a.m. When the night clerk asked if I had any bags, I realized that my only possession, other than the clothes I was wearing, was the toothbrush from the dentist appointment still in my shirt pocket. After an hour or two of fitful sleep, I returned to Red Cross headquarters in Bethel at 7:45 a.m. An experienced Red Cross Disaster Mental Health (DMH) Chief soon arrived to take command of the mental health activities. I briefed her on the previous day's operation and then returned to my hotel to rest. Later that day my daughter brought a "care package" from home, including warm clothes. Cold rain and snow were on the way.

During the next few days Red Cross greatly increased its DMH staffing levels as everyone realized that the entire community had been deeply affected by the tragedy. No one was spared its impact. Spontaneous memorial gatherings were occurring throughout the town, and planned events were held at several local churches. Red Cross DMH staff were on hand to help anyone who sought assistance. We also had a low-key and discreet presence at funerals of the victims, which took place over the next week or so. Red Cross workers at these events wore ID badges only and not their usual red disaster responder vests. Media reporters were everywhere. We assisted grieving parents who had questions about the advisability of having their surviving young children interviewed on camera, often suggesting that they demur. In addition to the intense grief they were experiencing, these parents were very fearful about their surviving children. We did our best to help survivors feel safe by dispelling the many rumors that were circulating in the first few days after the shootings. There were bomb scares and rumors of new shootings. We provided calm, reassurance, and accurate information to help survivors feel safe.

On Sunday, President Obama, who had been moved to tears in his televised press response to the tragedy, came to Newtown to participate in a multi-faith service at the town's high school. Prior to his public appearance in the school's auditorium, he met privately with the family of each victim. This was carefully planned by dividing the 26 families among six classrooms. After receiving Secret Service clearance, a Red Cross DMH worker was assigned to each room to support the families while the president went from room to room. I served in the classroom with the family whom I had visited on the night of the death notifications. During the approximately two-hour wait for the president, I had the opportunity to provide support for each of the families in the room. In this small sample, some individuals reported that the tragedy had increased their faith in God and that they had benefited greatly from the support of their faith community. Others were clearly still struggling and would need an extended period for their recovery. The President's interactions with family members were intimate and profoundly touching. He connected with each individual, expressed heartfelt condolences, and delivered a message of support from himself and from the American people. He shook my hand and offered his thanks for my service before moving on to the next room and then to the large public meeting.

In the auditorium, we provided emotional support to many members of the public and to the police who were among the first responders at the school. Some of the toughest looking officers were sobbing and shaking. Red Cross DMH and fellow officers helped to console them through soft words and a simple touch on the arm or shoulder. We discreetly passed out tissues and returned to our assigned stations. The entire public event conveyed great dignity, helped to galvanize and strengthen a deeply injured community, and demonstrated the degree of public support.

Disaster mental health interventions after events like the Sandy Hook School shooting are about simple, but nuanced actions. First, and foremost, it is essential to be authentic and completely present, in-the-moment, with the person you wish to assist. I spoke with survivors in a calm voice, maintained an unhurried cadence of speech, kept good eye contact, used reflective listening, and when I spoke with a child or someone who was seated, I dropped to one knee to be at their eye level. When I met with survivors, I introduced myself, and asked their name and how they wished to be addressed – "May I call you 'Henry,' or should I say 'Mr. Thompson'?" As I was granted permission in response to these small requests, it helped to restore a sense that clients have a bit more control in an environment where they previously may have felt completely overwhelmed and powerless. There are many similar examples in which I try to empower disaster survivors. Often, the smallest increase in the survivor's feeling of self-control helps to enhance their hope for recovery and confidence in the effectiveness of their own actions.

A few days after the shootings, Red Cross opened a Family Assistance Center (FAC) with staff participation from partner agencies like CTDBHRN, the FBI Office for Victims Assistance, and the Connecticut Judicial Department Office of Victim Services. The FAC location was not publicly disclosed and was accessible only to the immediate families of victims. Here, counselors provided mental health support and helped families complete application packages to cover funeral costs and address financial needs related to the tragedy. Other community members seeking psychological and emotional support were being sent to a nearby school where volunteer counselors from various organizations were providing assistance. In the coming months, substantial federal support from the Department of Education and the Department of Justice provided funding for ongoing counseling and recovery service related to the tragedy. Clearly, an event this brutal impacts the mental health not only of families of victims, but the entire community, for years.

My Post-Response Adjustment

I've provided mental health support in more than 20 major disasters in the continental United States and in other parts of the world. However, I've never had a disaster response experience that approached the emotional intensity that I felt at Newtown. And what I felt was a mere harmonic of what the families of victims experienced. Newtown had a profound impact on me, stripping away the superficial but often useful shielding that normally protects me, and I assume, most other people, from the emotional hazards of daily life. In this psychological state, my distance from the pain that I saw and felt in others was diminished, but with that loss came an extraordinary opportunity to understand and convey empathy to those I was seeking to help. I could sense that they perceived the genuineness of my support. This opened the door for my assistance amidst the cacophonous stimuli that these disaster survivors were experiencing.

After 10 days in Newtown I returned home to my family. I was exhausted, but believe that I assisted many people in a time of great need. Two important sources of support helped to sustain me during and after the deployment. The first was contact with my wife and children, who were very understanding and continually available while I was away and upon my return. And second, I received tremendous support from fellow Red Cross disaster mental health volunteers, both during and in the years since Newtown. This support is analogous to the way our men and women in military service build lifelong bonds forged in the face of adversity. Finally, part of my post-disaster adjustment has been facilitated by writing papers such as this one, as well as newspaper op-eds and letters, and by writing to elected officials about sensible gun control legislation.

Lessons Learned

- One of the foremost lessons of Newtown was the critical importance of developing close alliances before a disaster occurs. When I arrived on the scene I saw many familiar faces from Red Cross, but also had many competent responders on hand, some from Connecticut and some from other parts of the country. But the overall mental health response would not have been as robust without collaboration among a network of partner agencies. These were people I could trust to do competent work when Red Cross concluded its efforts and transitioned responsibility back to local resources. Also, assigning a state trooper to the family of each victim greatly increased the feeling of personal safety among deeply traumatized family members.
- While much interagency collaboration was successful in Newtown, the overall management of the behavioral health portion of the operation left much to be desired. The problem was that no single agency had the overall authority to plan and manage all family assistance activities. This meant that many freelance, unaffiliated mental health volunteers just showed up in Newtown and started interacting with community members. There was no background check or organized credentialing process, nor was there any supervision of these individuals. This problem exposed an already vulnerable community to unnecessary risks. The agreement between Red Cross and the National Transportation Safety Board that gives Red Cross overall responsibility for family assistance in commercial airline and rail passenger transportation disasters is one potential model for a solution.
- Another important lesson for the mental health responder is to recognize and accept that in the early hours following a mass casualty event there may be little we can do or say to alleviate the extreme emotional pain of survivors and family members. Nevertheless, we should not underestimate the powerful message conveyed by our compassionate presence: The community has rallied to help and will

be there in the days ahead to support them as they seek a pathway forward toward a new normal in their lives.

- Finally, nothing you've ever read, no training you've ever taken as a clinician or disaster mental health responder can fully prepare you to assist families and the community following the murder of so many small children and adults. Neither does this chapter presume to attain that goal. Instead, my hope is to better prepare you to provide effective and compassionate disaster mental health care in the face of unimaginable tragedy. One of my personal lessons – one that I had known prior to the Newtown shootings, but that was vividly punctuated by the unfolding events – is that a disaster mental health responder can feel significant pain as the result of what he or she sees in a disaster survivor. By maintaining and fully utilizing strong sources of personal support such as family, friends, and fellow disaster responders you can transform the difficulties of deployment into new awareness and renewed strength that can enhance your willingness to continue as a responder and improve your understanding of how best to serve others in their time of great need.

Chapter 13

2012 Shooting in Webster, NY

Steven N. Moskowitz

Unlike many who practice Disaster Mental Health, DMH is my "day job." As the Albany-based director of the New York State Department of Mental Health bureau that is responsible for Emergency Preparedness and Response, I oversee the maintenance and coordination of a state-wide cadre of DMH responders whom I can deploy following regional and large-scale disaster events. The position provides me with opportunities to engage in DMH work as both a practitioner and an administrator – a situation that allows the former to influence the quality and effectiveness of the latter.

Like most practitioners, I came into the work circumstantially rather than because of any planned career choice. As a Licensed Social Worker, my career arc has included stints as a family mediator, a therapist, and a community services agency administrator, a mix that proved valuable in negotiating the very delicate task of planning and guiding an intervention to assist the Webster First Responders from my position with a state agency. The work was delicate because my involvement in planning an intervention in Webster ran counter to a basic premise of emergency management – that disasters begin and end locally.

The Pre-Disaster Community

Named for the famous orator Daniel Webster, the village of Webster is made up of 5,500 inhabitants nestled on the shore of Lake Ontario, a short drive from the large metropolis of Rochester, NY in Monroe County. Originally an agricultural growing and distribution center, the town has been sustained in recent years by the presence of the Xerox Corporation which has research and manufacturing facilities in the village and the surrounding area. Growth in the business community continues to favor technology-centered endeavors, although the presence of a new craft brewery sourcing its ingredients locally harkens back to the town's agricultural roots. The village of Webster might be considered the poor cousin to the nearby town of Webster. The village has much lower incomes (family average is $50,00 vs. $70,00) and a higher poverty rate (12 percent for the village vs. 3.9 percent of total population).

The public safety structure in the Town of Webster includes the Webster Police Department with 32 paid officers. Fire protection for the west side of the town is provided by the West Webster Fire Department, a modestly sized, all-volunteer department consisting of 122 members who operate three fire stations with a total of 10 response vehicles.

The Disaster

In the early morning hours of Christmas Eve in 2012, members of the West Webster Fire Department (WWFD) were dispatched to a reported house fire on a spit of land just north of Rochester, NY along the Lake Ontario coast. First to arrive on the scene was the department pumper driven by a volunteer firefighter, who was also a lieutenant with the Webster Police Department. Close behind was the Emergency Medical Services "fly car" manned by a 19-year-old 911 dispatcher.

As they exited their response vehicles, both were shot and killed by William Spengler, Jr., age 62, who had set fire to his family home and then lay in wait to ambush responding firefighters and police. In the minutes that followed, two more Webster firefighters were shot and injured by the continuing gunfire, as was an off-duty police officer who was struck by flying shrapnel as he stopped to assist.

Firefighters were pulled back from the scene as police addressed the active shooter situation, a scene complicated by the fire that had now spread to multiple adjacent homes. After an initial exchange of gunfire with police, a tactical decision was made to hold positions until an armored vehicle could arrive. Eventually the shooter was found near his home, dead from a self-inflicted gunshot wound. In searching through his burned house, authorities found the body of Spengler's sister whom Spengler had killed before setting the initial fire. The fire destroyed six other homes, displacing those residents on the day before Christmas.

My Thoughts Pre-Response

The phone conversation that initiated my response was memorable as it illustrated the complexity that every DMH response poses for me as both the state's lead for our DMH program and as a trained mental health responder. As an administrator, I needed to quickly assess the particulars of what had occurred to guide me in crafting a response plan to support the Webster first responders in their recovery from an event that had shattered the thin veneer of trust they held that they would return safely from their next rollout. This assessment included not simply being familiar with the details of the shooting which had killed two of their brothers-in-arms, but I also needed an understanding of contextual dynamics as well: a working familiarity with the multiple emergency response and governmental jurisdictions, how to best apply the governmental resources at my disposal, and how to obtain buy-in from other mental health and emergency management stakeholders. All would be required if this effort was to be successful.

The administrative response was complex, and sometimes these managerial imperatives help me to avoid thinking or feeling too deeply about my personal and emotional reactions as a responder. In this case, I was acutely aware that I was a representative from the state capital going to a rural small town to bring mental health support to a community of firefighters and first responders – a group that experience had taught me tends to be skeptical of accepting assistance from the outside, and of the value of mental health support in general. So, the need to focus on management of the response and to work hard to put all of the pieces together offered ample opportunity to avoid thinking just how I would cope when, inevitably, I would be sitting with members of the fire company and confronted with the need to become an active DMH responder.

My Response Experience

Initially, emotional support in the form of Critical Incident Stress Management (CISM) Teams were provided for the dozens of police, firefighters, EMS personnel, and dispatchers who had participated in the response, in accordance with the Monroe County EMS plan. Four weeks later, the physician from the neighboring North East Joint Fire District (NEJFD) sought additional support as he felt that ongoing emotional and psychological challenges were affecting many of both the WWFD and other fire district volunteers who had participated in the response. This led to my involvement overseeing a multi-jurisdictional, coordinated intervention that included a community meeting of first responders and follow-up counseling assistance from county Disaster Mental Health responders.

This meant that my response to the shooting was initiated from outside of the local governmental structures that traditionally are responsible for post-event recovery operations and activities for events of this scale. This atypical situation was prompted by the concerns of the NEJFD's physician, which led him to seek assistance from experts in the U.S. Department of Health and Human Services, who in turn reached out to the NYS Office of Mental Health, Disaster Response & Emergency Preparedness Director – me.

The NEJFD physician explained that the standard county Emergency Medical Services (EMS) procedures for supporting first responders exposed to a traumatic event had been ineffective and as a result, members of the department had to deal with negative reactions to the events on several fronts. This first responder community was grieving the loss of two of "their own." While anyone close to the untimely death of a relative, friend, or co-worker experiences acute feelings of loss, that sense of loss is intensely magnified within the communities of first-response workers – be they paid or volunteer firefighters, police, EMTs, or 911 dispatchers. This is due in large measure to the risk inherent in first response work that is understood to place them in harm's way. Their personal safety is dependent on the man or woman working alongside them. Given that awareness, the ability of first responders to immediately roll out every time the alarm sounds or call comes in is empowered by the knowledge that the risk they face is shared among all the members of the response. The existence of this bond of inter-dependence among first responders leads to a deeply held sense that a loss to any one of their brother/sister responders becomes a personal tragedy for them all. Thus, the deaths and severe injuries inflicted on the firefighters and police responders brought collateral psychological harm to a large number of uniformed and civilian members of the response community – especially since, in this case, the injuries and fatalities were intentionally inflicted.

About a week following the funerals for the two fallen firefighters, I was contacted to assist the members of the WWFD because they were having difficulty maintaining operational readiness due to their feelings of intense sadness. The funerals were a testament to the tightness of the universal bond among the brothers and sisters in blue and provided the local responders with a sense of support, closeness, and even pride in the face of shared grief. More than 4,000 first responders came from across the country to attend the ceremonies and pay proper respect to the fallen. But once the funerals were over, many felt surges of sadness that simply overwhelmed their ability to deal with daily routine. Some of those first on the scene found themselves haunted by the memory of the body of one of the slain firefighters who had lain out in the open for more than four hours while police secured the active shooter scene. Others found themselves confronting the harsh reality of the risk of their service, leading to a sense of vulnerability accompanied by heightened anxiety and unexpected flashes of anger. Conflicts among family members and co-workers occurred more readily and frequently. These responders were easily overwhelmed by the mundane events of daily life.

Following the event, those directly involved in the response were offered the opportunity to participate in the County EMS CISM program. Unfortunately, many of the WWFD and NEJFD members did not feel the program was beneficial. They viewed the CISM program as inadequate, merely providing kindness and goodwill, reflected in the reference used by some of these first responders to the CISM program as "the hug squad." The hugs, although pleasant, did not sufficiently address the suffering of these responders. Instead of providing the intended opportunity for colleagues to share reactions to the event and offer each other support, participants remained silent, left to manage the emotional aftermath of the trauma that had shaken their world without the support needed not only by members of the Webster area Fire and Police Departments, but the EMS responders and 911 call center workers as well – a group that numbered more than 100 individuals.

The initial challenge I faced upon being brought into the situation was to chart a strategy that would overcome doubts and mistrust of those we sought to assist, including any lingering negative feelings toward the value of mental health interventions following their experience with the CISM team. I also needed to contend with the stigma of coming into this tightly knit group of responders as an outsider. Accomplishing these goals required input from multiple perspectives, so I began the process of identifying a group who would join me to determine what types of interventions might be effective, and who also possessed the experience to craft a sufficiently respectful approach to the culture of the first response communities we wanted to support.

To address those multiple challenges, the workgroup included DMH subject matter experts (SMEs) with expertise in working with first response communities drawn from the American Red Cross, the NYC Fire Department, and the SUNY New Paltz Institute for Disaster Mental Health. In order to build trust, the group also included members of the West Webster Fire Department and the Northeast Joint Fire District, the Monroe County EMS, and Department of Mental Health.

Our ad hoc work group began holding daily conference calls to plan the approach to identify efforts that would address the presenting concerns. We agreed that the interventions would be multi-faceted and delivered over time, beginning with a large-group information session open to the entire community of first responders. This would be followed by scheduling an ongoing presence of DMH counselors at the fire house, police department, and EMS for meetings providing follow-up information, and to be available for one-on-one counseling if requested. The goals of the initial session were two-fold: first, to establish confidence among the first responders that serious actions were being taken on their behalf to provide effective emotional support, and second, to provide psychoeducation to help them gain insight into the thoughts and feeling they were experiencing and to restore a sense of control that had been severely shaken by the trauma they had experienced.

As our intervention strategy placed a high degree of importance on building trust, we created opportunities for our DMH responders to interact with key leaders from the local community. This included organizing an informal dinner gathering immediately preceding the community forum where members of the WFD, county government, and the DMH SMEs had a chance to meet and begin to build the relationships intended to sustain the recovery process in a setting that encouraged casual conversation and open communication.

The community forum was held at a local hospital with facilities that were often used for community-based training, in a lecture hall that featured comfortable seating and warm lighting, creating a less stark environment than might have been expected in a municipal meeting room. About 120 attended, many more than expected, and almost all were first responders.

Given the multiple goals we were trying to accomplish, the workgroup paid careful attention to constructing the agenda. We were very mindful of the nature of the information being presented, who delivered each element, and in what order. First came establishing rapport between the first responders, local mental health, and the SMEs to create the foundation of trust that would enable the psychoeducational element to become effective. Thus, the opening remarks were made by the chief of the fire district – a figure of local authority and respect among those in attendance. He in turn introduced me as a representative of the State Office of Mental Health and allowed me to offer a message of on-going support and a commitment to continue to assist those impacted by the events.

Subject matter experts followed in succession to provide participants with information about the psychological impact of disaster and traumatic reactions. One presenter described the range of reactions that those present currently might be having or could expect to experience as they began their personal process of recovery. This presenter explained that these responses might include not only strong emotional reactions, but behavioral ones as well; that sleep could be severely disrupted; or they could find that they were becoming hypervigilant, with an inability to relax. The presenter also explained that they might see their peers becoming withdrawn socially or find themselves more frequently in conflict with family or co-workers. Care was taken to assure those in attendance that all these strong reactions were reasonable within the context of the events they had experienced and that they could expect to heal and move on.

The final presentation, by a member of the New York City Fire Department (FDNY) Mental Health Response Team, took the previous information on loss and grief and brought it home. Speaking with the authority that came from being "one of their own," the FDNY presenter assured those in the audience that the challenges they were encountering in managing emotions and feelings were not signs they were going crazy or losing it, and that acknowledging the challenges they faced and seeking out help when they became overwhelming was instead a step toward recovery rather than one of weakness.

Having hopefully provided insight into what they were experiencing, and why, through the psychoeducational presentations, we moved next to the more tangible aspect of our planned assistance by describing counseling services that would be made available to members of all the response organizations, including county DMH provider visits to regular department meetings and events. The follow-up activities would include additional psychoeducational print materials, resource and referral lists, as well as on-site individual counseling should that be requested.

As one sign of the effectiveness of our efforts, attendees did not all flock immediately toward the exits at the end of the presentations. Instead, many of the local responders came looking to engage with the presenters. Many had follow-up questions, but many seemed to simply want to extend their contact with these new acquaintances who appeared to offer the comfort of knowing where they had been, and who offered some hope about where they might be going. As it turned out, however, the conclusion of the public session was not to be the end of our response that evening.

After all the invited firefighters, police, EMS personnel, and 911 dispatchers headed back to home or work, several of the Webster firefighters we had come to know in putting the program together invited some of us back to the tavern where the company often "debriefed" and unwound after returning from a fire call. It was here, in the comfort of their home turf and with a sense that they had accomplished something positive for their peers, that the core group of Webster firefighters began to speak not of the needs of others, but of their own pain and the seemingly unbearable burden of grief that they felt. They spoke to me of the ties that bind firefighters to each other in ways that not even their families could fully understand, let alone people from outside of the community of first responders. With bodies held tightly as emotions welled up, they spoke of the emptiness that returning to the firehouse brought as the memories of the loss overwhelmed them. And so, I sat and listened. And they talked, never losing their composure but describing thoughts and feelings out loud that they struggled to comprehend and wanted so badly to master.

At no other time in my own disaster response experience was I more aware that my role in supporting these men was simply to sit and listen. It was also the most difficult intervention I had ever engaged in. Sitting still in the face of someone's grief and pain and doing nothing more than being there was hard, and it hurt. Eventually, the talk turned away from feelings and self, and began a transition to the safer topics of managing the firehouse and steps they would be taking to follow through on the visits from the county DMH teams. The energy that had driven the conversation began to dissipate and it became obvious that the time for leaving had arrived. As we parted, the appreciation for what had been accomplished was conveyed less in words than in looks of sincere gratitude, warm handshakes, and more than a few bear hugs.

My Post-Response Adjustment

Returning home following the effort in Webster brought to the fore the competing elements that the intervention represented for me. Professionally, there was a deep sense of accomplishment. I felt I had been successful in orchestrating a process that brought together the many different players who often don't find the way to work together toward the common goal of supporting those in need. I left Webster knowing that we had provided an effective psychoeducational session reaching many dozens of first responders, and that plans were in place for ongoing counseling support throughout the fire district.

In the days following my return, I leaned heavily on that sense of accomplishment to balance the other, less positive, emotions that came home with me – especially, an emotional hangover, a kind of numbness that I knew stemmed from the sense of powerlessness I had felt following my one-on-one time with the firemen who were close to those who had died. While my rational brain assured me of the value of sitting with them in the face of their grief, the experience of actually doing so left me feeling anything but effective. So, I leaned on my DMH training, acknowledging these competing feelings of pride and powerlessness and recognizing that both had been a part of the reality of my experience in Webster.

For me, returning home must always include this very conscious process of working through the ambivalence of conflicting feelings to ensure that all of me – the parts that are practical and objective, as well as those that can express compassion and empathy – make it out the door with me the next time I head out for a response.

Lessons Learned

- Know your official role in a response, but don't be limited by it. The experience in Webster combined my role as the organizer and facilitator of the overall process with that of responder when meeting in informal sessions one-on-one with the firefighters. This distinction is always present for me in the midst of a response, but it is ultimately a meaningless one, as the core elements of DMH guide my work in both.
- Sometimes the best way to provide empathetic mental health support is to begin by focusing on practical demands and realities. Planning and facilitating the Webster response first called for me to apply an objective, dispassionate eye to the organizational dynamics in which the response activities were to take place, which in turn, helped to define those activities as well. This is an example of my striving to maintain a balance of awareness of what I'm doing, and considering how to do it with sufficient empathy to appreciate the depth of loss and emotional challenges faced by those I'm working to assist.
- Related to the previous point, it's important to apply an objective perspective. In this situation, that meant that I looked first at the "who and what." Who were those most directly affected by the senseless murder of the responding firefighters, and what other individuals or groups should be included as the population in need of assistance?

To what degree and in what manner were those responding police, EMTs and even dispatchers affected? What services had already been offered by the existing assistance mechanisms and how beneficial did the recipients find those supports? Gaining that information accurately meant speaking directly to those affected by the shootings, and these conversations were often highly charged with emotions. By maintaining an objective manner throughout the course of those conversations I was able to create an appropriate response plan, being careful to appreciate the full depth of emotional impact of the event, without being overly influenced by the intense emotions generated by the process itself.

Chapter 14

2014 Mass Murder in Isla Vista, CA

Erika Felix

I first became interested in disaster mental health (DMH) service and research when I was completing my pre-doctoral internship for my PhD in clinical-community psychology. During my first few weeks of internship, the September 11, 2001 terror attacks occurred, and that changed the trajectory of my career. I happened to have a primary clinical supervisor with global expertise in DMH services who mentored me on gaining the clinical skills to serve in DMH response. After obtaining my clinical license as a psychologist in California, I volunteered in Sri Lanka following the 2004 tsunami, and in my home community through my local American Red Cross chapter. I also obtained a Research and Education in Disaster Mental Health research mentorship, funded by the National Institute of Mental Health, that launched my research career focused on studying the factors that affect child and family mental health post-disaster. I am on faculty at the University of California, Santa Barbara (UCSB), and as our department has the only other licensed psychologists on campus, outside of our counseling center, we volunteered to assist in staffing a satellite drop-in counseling center location for our students following the mass murder.

The Pre-Disaster Community

The mass murder occurred in the densely populated, one square mile community of Isla Vista, CA. Isla Vista is home to a large undergraduate and graduate student population from UCSB and a local community college, as well as families, some of whom have lived there for generations. As the focus of my disaster mental health services was with the UCSB students, I will describe my work with that population. However, many others were affected, including the employees who work at the local restaurants, bars, and convenience stores; the families who live there; and young people who were enjoying a show at a local theater that had to go into lockdown.

UCSB is a top public university and a global leader in science and engineering. In the 2013–14 academic year, UCSB had 19,362 undergraduate students and 2,863 graduate students, representing 77 countries.

Student ethnicity was 43 percent White, 24 percent Asian/Pacific Islander, 24 percent Latinx, 4 percent Black, 1 percent Native American, and 4 percent unknown. The UCSB community had experienced another mass murder in 2001, when a young man had driven into pedestrians in Isla Vista. Therefore, some faculty and staff on campus had experience with the previous tragedy, and alumni from that time who heard of the 2014 mass murder said that it brought back memories from 2001. In the 2013–14 school year, a meningitis scare occurred that greatly increased many students' anxiety, and a street party that turned into a riot had occurred in Isla Vista in April. So, faculty, staff, and students were already weary from the stressful events that had happened in that academic year.

The Disaster

On Friday, May 23, 2014, a young man who was not affiliated with the university murdered six students from UCSB and wounded more than a dozen others, across 17 different crime scenes, before killing himself. The attack occurred in Isla Vista, immediately adjacent to the university, where approximately half of the UCSB student population lives and where even more recreate, especially on weekends. However, it was the Friday of Memorial Day weekend, so Isla Vista was less populated than usual, as many students had gone home to enjoy the long weekend. The perpetrator stabbed, shot, and drove into cyclists and pedestrians with his car. The first 911 call was at 9:27 that evening. Events unfolded very quickly, and were ever-changing as the perpetrator drove through many locations, before taking his own life.

Students texted friends to provide warnings of the attack. The first official alert from UCSB was sent at 12:13 a.m. on May 24, 2014, saying there was no further threat and to remain indoors. The alert did not state what the original threat was; therefore, even though I was awoken from sleep by the text, I did not know what had happened until the next day. The tragedy reverberated throughout the grieving UCSB community and then the world, as national and international media attention descended upon Isla Vista for several weeks. The perpetrator left a misogynistic manifesto that was widely reported in the media, which caused distress for many of our students. This tragedy occurred towards the end of the quarter, shortly before final exams, which further compounded student stress.

My Thoughts Pre-Response

I learned of the tragedy through a friend, who was late to meet me because she was preoccupied with reading the perpetrator's manifesto. As she shared the horrific details, I was in disbelief. As soon as I could check email, I saw a flood of communications from the faculty in my department. Our department chair at the time was a school psychologist with years of crisis response experience. He quickly organized our department's efforts to support our counseling center staff. The tragedy occurred at the end of the week, and the counseling center staff were facing weeks of extended duties. So, as we were the only other licensed psychologists on campus, my colleague and I helped by staffing the drop-in center that Sunday, giving the center staff a day of rest. I was grateful to do this, as all I wanted to do was be with others from the UCSB community who understood what this felt like, and to support our students.

It felt surreal, doing my normal activities that Saturday, seeing people who were enjoying their weekend, when I felt such disbelief and grief. It was only when I arrived at UCSB on Sunday, saw my colleagues, and we began to share thoughts and emotions, that I felt I was in a community that understood what this meant. Given my prior training in Psychological First Aid (PFA), and my years of research and volunteer work in DMH, I felt confident in my ability to be a part of the coordinated response effort. I knew that several of our faculty were also trained and highly experienced.

My Response Experience

In addition to the regular counseling center office, the university decided to open a satellite drop-in counseling office in the Student Resource Building, collocated with the drop-in academic advising, financial aid, and emergency housing services they were already providing. I helped staff the satellite drop-in center for the first week post-tragedy. Along with other faculty in my department who were licensed psychologists, my department chair helped create and support an incident command system at our satellite location. He organized all of our response efforts for the weeks that followed, based on communication he was having with university officials. This included staffing the drop-in counseling center, outreach to student groups that had requested support (e.g., sororities), and returning the calls of concerned parents. Having that structure made me feel secure as a volunteer in the university's response, and confident that our students would get quality, coordinated care. This freed up our time to focus on responding to students. It felt good to serve with members of my department, and to share this experience with them.

On Sunday, we were the only ones staffing that location; later, for a short time, other community volunteers were allowed to participate. I felt a bit protective of our university community because I could not tell which of these volunteers was trained in PFA or a similar model, and which were not. There was one outside volunteer who made a comment after ending a meeting with a student that led me to believe that he was not trained in a crisis counseling model, and as the week passed another volunteer started to strike me as someone who was there because they needed to be needed. That made me uneasy. After a few days, the university stopped allowing non-university employees to serve in the crisis response, and I felt relief that those two volunteers had gone (although they could still serve in Isla Vista itself). Although that solved one issue, it meant that our department had more hours to staff at the satellite location, and that was stressful as we were volunteering and doing our regular job duties. Many of us just cleared our schedules to serve our community in its time of need.

As PFA is very flexible, I used it with all the students I saw over that week. It allowed me to tailor the focus to whatever the primary need was of the student in front of me. One of the most common interventions I used was normalizing a variety of emotional reactions to the tragedy. My first encounter was with a young man who was concerned that he was not having more of an emotional response, as he saw others crying and showing outward displays of grief. Thus, acknowledging that there are a variety of understandable reactions to extraordinary events, including numbing or a lack of emotion, was frequently needed. In almost every encounter, I also helped students identify helpful stress management and coping skills, including simple, tangible things such as making sure they took regular meals and had adequate rest. This was critical, as the tragedy occurred shortly before final exams, and some students were trying to balance the process of grieving with studying. One of the best interventions was informing the students of their options, and assisting with problem-solving, as necessary.

As many students were concerned about their ability to study in the midst of tragedy, UCSB allowed students three options: to take their grade as it was and leave for summer break; to stay and take final exams on schedule; or to take an incomplete and complete their final in fall quarter. Providing these options was very helpful, as students were then empowered to make the best choice for them. One student continued to ruminate, even after I provided the options, and it was clearly increasing her distress; being able to liaise with academic advisors, who were collocated in our building, was helpful in trying to alleviate her distress.

When groups of students came in together, two volunteers would meet with them. Following the PFA guidelines seemed to work with all the clients I saw, as meeting concrete needs, normalizing emotional reactions, providing information on healthy coping, and connecting to existing support systems seemed to satisfy all the students with whom I met. Even with a co-counselor, if one of us took one angle with PFA, the other might bring in another principle later in the conversation. Also, I usually ended with reminding students that if they were concerned for others, or were increasing in distress themselves, to be proactive and reach out to us, and perhaps consider additional sources of support. Afterwards, we would check in with each other, to provide feedback and support on applying PFA.

One group of students came to us because they were concerned for a friend who they reported had ongoing mental health issues prior to the tragedy, and they were now greatly concerned about how their friend was coping post-tragedy. We were able to help them identify tangible ways to support their friend that were within the expected boundaries of friendship, and to recognize when to reach out for help to a trained counselor. The friends were concerned that it was already at the level of needing a trained counselor, so we worked with them to call the student and suggest a friend accompany the student to the counseling center as soon as possible that day. As it seemed probable that this person would need ongoing counseling, we wanted to connect the student to the regular counseling center staff. We were able to arrange an appointment immediately.

Some students I saw wanted to be at UCSB, whereas others wanted to leave as soon as possible. For example, one student, away for the holiday weekend when the tragedy occurred, wanted to return to be around other people who understood what this tragedy meant. Others came to counseling distressed because they wanted to leave UCSB as soon as possible. One example was an out-of-state student, who unlike her California friends could not just go home for the weekend. She wanted to return home, to her family, where she felt safe. In contrast, an international student with whom I met was ending her time at UCSB in a few weeks. She wanted to stay near to support her friends as they grieved, but could not. She remarked how it would feel strange to return to her home country, where no one would understand what this event felt like to us. With all students, I offered empathy, and informed them of their academic options, which allowed them to go home early, if needed. For the international student, we discussed ways to stay connected with her UCSB friends.

Some students who came to drop-in counseling were simply trying to wrap their minds around this experience; others were already contending with a lot of life stressors before the tragedy, and were trying to figure out how to continue to cope with the additional stress. I was surprised at the compassion I heard from some students towards the perpetrator, as I was not expecting that. The students who expressed this commented on how hard it must have been to live with mental illness, and for his mother and father to parent someone with mental illness. At that time, they did not seem angry, but just saddened by the complete and utter tragedy of it, on all sides.

I noticed that as the media hype surrounding the perpetrator and tragedy continued, more students expressed distress related to media coverage, which included social media. Some students expressed how at first they had thought this was a relatively isolated event due to the perpetrator's mental illness, but they became increasingly distressed when they saw online that other men endorsed the misogynistic views of the murderer, and appeared to support him. I saw women who were fearful and angry over that. The #YesAllWomen hashtag and social media movement began in the days following the tragedy in response to the misogyny and entitlement that had seemed to be a motivating factor for the perpetrator.

I also helped staff the official campus memorial, which occurred four days after the tragedy. It was shocking to me to see how many different media outlets were there to cover the events. In fact, it was overwhelming, and I wondered why seemingly every news outlet in the world had to send its own team to cover the same event. It was also surreal to see people driving to the memorial in the same make, model, and color of car that the perpetrator had used as a weapon. I was startled each time I saw that type and color of car that day, and wondered how it was affecting our students, especially those who were in Isla Vista at the time of the murders.

At the memorial, we placed ourselves in areas where students could access us at any time and wore identifiers showing we were mental health support. I was able to walk over with my long-time departmental colleagues, who were also volunteering in the mental health response. It felt good to have time to connect with them, and talk about our own reactions to the events, as we walked to and from the stadium where the memorial was held. No students approached our particular support team during or after the memorial. Students were just hugging each other, and silently walked home. My colleagues goofed off on the way back to campus, as one ran a lap to race another back. Those moments of relief and camaraderie were needed.

During the week, several of us shared ways we were trying to take care of ourselves. I had to limit my watching of the news. When I saw the coverage on one 24-hour news network, which I normally liked, I was angry about the speculation and mischaracterization of our community that I perceived in the paid pundits on the network. Instead, at the end of the day, to decompress and transition into bedtime, I would watch some mindless, comedic reality TV show. It helped me laugh and focus on something silly, and it allowed me to get decent sleep that week. Supportive emails and texts from friends and colleagues around the world were also very helpful. However, at times, I was also disappointed in how many people did *not* check in on me, especially if it was a colleague in the DMH field. I was actually surprised at who remembered to check in and send words of support and who did not. I realize that people are busy and may not have seen the news, so it's not something I hold on to in a negative way. But I offer my initial reaction from that week, as I hope it reminds people that their emails, texts, and phone calls of support matter and are appreciated, even if it is weeks later.

My service ended after a week because of a planned vacation. By the end of the week, I was ready to get away and rest, but it also felt surreal to leave my community and go enjoy myself. While away, my mind would return to UCSB and to how people were coping. Again, it was strange to see life go on as normal for others, despite the devastating events that affected us. However, as my vacation progressed, I felt myself truly relax and decompress, which helped my mental health. The new school year started in October that year, and many people commented how it was good that students had more time away. UCSB planned around 18 months of memorial and remembrance events, including an interactive exhibit to remember the students whose lives were lost that was open throughout Fall quarter. There is now a permanent memorial on campus to these students.

My Post-Response Adjustment

I returned to campus in time for graduation. Our departmental response had ended by then. My colleagues and I who volunteered would sometimes discuss our experiences, and how it shaped our view of the tragedy and its aftermath. Summer started, and I began focusing on my role as a DMH researcher. The words of the students stayed with me as I designed a survey to try to understand the impact of the tragedy on our student population, and what was helpful to them in the initial few weeks that followed. I felt like I was truly living our scientist-practitioner values as a profession. The experiences students shared with me shaped the types of questions I asked in that survey, as I wanted our experiences to be helpful to other universities as they prepare for, and respond to, crisis events. I have been privileged and honored to share the voices of our students through research articles and presentations at conferences. I, like others, want this experience to have an impact for the better somehow. I do not want our tragedy to just be another statistic; I want us to know how to better support one another in the aftermath of these events.

Lessons Learned

- Make sure the volunteers you use are trained in crisis response; if not, they should receive a "just-in-time" training or they could be used later in the long-term recovery efforts, not for crisis response. I was not a part of the decisions about who was allowed to volunteer on-campus. Although many of us were crisis response trained and had experience serving in prior events, I suspect that some of the community volunteers did not. Communities and college counseling centers need to prepare for these events by offering regular training, and then keeping record of who is trained or not. This list can be used to call upon volunteers in the aftermath of a crisis. Questions about prior training and experience with crisis response could be a part of the screening process for volunteers that a volunteer coordinator could do. If someone is not trained, then they could be on the referral list for long-term mental health support, for affected individuals who will need trauma-focused treatment in the months and years to follow.

- It is different responding to an event affecting your community, versus being deployed to another community. I have done both types of responses, and it is just different when it is your own community. In practical ways, we did not have to work to build trust with the community, as we were already a part of the community. I probably also felt more protective of my community, and was concerned about well-meaning but untrained mental health volunteers inadvertently causing more stress. Also, in hearing student reactions to the event, at times it made me think about how similar or different it was to my own reaction, so I had to monitor my own reactions to be an effective crisis counselor in this situation, more than I had to in communities that were not my own.
- Know when a clinical referral is needed. Most students I saw had understandable reactions to extraordinary events, that would likely resolve on their own, and I reassured them of this. However, I also ended sessions with psychoeducation to be proactive and seek extra supports if they noticed their distress was lasting longer than several weeks, was growing in intensity, or impairing school, work, or relationships. If a student reported a prior mental health concern or stressor being exacerbated by the tragedy, I was more likely to encourage them to seek support from our counseling center.
- Know your limits. Towards the end of my service, I noticed I was getting weary, and needed more rest than I could get. I was not only volunteering but wrapping up projects at work to prepare for my vacation. By the last day of volunteering, I was thinking that I had been a better volunteer the very first day or two of the response than I was at the time. I recognized that I needed a break, and was glad I already had that vacation scheduled. I have also noticed this in the longer-term aftermath. Our community recently suffered a severe natural disaster, the Thomas wildfire and debris flow (2017). Our community again mobilized volunteers to serve, and I decided to *not* serve in the crisis response as a DMH volunteer, in part because of my demanding work schedule at the time. I decided that I could better serve our community by giving several practical public talks about ways to support resiliency and recovery in the community for the long-term aftermath. Those talks have opened doors to several opportunities to support disaster preparedness and response that I had not thought of before. So, there are a lot of ways to be useful to your community in the aftermath. Know what will work best for you and the community.

Chapter 15

2016 Pulse Night Club Shooting in Orlando, FL

Tara S. Hughes

I am a Clinical Social Worker, and first stepped into a Disaster Mental Health (DMH) role as an intern in my MSW program when I responded to a workplace suicide. I was immediately impressed by the effectiveness of supporting people after an incident with information and "normalization," and began to explore possibilities to do this kind of crisis work. I joined the Red Cross within months of 9/11 and have been involved in a number of responses since then, including hurricanes (Katrina, Super Storm Sandy, and others), deadly tornadoes, airplane and bus accidents, the Sandy Hook School shooting, and the Boston Marathon bombing. My "day job" is Coordinator of Human Trafficking Service Programs at the International Institute of Buffalo.

On the morning after the Pulse Nightclub shooting, Red Cross asked if I was able to deploy to Orlando, Florida. After initially saying no because my children were home from college on break, my kids' insistence that the people in Florida "need you more than we do right now" made me change my mind.

The Pre-Disaster Community

The Orlando Metro area has a population of just over 2,387,000. Orlando is known for its tourist attractions, and for hosting conferences and conventions, but the city and surrounding area is vibrant in its amenities for residents and known for its support of the Lesbian, Gay, Bisexual, Transgender and Queer (LGBTQ) community.

Orlando's population is just over 30 percent Hispanic, including the largest Puerto Rican population in Florida. The Hispanic community is fast growing, with an overall increase of 68 percent between 2000 and 2014. This large increase has brought with it many Latino agencies and businesses that cater to and represent this population.

There is also a relatively large (4.1 percent) self-identified LGBTQ population in Orlando, which has open support for LGBTQ businesses and people. However, the Governor and Attorney General of Florida both have expressed outspoken opposition to the legalization of same sex marriage, continuing to vow to fight US rulings that declared as unconstitutional the 2008 state ban on same sex marriage.

The state of Florida has a long history of responding to natural disasters, and has done so effectively. While Orlando law enforcement and medical professionals had not received more than average training to respond to an event like the shooting at Pulse, the community had confidence in the abilities of the first responder organizations and emergency management personnel.

The Disaster

The Pulse Nightclub was founded in 2004, and dedicated to the memory of a gay man named John Poma who died of complications of HIV in 1991. John's sister and friend opened the LGBTQ nightclub and chose to name it Pulse as a tribute to John's heartbeat, which would continue to "beat" in a club that personified his joy for life. The club catered to the LGBTQ population, although LGBTQ allies were welcomed and seen there routinely.

In the early morning hours of June 12, 2016, gunfire broke out in the club resulting in 49 victim deaths, the shooter's death, and at least 53 injuries that required treatment at a triage center or hospital. The nightclub was hosting its weekly Latin Night at the time of the shooting and there were approximately 300 patrons in the building and on the patio.

The perpetrator, Omar Mateen, entered Pulse at 2:02 a.m. and began to shoot and kill random patrons. He used multiple guns, and took time to reload those guns several times. He used his smartphone to make multiple calls, and reportedly searched the internet for news of the shooting while it was still in progress. He spoke with a hostage negotiator three times, called his wife once, and called a local news station. He claimed allegiance to ISIS, and stated he was strapped with explosives and that there was a bomb in a car in the parking lot of the club. He remained in the building along with terrified hostages for just over 3 hours, and was killed at 5:14 a.m. The investigation showed that the shooter had no long-term connection to ISIS, did not have explosives on his body, and had not put explosives in a parked car. As a result, there were questions about the time it took for the shooter to be killed by the police, and therefore, the amount of time that those who remained in the building had to wait for rescue.

My Thoughts Pre-Response

When mass casualty incidents occur, I always think: "I wish I could do something." In this case, the inclusion of the LGBTQ population as a target of the attack was a definite pull to want to be a part of the solution.

My personal relationships and professional life have led me to be a staunch ally of those who identify as LGBTQ, and I wanted to do what I could to ensure that a person's sexual or gender identity wouldn't have a negative impact on their care. I wanted to assist the Red Cross in its universal, impartial, and neutral humanitarian mission.

My desire to deploy was complicated both by having my children home from college and by the responsibilities of my regular job. I wanted to spend the time I had set aside to be with my children, but was quickly reminded by them that they would still be my kids when I got home, and that I could help many people by going to Orlando. I guess I was "schooled" by children whom I had raised to give back to their communities when they have something to offer!

Although my agency leadership is very supportive of my deploying with Red Cross for several weeks a year, I have to take personal and vacation time in order to leave. When I do not have enough time to cover a full two-week deployment, I take unpaid leave. This is not a huge hardship, but does make paying the bills more of a challenge.

My Response Experience

The Family Assistance Center, called the FAC, is the location where victims and their families can go to get access to a variety of services. The location is protected from the public and the media, and is set up to provide a calm and sensitive atmosphere for those directly impacted by the incident. DMH and Disaster Spiritual Care support is at the forefront of the available services, but victims and families also can access Victim Compensation applications and funds, as well as other relevant services. I was asked to be the Red Cross FAC Lead.

The City of Orlando, in conjunction with the FBI's Office of Victim Assistance (OVA), chose Camping World Stadium as the location for the FAC. The Club Level was used as a gathering area for the majority of services, with quiet spaces for support and the return of personal items a floor above in the suites. I would never have thought a football stadium would work as a FAC, but it was perfect in many ways. The one ongoing personal challenge was that the volume of voice prompts on the elevators was set for loud football games with large crowds. I repeatedly asked if she had an "inside voice" because she sounded like she was screaming in the relative quiet!

The first person I met from the City who was taking the lead for running the FAC said "Hi! I'm Kathy and I have no idea what I'm doing." To which, I responded, "Hi! I'm Tara, and I am an experienced Red Crosser." I told her I had helped to open and run FACs in Newtown, Boston, and after airline disasters. She hugged me. Being able to share my experience with people who are "on the spot" and don't have it is one of the reasons I do this work. Experience allows a response to meet the typical needs while remaining reactive to the unique challenges faced in each event.

A FAC is generally run by a government or community organization, and Red Cross generally plays a support role. The integration of Red Cross into the overall response at the FAC is the responsibility of the FAC Lead, as is the management of Red Cross personnel on site. From a DMH perspective, this position lends itself to supporting the Red Cross workforce and the workforce of our external partners. As FAC Lead I provided information, managed expectations, worked with multiple systems and addressed the understandable reactions of victims, families, and workers on a daily basis. Although I had many interactions with those directly impacted by the shooting, my focus was to support workers, both internal to Red Cross and representing external partners, so they could effectively do their job to support those who were directly impacted. Again, bringing the experience of prior mass casualty responses and prior FACs to this job gave me the opportunity to predict the potential challenges that could be faced by workers, and to support them as they struggled with the incident, the losses, the lack of sleep, and the frustrations that were inevitable. In addition to spending a great deal of time with individuals from various agencies, I was able to facilitate Psychological First Aid (PFA) training for several agency groups in an effort to care for their workers.

The Orlando FAC brought together 35 organizations to offer services to the victims and families, including concrete services like travel assistance, Consular Services, state and federal Victim Assistance, and emotional support in the form of DMH and Disaster Spiritual Care (DSC). The FAC was staffed by several hundred people at a time, and could have been chaotic. There were great efforts taken to set the expectation of quiet and calm, and reminders throughout each day to reduce noise and visual chaos as much as possible. Each morning began with a FAC meeting of all agencies during which behavioral expectations were reiterated, questions were answered, and new information was given. The FAC Leads from various agencies monitored the atmosphere of the FAC continually, and made adjustments as needed in terms of noise level and number of people present.

In the eight days that the FAC was open, 956 individuals and 298 families came and received services. Services were available to family members of the deceased, those suffering physical and emotional injuries, club staff and patrons, and others directly impacted by this tragedy. We saw many wheelchairs, crutches, bandages, and casts on those wounded in the attack. People expressed a variety of emotions. Some were numb – from tiredness, from medications, or from dissociation. It was hard to tell. Some cried quietly when they saw friends or others who were injured. Many expressed anxiety about many things – safety, the loss of a sense of security, housing difficulties, job loss, and managing family relationships that were difficult prior to the shooting due to sexual or gender identity issues and/or estrangement. When working with LGBTQ clients DMH needed to be sensitive to the potential negative impact of unaccepting family members. A common query like "have you spoken with your mother and father about the tragedy?" might be a particularly insensitive question for this population. LGBTQ partners of the injured were not all aware that they would be treated respectfully and appropriately by area hospitals. DMH made sure to get the accurate information out to concerned loved ones that they were welcome to visit their friends and partners.

The fear from this shooting was wide ranging and focused not only on prejudices against the LGBTQ population, but deportation threats for undocumented people. All staff were encouraged to discuss these issues openly, maintaining a good flow of information about predictable and "normal" reactions for survivors and families. We publicized and made sure that immigration lawyers were present at the FAC. These lawyers could assist clients in obtaining immigration relief because they were a victim of a crime, and also helped them obtain available victim assistance benefits safely.

Loss was everywhere. One worker from a local LGBT Center was close friends with 24 people who died, and knew others who were now permanently disabled. His experience was not unusual, and speaks to the profound grief that surrounded people in those weeks. I talked multiple times a day with this worker, giving support focusing on the need to take care of himself while he served his community. I checked in about drinking water, eating routinely, and sleep. I met his partner and we talked about what they were both experiencing and how people manage grief and stress differently. I encouraged them to tolerate each other's different grieving styles. I set up a PFA training for the staff of the LGBT Center so that all workers were exposed to information about mass loss and grief.

Latin Night at Pulse brought together two populations that were in some ways vulnerable – Latinos and those who identify as LGBTQ. This complicated the community response in some unique ways. When the FAC opened, several organizations representing local Hispanics were invited to provide services. It came as a surprise to many of us, but this caused problems because of a pre-existing rift in the community about which agency truly represented the needs and rights of the Hispanic population. Fortunately, Red Cross deploys workers who focus on external relationships with community and government partners. Although this challenge was being played out at the FAC, the task of facilitating a solution to this time- and energy-consuming collaboration was handed off to External Relations as they had the time and expertise to meet this challenge.

Politically, there was local support for the LGBTQ population, but at the state level, the Governor and Attorney General had spent years fighting against same-sex marriage initiatives and laws, and were vocal in their opposition to LGBTQ rights. After the shooting, the Governor expressed condolences for those impacted but took days to acknowledge that the attacks were targeted at the LGBTQ population. The Attorney General expressed her support for the LGBTQ community in her comments, but in interviews was unable to reconcile this support with her prior statements. All of this could have remained in the background, but both politicians coming to the FAC on numerous occasions, wanting to be seen as supportive and involved, brought it to the forefront. It was difficult for the victims who were present and for those working at the FAC to have to interact with either individual or their staffs. Knowing the likelihood of these politicians appearing at the FAC, continual efforts were made to talk with workers about how to cope effectively with people and groups that may be supportive in this instance, but may not be supportive overall to their interests.

It is always a challenge for the Red Cross workforce when we are working as a support in someone else's "house." We can give suggestions, talking about best practices and what experience has taught us, but many decisions are not ours to make. In this case, DMH and DSC workers were not used in the traditional sense. As this was a federal crime, the use of Victim Specialists was the choice of the FBI, and we had to work within that structure. These Victim Specialists are trained to work with victims of crime and assist them in accessing services. They were paired with families and individuals as they came into the FAC, and Red Cross DMH and DSC were used if there appeared to be a need for more than PFA. DMH and DSC helpers expressed frustration that they were not being utilized as they could have been. It became difficult at the leadership level to have to repeatedly reiterate the structure and why we were functioning the way we were with some disgruntled DMH and DSC workers.

Another challenge arose with the discussion of a site visit for the families. A private visit to the site of a mass casualty incident allows families a somewhat intimate moment to experience the place where their loved one was last alive. It is also a chance for a survivor to return to the site of their potential trauma without having to worry about people watching or taking pictures of their reactions. Those of us who were working with survivors and families were in agreement that a site visit was needed and was appropriate, but a decision was made by officials outside of the building that a site visit was not going to happen. That was highly frustrating, but advocating on behalf of the families did not change the decision.

When a FAC is successful, it is difficult for those in charge to think about closing it. The FAC at Camping World Stadium met the concrete basic needs of the survivors and families. It also allowed for an observable easing of anxiety for people as they were able to talk about their challenges, connect with others who were experiencing similar emotions and thoughts, and experience support in this time of great need. Seeing and hearing about the good being done at the FAC made those running the center for the City of Orlando resistant to closing it. However, the benefits of a FAC are immediate and short-lived, and if left open too long, issues of fraud and dependence can begin to manifest. This is very hard to see when the FAC is serving many people and you have yet to see the difficulties arise. Conversations around closing the FAC included many more community agencies and organizations since the long-term assistance plan has to be developed by and supported with community resources. In the two weeks I was in Orlando, the only discussion that involved screaming focused on not wanting to close the FAC. Here again, experience was key in convincing those in a decision-making position that the FAC had a "life expectancy" and next steps needed to be planned.

This work cannot be done in a vacuum, and one of the reasons that I am able to continue it is the people I meet while I do it. In my role as a FAC Lead, it was my privilege to find special friendships both in and outside of the Red Cross. In Orlando, the people who I will be #foreverconnected to come from many organizations: the Red Cross, the FBI, the Department of Justice, the City of Orlando, and Orange County. This was the group that I worked with every day, who allowed me to "take a call" (what we said when we left a meeting because we had started to cry) and to laugh, both of which made me able to keep doing the work in the face of intense pain and loss. In addition to these people, calls to my children and to Red Cross friends who had responded to similar incidents were invaluable in keeping me connected to the world outside of the FAC "bubble." Maintaining the lifeline to normal life brings both perspective and connection that allows for transition away from the response and back to daily life.

My Post-Response Adjustment

Returning home after a deployment is always a challenge. The intensity of a mass casualty response makes normal life seem slow-paced and monotonous. The opening of the Orlando United Assistance Center two days before I left helped with my having to leave, as it seemed like a natural transition point for many things. This did not necessarily mean that arriving home "made sense." I was collected from the airport by my daughter and, as is usual, she wanted to catch me up on what had been happening at home for the past two weeks. One of the biggest challenges of returning from an intense deployment is that family and friends can't fully understand what I have experienced. The details of individual situations fall flat without the visceral awareness of the intensity, the immediacy of need, and the personal connections that form quickly and with great intensity.

Before I left Orlando, I was able to spend time with new friends from the City and Orange County, processing what we had accomplished at the FAC, and what the next weeks and months might look like for them.

Multiple times in those days, we spoke about how we would be #foreverconnected by this response. In returning home, there needs to be a balance between letting go of the response and holding on to these relationships. You need to honor what you have done, as well as the home life that allows you to do it.

Lessons Learned

- Experience matters. If you're interested, find a way to get some. Begin volunteering with your local Red Cross chapter or another organization so you can gain exposure to small events in order to build your skills and confidence, so you're ready for your first deployment to a major disaster. At the same time, it's important to remember that if you have responded to a disaster, you have responded to one disaster. Each situation will be different, and demand different things from you and the impacted community.
- Emotions will flare in both predictable and unpredictable ways and times – including your own emotions, especially frustration. DMH must be flexible and ready to react in any and all ways that are required. This flexibility is never more important than when a mass casualty incident occurs. Trust those in leadership to know the full picture and how to best use you. Questioning decisions and complaining about what you are being asked to do does little good, and causes frustration on all levels.
- Sneakers are important to take on deployment, as is stretching your calves daily when you are walking on concrete. I make sure that I get a good cup of coffee in the morning on the way to the job. (There is a lot of bad coffee made during disaster responses!) I surround myself with people who can laugh when that it possible, listen to music before and after my work shift, and bring a book to read.
- Partnerships can be challenging, especially when people want to be seen helping their people, but an effective response takes all organizations collaborating and putting the needs of survivors above politics or publicity.
- Gaining the largest understanding of all that is happening (the ten-thousand-foot view) is vital to understanding the importance of what you are doing. Enter the experience believing that you don't know anything about the place where the incident occurred or the people involved. True curiosity about both will open conversations that you never dreamed possible.
- It is vital to stay connected to your supports, and know who they are before you leave. You'll have times when you just need to call and talk. Having people who get that means they don't expect it to be a two-way conversation, and that's OK.

Section III

International Disasters

Chapter 16

International Disasters Section Introduction

Amy Nitza

Disasters shatter assumptions about the nature of the world and one's place in it. Thus, the reactions that individuals and communities experience after a disaster are not just a result of the event itself, but also of the world around them. Culture, context, and history shape all aspects of a disaster, including the attributions that individuals and communities make about its causes, how they express distress, and how healing and recovery occur, including how, and from whom, help is typically sought. As described by Miller (2012), "What is most salient for disaster responders is having an understanding, within a sociocultural context, of the subjective experiences of individuals, groups, and collectivities that have lived through disaster and recognizing the many stories, meanings, reactions, and needs engendered by a specific disaster" (p. 7). Some concepts to consider in developing such an understanding include sociopolitical history and climate, worldview and communication patterns, and traditional and indigenous healing practices, among others.

The authors of the case studies in this section include two who were responding to a disaster within their own cultural context, two who were from outside the culture and were deployed to the disaster setting with an international response organization, and one who responded to a disaster that took place locally, but which involved survivors and responders from multiple countries and cultural backgrounds. They highlight key lessons learned from within those different perspectives, and together offer a range of cultural considerations for effective disaster mental health work.

Sociopolitical History and Climate

Community reactions to tragedy reflect and are shaped by the social and political forces around them. Pre-existing social inequities continue to play out in the aftermath of a disaster. Because traumatic experiences induce a sense of powerlessness and loss of control (both real and perceived), an individual's understanding of a traumatic event will be shaped by their experiences of privilege, oppression, colonization, and other social factors.

At a broader level, any specific event is situated in the in-group/out-group divisions, and other racial, ethnic, religious, or social tensions that exist in a place. Understanding these complexities is crucial to understanding the event itself, as well as the reactions and needs of survivors, and to developing a plan for responding in culturally appropriate ways.

A number of the case studies in this section highlight the significant influence of sociopolitical context on disaster response. The massacre at Raba'a in Cairo, Egypt (Abdelaziz, Chapter 20) was embedded in a deep and complex set of historical, political, religious, and ideological differences within the country. Likewise, the multiple social and political contexts that converged on the island of Nauru (Brooker, Chapter 19) played a direct role in sparking the riots there. To fully understand that event, one must consider the political history and climate in Australia that led to the asylum seekers being held on Nauru, as well as the social and political climates of the countries from which the asylum seekers fled.

Postcolonial countries, and/or countries such as Haiti with a history of being invaded by Western nations, are likely to have a historical mistrust of outsiders that carries over to any influx of outside responders following a disaster. There is potential harm associated with working in these settings without an understanding of the history and modern-day consequences of colonialism, invasion, or occupation. This may occur through power dynamics in relationships between Western agencies and responders and their international clients or colleagues. For example, Jean-Charles (Chapter 18) notes that the arrival of overwhelming numbers of outside responders following the 2010 Haiti earthquake, many of whom were inexperienced and had an insufficient understanding of the Haitian culture and context (including its history of invasion and occupation by the United States), resulted in additional and unnecessary suffering.

Worldview and Communication Style

Worldview shapes how people make meaning of their experience – how they conceptualize and solve their problems. Many psychological theories and the intervention models on which they are built are based on a Western worldview of individualism. The underlying assumptions in many of these models about the primacy of individual wants, needs, and goals, and the importance of self-determination, self-reliance, and an internal locus of control, may all be incompatible with a collectivist worldview. Yet approximately 70 percent of the world's population comes from collectivist societies (Chung & Bemak, 2012). When not carefully taken into account by responders, worldview differences can create mismatches that impede their best efforts at helping.

Communication patterns are often a reflection of worldview, and are another crucial consideration in the provision of DMH services. As described by Brown (2008) "… the ways in which humans translate their inner biological states of disequilibrium into outward expressions of distress are strongly affected by culture and context" (p. 7). The construct of low- and high-context communication patterns, which are linked to individualist and collectivist worldviews, has particular relevance to responders. In the low-context communication patterns common among Western individualist cultures, the verbal code is the primary source of information; intended messages are conveyed using the words themselves. Communication is done directly and explicitly, and is done in ways that are consistent with one's feelings. These patterns may be a mismatch when working within a culture with high-context communication patterns characterized by a more restricted code system, in which words are less necessary to convey meaning as messages are interpreted through social cues and an accumulation of shared experiences and expectations. High-context communication is less direct, and is typified by politeness, discretion, and the importance of "saving face" – an important concept in collectivist cultures. Notably, putting feelings into words is not seen as an important goal, as it may be seen as lowering or spoiling their value.

In situations such as these, the concept of providing a compassionate presence when there are few words that can offer much comfort – a theme that runs throughout this book – takes on even greater significance. Whether it is being done at an Ebola patient's bedside while dressed in a complete set of personal protective equipment, or while maintaining a physical presence in a prison to help ensure that imprisoned asylum seekers are not physically assaulted, the authors in this section found ways to connect with those they were helping. Addressing survivors' interrelated physical and practical needs along with their psychological and spiritual needs also takes on a unique importance in such settings. Examples from the authors in this section include ensuring that an Ebola patient was able to receive her favorite beef feet bouillon soup, and handing out pain-relieving medication to suffering asylum seekers as they sat in the rain. These moments of human connection and support can transcend cultural differences.

Traditional Beliefs and Practices

A related consideration is the question of how and from whom help for personal and social problems is typically sought. Natural help-giving networks can be disrupted or delegitimized when traditional beliefs and practices are overlooked. At its worst, Western mental health providers "parachuting in" to an international disaster setting and providing Western-based interventions, without regard for the local traditions that shape a community's response and needs, can become what has been referred to by Bemak and Chung (2011) as *psychological colonialism*. The picture portrayed by Watters (2010) of the "invasion" of Western mental health professionals after the 2004 Asian tsunami, utilizing Western interventions that made little sense to survivors and disregarding their healing and help-seeking practices, is a cautionary tale in this regard.

Working to build trust with local experts and authorities and seeking their guidance and input on intervention strategies not only helps to ensure the cultural appropriateness of those strategies, but also helps to establish the local credibility of the overall response effort. In her experiences during the Ebola outbreak in Guinea, Lebel (Chapter 21) describes the mistrust and stigma that the Western response team, and infected patients, faced from the communities in the area. Her team worked to establish trust with the local communities by making visits to these communities to meet with village elders, chiefs, and traditional healers to discuss their concerns; they also invited these leaders to visit the treatment center to demystify the process and counter the many rumors that were being spread among the population. The team's efforts to incorporate traditional funeral practices into the sanitary burial procedures that were necessary to prevent contamination played an important role in their efforts to promote healing and recovery. In his response in Nicaragua, one of Diaz's (Chapter 17) first orders of business was to identify and meet with local elders and other religious leaders to learn about the needs of their communities; he built on these relationships later to plan support activities and coordinate service delivery.

Building Local Capacity through Training

In low-resource settings or settings without an existing infrastructure of mental health providers, a DMH response must support and build up local capacity without undermining existing community structures and support mechanisms. Training local people, including those without previous formal mental health training, to provide basic supportive services in a culturally appropriate manner as well as to provide additional training to others, is an important component of disaster response in such settings. Sometimes referred to as "task sharing" (Eaton, De Silva, Rojas, & Patel, 2014), training non-specialists to provide basic mental health interventions has been demonstrated to be successful in a number of settings including Pakistan, India, and Uganda (Eaton et al.). An emphasis on this type of sustainable approach is consistent with the *Guidelines for Mental Health and Psychosocial Support in Emergency Settings* established by the Inter-agency Standing Committee (IASC, 2007) which emphasize maximizing the participation of local affected populations in the response, including working to "identify, mobilize and strengthen the skills and capacities of individuals, families, communities and society" (p. 136). Similarly, Miller (2012) has detailed an approach called "psychosocial capacity building" which emphasizes building on existing community resources to create sustainable local capacity for recover.

These approaches can be contrasted with the numerous problems associated with outside mental health volunteers rushing in to provide direct services for a limited time, and then leaving. In Chapter 18, Jean-Charles highlights the challenges posed by the overwhelming number of outsiders seeking to provide assistance and describes the approach he and his colleagues (both Haitian and American) took to establishing a sustainable local mental health response by training local responders using the IASC guidelines. Similarly, Diaz describes a training program for local personnel that created a tiered system of community-based responders. Developed in collaboration with village elders, this program created capacity for community outreach, psychoeducation, assessment, and the provision of Psychological First Aid.

Additional Considerations

There are numerous other considerations when responding to disasters internationally. No article, book, or training program can answer all of the questions that come up for DMH providers in all of the unique and challenging settings in which they find themselves. Perhaps what is most important, then, is for well-trained DMH responders to have sufficient awareness to be able to identify and ask the questions, rather than making assumptions that may lead a responder down a non-helpful path. Examples of questions to be considered in developing this understanding include (Miller, 2012; Summerfield, 2004):

- How are tragedy and loss understood?
- How are risk and adversity faced and managed?
- What allows people to feel hopeful?
- What are acceptable reactions after a tragedy?
- What are acceptable ways to express distress?
- What are acceptable forms of help-seeing?
- What serves as just compensation?

Another frame for considering the appropriateness of Western response interventions in non-Western settings was proposed by Hanlon, Fekadu, and Patel (2014). These included feasibility, equity, sociocultural acceptability, contextually acceptable outcomes, and affordability. Feasibility involves ensuring that the intervention can be implemented and sustained appropriately with the existing mental health resources available in a given location. Equity refers to the importance of making services available to vulnerable and disadvantaged groups so as not to reinforce the inequalities that exist between and within communities. This may necessitate moving beyond what is convenient in order to overcome barriers to services for these groups. Sociocultural acceptability involves considering how the intervention fits, or does not fit, with the worldview of the people involved, including their conceptualization of the causes of disorders, patterns of help-seeking, and modes of intervention and healing. Relatedly, contextually acceptable outcomes refers to targeting the interventions toward outcomes that are meaningful and important to the people being helped; that is, while symptom reduction is often the focus of Western-designed interventions, this may be less important to the people receiving the intervention than other potential outcomes such as improved social relationships, poverty reduction, etc. Affordability in terms of both direct and indirect costs to individuals, caregivers, and health systems should be considered.

Finally, it is essential that DMH responders enter each setting with a sense of cultural humility in which they are aware of their own culturally embedded assumptions about the world, and then suspend those assumptions in order to understand the subjective experiences of the people they are there to help. This awareness of one's own cultural assumptions is difficult yet critical. As described by Edward T. Hall:

> Culture hides much more than it reveals and strangely enough what it hides, it hides most effectively from its own participants. Years of study have convinced me that the real job is not to understand foreign cultures, but to understand our own.
>
> (Hall, 1959, p. 39)

References

Bemak, F., & Chung, R.C.-Y. (2011). Post-disaster social justice group work and group supervision. *Journal for Specialists in Group Work*, 36, 3–21.

Brown, L.S. (2008). *Cultural competence in trauma therapy: Beyond the flashback*. Washington, DC: American Psychological Association.

Chung, R.C.-Y., & Bemak, F.P. (2012). *Social justice counseling: The next steps beyond multiculturalism*. Thousand Oaks, CA: Sage.

Eaton, J., De Silva, M., Rojas, G., & Patel, V. (2014). Scaling up for mental health services. In V. Patel, H. Minas, A. Cohen, & M. Prince (Eds.), *Global mental health: Principles and practice* (pp. 297–334). New York, NY: Oxford University Press.

Hall, E.T. (1959). *The silent language*. Greenwich, CT: Fawcett.

Hanlon, C., Fekadu, A., & Patel, V. (2014). Interventions for mental disorders. In V. Patel, H. Minas, A. Cohen, & M. Prince (Eds.), *Global mental health: Principles and practice* (pp. 252–276). New York, NY: Oxford University Press.

Inter-Agency Standing Committee (2007). *The IASC guidelines on mental health and psychosocial support in emergency settings*. Geneva: IASC.

Miller, J.L. (2012). *Psychosocial capacity building in response to disasters.* New York: Columbia University Press.

Summerfield, D. (2004). Cross-cultural perspectives on the medicalization of human suffering. In G. Rosen (Ed.), *Posttraumatic stress disorder: Issues and controversies* (pp. 233–247). New York, NY: Wiley.

Watters, E. (2010). *Crazy like us: The globalization of the American psyche.* New York, NY: Free Press.

Chapter 17

1998 Las Casitas Mudslides in Nicaragua

Joseph O. Prewitt Diaz

As I was growing up in a small town in Puerto Rico, my grandparents encouraged me to get involved in helping people after a storm, a fire, or a flood. My mother called this work "civic tithing." I carried this lesson with me into my post-secondary studies in the fields of religion and counseling, and my doctoral studies in Educational Psychology.

Since 1990, with the establishment of the Disaster Mental Health function in the American Red Cross, I have served as a volunteer and deployed at least twice a year. I served as an International Delegate for the American Red Cross International Services from 1999 to 2010. During this period, I responded to human-caused and natural disasters on three continents. I was awarded the American Psychological Association International Humanitarian Award in 2008.

When not involved in disaster response, I served as a professor at Penn State for 12 years. At the time of the call I was the Director of Psychological Services for the Chester-Upland School District. On the day of the mudslides, I was serving as Disaster Mental Health Coordinator for Hurricane Georges in Puerto Rico.

The Pre-Disaster Community

The mudslides occurred in the Chinandega District of Nicaragua. New towns were built there after Nicaragua's revolution (1979–1990); most of the population had relocated from the Atlantic side of the country. The Nicaraguan government reported that approximately three-quarters of the population in the affected area came from the Autonomous Region of Nicaragua, comprising indigenous groups including Misquitus, Mayangnas, Ramas, and Garifunas. The two predominant languages among this population were Misquito and Wiswis. They were by and large involved in agrarian tasks, and most lived in extreme poverty by Nicaraguan standards.

The majority of the disaster-affected population was Catholic, while smaller groups were members of the four Apostolic Churches, and yet another group of healers and "espiritistas" (people who communicated with the spirits and were able to cast spells to alleviate "evil eye") were affiliated with the Yoruba tradition. There was an itinerant priest, and two local pastors in the community. Many of those impacted were farm workers whose only access to survival was the weekly acquisition of basic staples from the farm owners' stores. The population lacked a public health system. Although there were visiting nurses, most health issues were dealt with by local healers. Issues of behavioral health were dealt with by local counselors or "espiritistas." Most of the emergency services were provided by the Nicaragua Red Cross.

The Disaster

On October 30, 1998, as Hurricane Mitch passed through the area, the excessive rainfall triggered a catastrophic landslide – a flank collapse of the Las Casita volcano. Las Casita is a complex and probably dormant volcano located 4,600 feet above sea level with a crater that is about one-half mile in diameter. The mud covered an area about 12 miles long and one-and-a-half to two miles wide, on the southwest side of the volcano. The towns of Rolando Rodríguez and El Porvenir were the first to be hit by the mud, which continued to flow down the side of the volcano, destroying villages, settlements, houses, and farmland in its path. The municipality of Posoltega and the town of El Porvenir were completely destroyed.

Approximately 2,000 people were killed. Another 8,000 were displaced, of which 3,448 were housed in extended shelters. In terms of property damage, 653 homes, 10 schools, and the regional health center were destroyed. The affected area had lost its human, social, cultural, financial, and built capital. Most of the agricultural lands, and thus the major source of employment, were lost, as were family and community heirlooms. The survival of the affected area was now dependent on external governmental and non-governmental stakeholders.

My Thoughts Pre-Response

I was sitting at the Disaster Relief Operation for Hurricane Georges in San Juan, writing my final report, when I received a call from the Red Cross HQ. The voice on the other side wanted to know if I spoke Spanish and had an updated license and a passport. I answered in the affirmative, and the next sentence was "Well, we need you in Nicaragua." I was then offered a one-year appointment to become an International Delegate to Nicaragua with primary disaster mental health duties.

For me personally, it meant going back home and dropping everything: taking a leave of absence from my job, putting my things in storage, and renting out my house. This phone call changed my life – what to do?

I was going to a country in Central America that had just been through a civil war, had a depressed economy, and where most of the population didn't speak Spanish. I found out that mental health professionals were not readily available; there was one sole facility in the country that had a mental health clinic and ward. I was confronted with the possibility that every theory that I had read about, every practicum that I had experienced, and every consulting experience might be worthless in the setting where I was going to be deployed.

During my briefing, I was informed that I would have an experienced counterpart from the Spanish Red Cross (SRC) joining me. We would be working in tandem with the Nicaraguan Red Cross as external consultants. As my emotional reaction began to dissipate, I began to think about what we would do in the first 72 hours, in the first week, in the first month. Of all stupid things, I wondered whether my blazer would be crushed in my bag, and what the people there would think of me.

My Response Experience

I met my SRC colleague, a psychologist, who came with a lot of experience dealing with human-caused disasters in Africa. During the flight from Miami, we prepared a work plan. Our first order of business was to meet with the pertinent authorities in Managua and get our marching orders. We both agreed that once we reached the target site we would spend some time conducting an environmental assessment focusing on resources (human, social, environmental, and built).

After two days in Managua and a three-hour jeep ride we finally arrived in Chinadega on November 5, 1998. We were assigned a "champa" (a blue tarp with sides in a central area reserved for responders). We were to be deployed for at least 10 months to support the immediate response and early recovery. We then began our tour of the five shelter sites: Los Tololares, El Tranon, Betesda, El Bosque, and Santa Maria-El Tanque. The sites seemed to have been established where they would have greater access to roads, communication, public health and health services, electricity, and educational opportunities.

We held small focus group meetings. Our objective was to identify the elders, healers, and counselors in the community. We then appointed individuals, who we referred to as community facilitators, whose primary role would be to mobilize the members of the shelter sites. Each shelter site had up to five community facilitators who were trusted by their immediate neighborhood group and were the bridge to external stakeholders. These personnel received a 32-hour operational training that included the following topics: (1) community mapping, (2) needs assessment, (3) nonverbal communications, (4) listening skills, (5) Psychological First Aid, and (6) simple psychoeducation strategies. Our expectation was that each community facilitator would be respectful, sensitive to the need of each community group within the shelter sites, aware of and sensitive to cultural and traditional boundaries, and willing to learn from what the established elders wanted to share.

To address organizational issues, we asked for a planning meeting with all of the organizations that were working with the affected population in order to get to know each other, develop a service map, and foster a harmonious environment. We were not trying to bring proposals from different groups to the table, but rather to create an environment of reflection focused on the theme of rebuilding a safe and healthy community. By the fourth day we had a community service map with five sites, and a schedule of who would be in each site and what activity they would be undertaking. As we completed the preliminary community assessment there were 22 non-governmental organizations providing some type of mental health and psychosocial support. The Ministry of Health took over the responsibility of keeping administrative control of the recovery process.

There were at least two immediate challenges regarding survivors' mental health. First, there were referral needs, but nowhere to refer survivors with pre-existing mental health issues. Second, while well-intentioned, local organizations' efforts were short-lived, usually only lasting one to two days or through a weekend clinic.

We spent a good part of the first month meeting with survivors and in groups with helpers who were emotionally overwhelmed with the nature of the disaster. We used Psychological First Aid, emotional defusing tools and activities, and referrals to the Military Hospital in Managua (some three hours away). By the second month we found that the population of helpers had reduced significantly. Thus, we recruited a cadre of local volunteers, and initiated an operational training that included Psychological First Aid, community assessment, and the use of locally developed tools in the form of brochures ("Share your Feelings"), posters, and community plays (a simplified version of psycho-drama). The basic messages were: rest, eat, talk, recreate in groups, and work together. We addressed two basic sets of feelings: (1) survivors' feelings of loss, grief, and fear; and (2) expectations for the future. We assumed that the mudslides caused a temporary state of emotional upheaval where the majority of the people would cope in a healthy and normal fashion. Providing a space where the disaster-affected people were able to talk about their response, to recreate, rest, and work together would set them on the road to recovery.

We also had to consider the emotional needs of the helpers. Over the course of two months, over 100 spontaneous responders showed up at the recovery sites. Most of these people came from the capital in small brigades. They were not prepared to experience what they saw. They lacked the language skills to communicate with the affected people and thus they experienced both guilt and compassion fatigue. My colleague met with these day-volunteer groups as they were leaving and assisted them by conducting informal debriefings. One of the problems that emerged was that many of the spontaneous volunteers saw the disaster as an opportunity to show up for meals with small groups of survivors, to get rid of old clothing, to proselytize a religious belief, and in some cases to offer to hire young girls as house servants in their homes in Managua. The matter was reported to the personnel of the Ministry of Health; many of these groups left, never to return.

In the third and fourth weeks two medical brigades from the U.S. Navy and the Honduran Army provided assistance. They attended to health needs, and dispensed vitamins, antibiotics, creams for mosquito bites, and some anti-anxiety medication and sleeping pills. Several weeks after they left there was an underground market of un-prescribed medication in the sites. Red Cross was informed about this situation by the Ministry of Health dispensary staff. We immediately began a campaign of psychoeducation on the effects of non-prescribed medication in all the sites.

We organized a number of focused activities to meet specific groups' needs. One involved creating safe spaces for children. The teachers and caretakers were women or men who had lost limbs and couldn't work in the fields, or in carpentry or road construction. This became a much-celebrated activity in the area. People who had thought that their life was through were now called "professor" by the children and parents alike. In conjunction with the World Health Organization, we organized a project called "Return to Happiness" where small groups of children wrote, drew, and acted out their stories, and small groups formed teams and played.

We also created safe spaces for community groups. One was for people who had lost limbs and were now adjusting to a new lifestyle. Another group was composed of widows and widowers and their respective families. The identified problem was that this population was dedicating all their time to helping family members adjust to the losses rather than addressing their own needs. We funded a Fun Day for this group, including a discussion about missing a significant other and letting go. They would have lunch and then some space to reflect and talk about their feelings, and at the end of the afternoon everyone would draw or compose a letter to the lost loved one which was then sent either in a balloon or through fire to their dear one in heaven. These "encuentros" (encounters) became very popular among adults in that it allowed them to share their feelings openly and normalized their "new normal" in the emerging communities.

We paid a great deal of attention to the importance of spirituality in the recovery process. Survivors struggled with difficult questions such as "why am I alive," or "why did I lose my dear ones, property, and source of work?"

We were able to help them address these issues through the different religious groups and the Yoruba tradition best represented by Santeria, Orswha, and Candonble practices. This was an essential task for us: The sooner we could contact elders, healers, and cultural counselors, the sooner we could begin providing support activities.

We had a request for a tarp where the Catholic Church could hold mass during Christian holidays. The Apostolic pastors protested, and as a result, we all agreed to the construction of a large tarp that would be used at different times of the week for different religious experiences. The Yoruba followers would hold their meetings in their residential tarps; the focus was to communicate with the spirit of lost loved one.

One essential part of our entire response was working to augment mental health and psychosocial support through local personnel. We needed to multiply the trained local community facilitators so that they could use simple tools to alleviate fear and foster resilience. Most of the tools for training were locally developed with the advice of the elders and counselors. The training was composed of assessment and community mapping; Psychological First Aid; and psychoeducation.

For the assessment and mapping, common reactions to the disaster were elicited from community elders representing each of the language and cultural groups. The community facilitators elicited information about what situations were causing stress; was there a local name for the problem; how does it manifest itself, what causes it, and who gets it; how is it treated and how effective is the treatment; and how can the problem be avoided.

PFA was described as a first order intervention designed to reduce disaster related stress. Our model consisted of five steps: (1) intervene immediately; (2) listen, and respond with words that provide a sense of hope; (3) validate the person's feelings; (4) plan for next steps (encourage the affected person to begin to identify a personal strategy to move forward); and (5) refer to existing community network.

Three non-verbal psychoeducational tools were developed and used in Las Casitas. Each tool consisted of five parts so that the participants could use their fingers as a learning aid. The first, "share your feeling," was a pictorial trifold with five basic suggestions: talk to your friends, eat, rest, recreate and play sports, and work with your friends. The second tool was a pictorial trifold for "Psychological First Aid." The components were PIES interventions (proximity, immediate, experiential, and simple): listen, validate feelings, plan, and refer to community support group. The third tool was a six-page booklet used for planning small community resilience-building activities.

The methodology used in the training sessions was participative and interactive, with more emphasis on brainstorming, group work, role-plays, and the workshop method rather than lectures and presentations.

This encouraged discussion and led to interaction between participants on the one hand, and with the facilitator and the community on the other. Each group made a list of psychosocial supports and self-care activities, as well as the mechanics of organizing group meetings and community activities.

Building on those initial capacity-building activities, my colleague and I identified the most advanced of our community volunteers, government community aides, and some of the community facilitators, and began a course for mental health technicians. The focus of the two-week course was to help people understand the loss of place and how to develop a psychosocial recovery plan through community initiatives and participatory techniques. We trained a group of 20 technicians who could conduct participatory assessment, engage specific marginalized and vulnerable community groups, organize community activities that improved emotional well-being, and engage community members in "resilience enhancement brigades." Three months later we opened a course for community mental health specialists who had a basic professional degree (teachers, nurses, psychologist, social worker). These personnel were trained in PFA, stress management and self-care techniques, non-verbal communication, and resilience development with diverse sectors of the communities. Seventeen people graduated and were left in charge of the psychosocial support program in Las Casitas as we completed our assignment ten months later. The role of the specialist was to involve the affected people in a process that is controlled by them, and responds to the resources and needs of the community. With time, this process improved community mental health using strategies selected by the people.

Our final psychosocial capacity-building initiative involved creating a "resilience support brigade" composed of affected people who provided cultural, linguistic, and contextual competence by identifying human and social capital among the affected people. They worked with members of the Nicaraguan Red Cross who provided management, administration, and technical support to the program. This cadre conducted rapid environmental assessments, reunited loved ones into specific camps, conducted small group activities to facilitate sharing of feelings, conducted recreation activities for diverse community groups, and organized and funded resilience projects in the community.

My Post-Response Adjustment

It is always difficult to adjust to the back-home scene after working in a major disaster. The most difficult thing for me is to share the sights, sounds, and action during the disaster with people back home so that it doesn't sound like a series of scenes from a horror movie. One thing that helps quite a bit is taking time off to do something different. I try to take breaks during the day, and take every third day off, away from work.

I try to switch channels to the home front – to understand what happened to the relationships that were left behind. It's like you will never be the same, but the people who are around you have also had their experiences and will never be same as you left them. I feel like I must re-construct my physical and emotional center every time I return from a disaster experience.

Probably the most important thing I do is to keep a diary. I use my daily reports to reflect back on my own feelings, what I learned, and how I would do things differently. I check myself so that my role as a technical assistant doesn't get intertwined with the population I am serving, in this case the Nicaragua Red Cross. It's kind of difficult to be in the recovery site, share meals and living accommodation with the affected people, and not get personally involved with the situation, the people, and my knowledge of the steps that need to take place to achieve the goals of community-based psychosocial support.

Lessons Learned

- Factor in a gestation period before jumping into response activities. My role was as an external technical advisor, not a direct provider to the affected people, although I was living in the field with the Nicaragua Red Cross personnel. It was important to conduct an environmental assessment to figure out population, including diversity in culture, language context, age, and marginalized groups. It's also important to figure out your team's strengths and weaknesses: How people learn, common cultural manifestations, diverse problem-solving skills, and solution-focused approaches. More importantly, what is expected of you as mental health workers? Define your operational parameters.
- Tailor the psychosocial response to the specific disaster. Identify social, human, and political capital. Identify strategies and activities to provide multi-dimensional psychosocial care that is considered appropriate by the diverse community groups (ethnic, cultural, social) of affected people and that also meet national and international standards.
- In your immediate response plan and moving forward into recovery, identify and proactively address barriers in access to care. But also recognize the social dimensions and sources of resilience, including utilizing community elders, healers, and religious leaders as your allies in developing a service plan that is appropriate for the whole community.

- Coordinate and integrate disaster response services into the country's mental health response plan, and where possible integrate the World Health Organization and other international groups that advocate for mental health services, psychosocial support, the protection of women and children, and the reduction of stigma toward those considered different and "less-than" in the affected area.

Chapter 18

2010 Earthquake in Haiti

Wismick Jean-Charles

I was sitting in the middle of a meeting of the International Association of Applied Psychology (IAAP) at the United Nations (UN) when the devastating earthquake struck Haiti on January 12, 2010. I was in New York to pursue my doctorate in psychology at Fordham University. Previously, when serving as a training director of the seminarians in Haiti for my religious order and as a principal of a high school in the northwest of the country, I had personally experienced the devastation from Hurricane Jeanne in 2004 and worked with survivors who had been traumatized. After this experience, I had decided to attend Fordham University to complete my PhD, and to receive specialized training in trauma studies in order to learn innovative approaches to address the psychosocial needs of trauma survivors, and then to return to Haiti to continue my work.

The Pre-Disaster Community

Haiti is no stranger to disasters. Historically, Haiti has experienced decades of political conflict both prior to and after its independence in 1804. During the Duvalier dynasty (1957–1986), severe human rights abuses were documented. When, in 1986, "Baby Doc" Duvalier was forced to leave the country, political instability continued with several coups d'état followed by widespread violent crime. To this day, death threats, murders, armed robberies, home break-ins, car-jackings, and kidnappings are not uncommon.

Haiti has also suffered from cyclones, hurricanes, floods, and earthquakes throughout its history. The island nation was ravaged by Hurricane Hazel (1954) that affected every part of the country, killing several thousand people. Hurricane Flora (1963) struck the south and west regions, causing over 5,000 deaths. These were followed by powerful hurricanes in 1966, 1980, 1988, 1994, and 1998. Hurricane Jeanne slammed into Haiti, killing thousands, in 2004. My hometown of Gonaives, the port city where Haitians declared their independence from France in 1804, was particularly hard hit by Jeanne. Overall, about 3,000 people were killed by this hurricane and hundreds more were reported missing and never found. Mass graves were filled with corpses.

Although Haiti is familiar with disasters, it remains unprepared to deal with their aftermath. To this day, Haiti has no clear disaster preparedness programs, or local first responders who have specialized training and proper equipment. Eight years after the 2010 earthquake, local governments still have not yet communicated realistic planning and mitigation measures. Local communities and neighborhood organizations are still not fully aware of proactive measures they should implement in the event of disaster. While the Haitian Directorate for Civil Protection is responsible for risk management, the country unfortunately continues to only react after disasters occur, and to rely heavily on the response of the international community.

The Disaster

Not since the 18th century had the nation been hit by an earthquake of the enormity and intensity of the one that occurred in 2010. The earthquake hit at 4:53 p.m. some 15 miles southwest of the Haitian capital of Port-au-Prince. The initial shock registered a magnitude of 7.0 and was soon followed by two aftershocks of magnitudes 5.9 and 5.5. More aftershocks occurred in the following days, including another one of magnitude 5.9 that struck on January 20 at Petit Goâve, a town some 35 miles west of Port-au-Prince.

Approximately three million people were affected. The UN and the Haitian government estimated that the death toll was between 250,000 and 300,000, and an equal number were injured or permanently disabled. Hundreds of thousands of men, women, and children saw their homes destroyed before their eyes, and the earthquake resulted in 1.5 million internally displaced people.

The nation's capital suffered widespread devastation. Countless dwellings were reduced to rubble, while hospitals, churches, and schools collapsed, and roads were blocked with debris. Numerous government structures were heavily damaged or destroyed, including the presidential palace, parliament building and main prison.

Thousands of volunteer non-governmental organizations (NGOs) responded with the good intention to save Haiti. Our country is said to be home to over 13,000 NGOs. Churches, community groups, small organizations, large multi-national organizations, and several foreign militaries and governmental actors promptly arrived, all intending to provide basic services such as water, sanitation, nutrition, and health services relief. Medical and surgical teams from almost all over the world arrived to provide assistance. While it is certain that many lives were saved by these first responders, it is also evident that some people suffered at the hands of inexperienced aid providers who had an insufficient understanding of the Haitian context, culture, and heritage. Despite the massive presence of these NGOs and the huge financial commitment to mitigate and respond to the disaster, to date there is little evidence of positive impacts of these investments.

My Thoughts Pre-Response

When I saw the terrible scene and heard the rumors (there was no way to confirm the information as all phone access was cut off) that the seminary where I had lived for seven years was destroyed, and 10 seminarians whom I had trained were trapped in the rubble of the collapsed school theology building, it became clear to me that I must return to Haiti and get involved. At the same time, I was not sure what I could concretely offer. First, academically, I felt ill-equipped to work with children, the most vulnerable group in need of assistance and comfort, since I was still in training. Second, emotionally, I felt that I was unprepared to face the damage, particularly the destruction of the seminary where I had lived, the theology school where I had studied, and the church where I was ordained as a priest. Third, ethically, I was not certain how I could negotiate my absence with the church in New York where I was working full time as a student and parish priest. Lastly, socially, as no general policies to guide interventions existed, it was not clear for me how I could bring healing and hope into this desperate situation.

I learned that my family members who lived in Port-au-Prince were safe only on the day of my departure, though their house was, like many others, damaged. I experienced some significant tensions between my personal losses and my professional role, which meant that I was often dealing with other's people pains and traumas and not taking much care of my own. In this situation, I felt so emotionally overwhelmed that I decided to seek help from a psychologist before my departure.

My Response Experience

After three days of emotional and practical preparation, I traveled to Haiti as a member of the response team of the IAAP. On Saturday evening, January 16, we arrived in Santo Domingo, the capital of the Dominican Republic, since there were still no flights landing in Haiti. We then caught a six-hour bus ride to Port-au-Prince, arriving on Sunday, January 17, almost 24 hours after we left New York. We deployed into two major settings: La Paroisse Saint-Louis Roi de France de Turgeau and l'Hôpital de la Communauté Haïtienne, de Pétionville.

La Paroisse Saint-Louis Roi de France

The church *Saint-Louis Roi de France*, a parish in Port-au-Prince, is staffed by my religious order, the Montfort Missionaries. Long ago, when I was both a student at the Université d'Etat d'Haïti (State University of Haiti) pursuing my bachelor's degree in psychology and a seminarian in training for the priesthood, I lived there. On this trip, I once again stayed at the church property, this time outdoors under a tent, alongside hundreds of survivors, since all the houses and the church building were destroyed. Some of the survivors had been injured; most were traumatized by the experience, uncertain of the future. They were all left without adequate necessities to sustain life. At our makeshift churchyard camp, they were living and sleeping side by side on blankets. Food and water were scarce, but we were fortunate enough to have a meal after two days, consisting of rice and beans provided by the priests and nuns.

In this camp that became our home for seven days, children sang songs at night, and survivors began their days early in the morning with prayers and spiritual devotions. We quickly understood that religion and spirituality were a part of their cultural healing practices and that we therefore needed to incorporate their spiritual resources into our response.

Indeed, the religious and spiritual context of Haiti is a unique one, inspired by the practices of the indigenous Taino people, the Roman Catholicism of Spanish and later French colonizers, the beliefs and practices that enslaved people brought from Africa, and more recent additions from Protestant Christianity and other faith traditions. Spirituality is an integral part of daily life for the vast majority of Haitians of all social classes. The majority of Haitians are Catholic, and a significant number either practice or are shaped by the beliefs and practices of Vodou. Faith communities are the places most Haitians receive both spiritual and psychological support when facing trauma.

In my interventions, I considered how their spirituality and religion might be useful to them, while I remained cognizant that some can also use religion or religious beliefs to deny reality. Of course, I carefully kept in mind the ethical responsibility that I had to respect and accommodate each person's values in order to avoid unnecessarily offending anyone. I tried to help those with religious beliefs to draw on spiritual resources for meaning-making, purpose in life, healthy interpretations, new perspectives, and a sense of order and coherence in this chaotic and confusing situation. Since the integration of psychology with spiritual and religious approaches was so new in Haiti, I exercised caution, respect, sensitivity, and flexibility when incorporating spiritual resources and when consulting with secular psychologist colleagues.

My formation as a priest and training as a psychologist had prepared me for this integration of spiritual and psychological support and I was very comfortable integrating religious rituals into my work with the survivors at the camp. For instance, in a session conducted for 35 traumatized nuns, the Daughters of Wisdom, I gave each one a piece of the rubble that I retrieved from the ruins of their destroyed houses and schools, and one by one they placed the rock in the pot of a beautiful plant, and poured water over the pot, in a symbolic gesture of life arising out of death. In addition to religious rituals, we also used creative arts and songs with the children who lived at the churchyard, which have been shown to be effective in their healing.

Haitian culture is one in which people are frequently skeptical of talking about their feelings. However, as we worked in the camp it became apparent that there were those who found talking helpful – I assume because of the extreme situation of the earthquake. For example, as soon as one family heard we were in the churchyard, the father of a teen who had pulled herself out of the rubble asked for a "session." Many of the survivors who were not familiar with exploring deeper emotions welcomed the opportunity to explore the meaning of this terrible event. A Haitian psychologist in our church campground referred poignantly to his reliance on Viktor Frankl's "logotherapy" – a search for meaning in the midst of total disaster, which was the only way Frankl survived the Holocaust. At the church camp, the majority of survivors reported being scared, depressed, panicked, and even angry about the tragic event. Some interpreted the disaster as "God's will," explaining that God is angry at people's sins or at evil-doers. Others, however, believed that the event was an act of nature.

In any disaster response, building local capacity is crucial. Since we were there on just a seven-day mission, we quickly determined that it would be crucial to train local people to continue the work. However, deciding who to train and how to train them presented significant challenges. While I myself experienced doubts and concerns about the feasibility of such an endeavour, my colleague had significant experience in this area, and relying on the Interagency Agency Standing Committee (IASC) Guidelines on Mental Health and Psychosocial Support in Emergency Settings (IASC, 2007) we rapidly determined ways to train local people in some trauma survival skills.

With the help of the parish priest who was the informal community leader, we mobilized the church camp resources (people, especially the young people, and other assets) and coordinated with the church network to address the needs of the community. We instructed the priest that we needed to recruit people who were warm-hearted and who cared about helping others, since doing simple acts of kindness did not require years of professional training. We immediately gathered a group of Boy and Girl

Scouts aged between 20 and 22 years and trained them in some simple Psychological First Aid techniques, as comforters and helpers, so that they could then pass the techniques on to others in the church camp to create sustainability until other professional teams could come to offer further trainings and assessment of needs.

L'hôpital De La Communauté Haïtienne

We came from New York with five suitcases stuffed with medical supplies, and we went to the local hospital in Pétionville to deliver them. There we were greeted, to our surprise, by a group of 35 Haitian undergraduate psychology students, gathered by a local social worker who just the day before mentioned his plan to send a message to a few students to come learn support skills and to spread the word to other students. I marveled at the large group of young people who came so willingly to help, assembled within so few hours. We set about training the students to use tools and techniques for dealing with their own and others' trauma, relevant to the Haitian culture.

The workshops consisted of information about trauma, including physical, psychological, behavioral, and spiritual symptoms. To help others, they were instructed to be "comforting" – to listen, but not to attempt to conduct "therapy." We based the training on the IASC Guidelines; we emphasized involving local people to help, being culturally sensitive, working in the local language, and being sustainable (IASC, 2007). The training consisted of elementary techniques that do not require advanced clinical skills, such as breathing exercises for relaxation, stress reduction, and support to promote the process of recovery and the development of resilience.

We embellished the lessons by adding spiritual and religious rituals. Drawing from my theological background, I have created a number of rituals to teach lessons on resilience. Most of the rituals include symbols of rocks, water, candles, and flowers. For instance, I used a lighted candle to teach them to stand in the darkness created by this disaster, to navigate this darkness and walk through their "nights" with a new sense of openness. Then, they were invited to pass on the lighted candle to represent helping others to find light and becoming beacons of hope and light for others. I also used the symbol of a flower to help them develop a deeper sense of gratitude for what is truly important in life by facing the loss, trauma, and sadness with openness and possibilities. The symbol of a flower in this context of disaster and despair was intended to teach them that beauty can come from chaos.

Modeling the self-care lesson of our trainings, we asked the students to go around in a circle and share something they plan to do for themselves that would represent "being good to yourself." Certainly, many people might answer that they would go to the movies or eat pizza, but there were hardly pizzas and movies available in Haiti then for those students, nor could they treat themselves with anything that would cost money. To vividly illustrate this, we gave non-material examples such as "I'd ask for a hug from my friend." However, despite our attempts to get them to focus on themselves, the main response was, "Je veux devenir plus fort pour aider plus les autres" ("I want to become stronger to be able to help others more"). At first, we tried to get them to pick something else that would more clearly be for themselves, since they were already doing so much for others. But when they persisted with that answer, we understood the depth of their dedication. To these youth, asking for strength to help others was as legitimate or comforting as treating themselves to pizza or a movie. I was personally moved and massively impressed by their intention to be empowered to serve. As we continued around the circle, hearing more wishes for strength and courage to help others, we asked the group to encircle each other with that strength and courage. Some lifted their arms in a universal sign of victory. The group laughed in a spirit of togetherness and hope.

Each training workshop ended with a ritual ceremony of gratitude that consisted of passing the lighted candle to understand that light that can emerge from terrible darkness. Each person was given the opportunity to make a concluding statement. "I am grateful for being here with you all," one student said. "Thank you for my new friends and the chance to do something for others," another student said. Everyone hugged each member of the group and left the hospital.

After the training, they were sent to give the traumatized people encouragement, comfort, and reassurance through acts of giving them water, holding their hands, and offering an "ear," a "heart," and a "hand." The group was all very excited to apply their new skills to care for those suffering.

Despite our fears that seeing the extent of the wounds and pain of the hospital patients would keep these trainees from returning to do the work, all 35 of them signed up for more shifts, some even committing to daily service. As a priest and psychologist, I know how important it is to make a consistent and long-term commitment. When I returned to New York, it was exceptionally rewarding to hear from the hospital social worker that the youth helpers continued to keep their schedules. There was hope.

This was the beginning of what would become today the Center for Spirituality and Mental Health (CESSA for its French acronym; Centre de Spiritualité et de Santé Mentale). CESSA was born with these local students who were dealing with their personal losses of homes and schools and who had deaths in their own families. But they were willing to learn new skills and committed to serving others.

My Post-Response Adjustment

I returned from my seven-day mission on January 23, 2010. The return to "normal life" was both challenging and rewarding. On one hand, it was very hard for me to get back to a comfortable life in New York when I recalled the hardship of my people in Haiti. On the other hand, it was very rewarding to return to New York when I saw how many people and institutions wanted me to talk about my experiences.

To reach the broader diaspora and non-Haitian community to educate them about mental health in Haiti after the disaster, I talked about my response experience on a radio show, at the UN, and at several academic conferences. Various videos were also produced about my responses.

I truly experienced a feeling of fulfilment during this post-response period. As a first-line responder, I felt honored to be an ambassador for my nation with the mission to spread the word that all those impacted by the disaster and who experienced trauma did not have access yet to the mental health support they needed. I took those opportunities to inform the international academic community about the lack of available resources to provide Haitian people with the psychosocial support that they needed. These academic and social events were powerful vehicles for me to communicate about Haiti's needs for healing. I felt privileged to make valuable connections for Haiti and to keep global attention focused on this previously forgotten country.

Lessons Learned

- Local students can be a valuable asset in low-resource countries to aid communities in recovery. Students should be recruited, equipped with simple psychosocial support techniques, and involved in recovery efforts.
- Relatedly, disaster responders must create sustainable programs and adopt innovative approaches that engage local people and communities. This was essential since many aid organizations that came to help after the earthquake left the country when the media had gone, while in Port-au-Prince, people impacted by the disaster who experienced multiple traumas were trying to get back to normal life without really having access to the mental health support they needed.
- Helping people to draw from healthy religious beliefs and spiritual practices can be beneficial in disaster mental health response. Disaster responders should find ways to support people's spirituality and to integrate local spiritual practices into the response plan when appropriate.
- To address the need for sustainability, CESSA was founded on the first anniversary of the earthquake in 2011. Its mission is to use both

spirituality and psychology to promote the resiliency of the Haitian people. CESSA has great promise to grow (1) to provide more services to Haitian communities; (2) to offer more professional trainings for Haitian students of psychology, nursing, medicine and related fields, early career professionals, and even established professionals; and (3) to form more partnerships with both local and international organizations with similar missions. The success of CESSA in Haiti, one of the poorest countries in the world, can be used as a model for disaster response in other low resource countries.

Chapter 19

2013 Asylum Seeker Camp Riots on Nauru

Stephen Brooker

Nursing was an accidental career choice stimulated and sustained by an innate desire to help those most in need, to fight for human rights and play my part in making the world a better place. My previous career within the legal profession had taught me lessons about crime and criminality, power and money, influence and control; nursing, on the other glove, taught me compassion and respect, teamwork and excellence, vigilance and calm.

After RN training in the UK, I travelled the world. Recognizing my skills dealing with the physical body were limited by skills with words and emotion, I studied a Diploma in Mental Health, then worked in Hong Kong for Médecins sans Frontières (MSF) with Vietnamese refugees; then in India, volunteering on an HIV/TB care and support project.

I hit another barrier: culture. Efficient in care of the body, culture was a sea and I was caught in a storm, so I studied for an MA in Medical Anthropology before emigrating to Australia. After working in immunology for 15 years, I took an opportunity to run a mental health facility before being appointed Director of Mental Health Services (DMHS) for the Detention Health Network (DHN) of the International Health and Medical Services (IHMS) in early 2012.

The Pre-Disaster Community

As an old indigenous land colonized by Europeans in 1788, the intertwining of politics and refugees/asylum seekers in Australia has deep roots. In the modern era, different government administrations have brought with them a changing string of immigration/refugee/asylum seeker policies. After the Vietnam War, Vietnamese refugees began arriving, followed by other waves of "boat people." The first Immigration Detention Centers (IDCs), short-term facilities with basic accommodations and services, brought with them the symbolic introduction of fencing. Discussions around the benefits of community detention were overshadowed by politics, which resulted in detention within designated, controlled centers. In the 1990s, the Howard government introduced the use of offshore processing of refugees and asylum seekers on the islands of Nauru and Manus – a practice which was re-introduced as the number of asylum seekers and boat arrivals rose throughout 2011–2012. The Regional Processing Center (RPC) where I worked was reopened on Nauru in 2012.

Nauru is a remote independent nation in the South Pacific with around 12,000 residents – the third smallest state in the world. Known for phosphate mining, most necessities are imported; the economy is poor with high unemployment, morbidity, and mortality. Desperate economic pressures have resulted in continued dependence on Australia as a significant source of income.

Once the RPC opened, there was an immediate transfer of asylum seekers from other detention facilities. The first transferees were hundreds of men from a variety of different countries and ethnic backgrounds: Iranians, Tamils from Sri Lanka, Afghans, Iraqis, Bangladeshis, Rohingyas from Burma, and Palestinians. Many had a background of escaping persecution, torture, and trauma; they were of different ages, educational backgrounds, and social status. Most had been detained from between a few weeks to a few months.

The original facility was in considerable disrepair. While new facilities were being built, many asylum seekers were housed in tents in tropical conditions with no respite from the sun and heat. Meanwhile, Australian staff were housed in the local hotel or in "dongas" (temporary, transportable dwellings) some 10 minutes away from the RPC. The local hospital was dilapidated and although the hospital staff were willing to help, they struggled to meet the demands of the Nauruan population. One vitally important skill base that failed to meet Australian standards was in the area of emergency response.

My Thoughts Pre-Response

When I started with IHMS, I found:

- A distinct lack of systems and processes.
- A rise in self-harm and self-injury.
- A demoralized mental health workforce.
- A medically-driven model of care.
- No set client-staff ratios.
- Inexperienced managers in the area of mental health.

Increasing boat arrivals, rapid flux in center numbers, and rapid recruitment and rotation of staff made for a volatile mix under intense political and media scrutiny. It was clear to me that although IHMS was contracted to provide health services through the DHN, it had no expertise in running such services. IHMS's main loyalty was to the government (its sole contract) and not to the clients it was employed to provide a service to: the asylum seekers. As a clinician, my duty was to the clients and I knew that to survive in a clinically toxic environment I would have to tread very carefully.

In mid-2013 I was asked to cover the Health Service Manager (HSM) on Nauru who was going on leave. I had already travelled to Nauru, helping to set up and support the team there and deal with some critical clinical issues, such as mass outbreaks of potential self-harm manifesting in so-called "protest behaviors" like hunger strikes.

Arriving 10 days before the riots, I had a sense of familiarity and camaraderie. I knew the team, the situation, the response, the systems, the processes, the stakeholders, the clients. What I didn't see or anticipate was the combustible mix that was developing in the newly-built RPC: A tinder-box had been created that a spark was going to ignite. I could say that the riots started without warning, although with hindsight the warnings were everywhere. They had just been underestimated, ignored, or dismissed.

The Disaster

Amid gradually building tensions in the RPC, peaceful protests by the detained asylum seekers finally erupted into violence on July 19, 2013. The actual riot started just before sundown and involved detainees setting fire to buildings (the medical center and their own newly built accommodations) as they armed themselves with rocks and sticks, and in some cases knives and steel bars. The situation unfolded quickly, with many unknowns (who instigated, who were the leaders, what degree of preparation was involved, when did negotiations break down, etc.) as the security personnel struggled to contain the situation. The detention center was not huge, but as the sky darkened there was a sense of chaos and things spiraling out of control.

Police and security personnel reinforced the perimeter, holding the line as the asylum seekers tried to push forward, throwing rocks and chairs and anything else that could be thrown. Inside the center, no one could really determine what was taking place as it was getting too dark, too dangerous, and too violent, even as hundreds of local Nauruans, some carrying machetes and steel pipes, started to arrive after emergency calls were put out on radio and local TV.

By the time the riots were over several hours later, 80 percent of the buildings in the RPC were destroyed, including the accommodation buildings, the health center, and the dining room, resulting in an estimated \$60 million in damages. Of the approximately 575 detainees being held at the time of the riots, 129 were identified as having been involved. Some 60 were held at the police station and four were hospitalized, while others were treated on-site for mainly minor injuries. The vast majority were in some kind of distress.

My Response Experience

On the day of the riot, we held an education event in the clinic with a visiting psychiatrist on "Detention Fatigue." Security briefings whispered rumors of discontent, but nothing out of the ordinary. The number of clients on hunger strike had lessened recently and the atmosphere seemed calmer and safer. However, there had been a few occasions when the clinic had been hit with a significant number (anywhere from a few people up to around 30 to 40 when the situation had really deteriorated) of people engaging in self-harm activities, so we instituted a series of emergency response drills. Something could happen at any moment.

At about 1 p.m. my emergency phone rang: called to a briefing. This was not unusual. There were constant alerts, briefings, communications around protest behaviors, rumors of marches, demonstrations, some kind of disruption. Eight to 10 people from all the major stakeholder groups were briefed on intel that "something" was going to happen. The asylum seekers were gathering; they knew that Kevin Rudd, the recently reinstalled Prime Minister, was due to make an announcement on off-shore processing of asylum seekers later that day. With an Australian election imminent, this was big political news.

I'd expected to be in the emergency briefing for a short time, but 1 p.m. turned into 2 and 3 as the afternoon drifted on. Towards the main entrance, staff were leaving in dribs and drabs. Some were in lines, others in clusters, most in emergency vests in orange and yellow. This slow-motion evacuation was unusual because the emergency committee should have triggered evacuation procedures, but we hadn't. We watched our staff file out.

The security personnel were engaging with the asylum seekers, seeing what they wanted. Of course, this was freedom and justice, to return to Australia and have their applications for asylum dealt with under the obligations of the treaties Australia had signed, but this was nothing that the people on the island could help them with. This was the responsibility of politicians sitting in offices in the capital, Canberra, the announcement from Rudd hanging like a storm cloud.

Around 4 to 5 p.m. the emergency briefing ended. Discussions with the asylum seekers were not paying off; there was a feeling of urgency. Even so, there was a languidness in the response reflecting the sullen tropical heat, like we were drifting into a fire. I left the camp and spoke to our medical staff outside. An ambulance was in place; a medical tent set up. It was mundane in some way – toilet breaks, food, "how are you doing?", "this is what we know." Waiting, waiting, waiting.

Outside the RPC, on the phosphate covered roads, it seemed settled and calm. Inside the RPC the situation was escalating. The security firm's attempts to engage the asylum seekers were still stymied by Department of

Immigration and Border Protection (DIBP) personnel who gave a verbal report that they had "refused to negotiate" with asylum seekers requests around "continued detention on Nauru" due to perceived "threats to property." The refusal to negotiate was one of the worst mistakes I've ever witnessed in 25 years in professional settings for, as the sun began to set and red clouds crossed the sky, Rudd made his announcement that all asylum seekers who arrived in Australia by boat would be sent to RPCs for processing and resettlement, none allowed to stay. Australia was closed to refugees.

The riot started. From the ambulance we had a clear view of the main gate: men shouting and yelling, things being thrown, security guards pressing back. In a few short seconds the whole atmosphere changed. We drove the ambulance down to the medical tent a short distance away, briefing the team and listening to the noise: a low human rumble, bursting with violence. It seemed a gunshot went off – not a gun, although it sounded like it. The medical center was on fire and oxygen cylinders were exploding.

The situation was acute yet strangely calm. We were in "the zone" where clinicians focus on the work in front of them, even as the sky grew darker and reddened again as fires took hold. We remained practical and authoritative, liaising with other stakeholders and assessing what we were dealing with: a few injuries and other clinical priorities. Nothing life-threatening, no broken bones. Cuts, scrapes, a few bruises.

Being so near the epicenter of the riot, our staff were at risk, as was the ambulance and the equipment. At this point, not knowing whether the riot would spill out onto the road or how the Nauruans or security would handle the asylum seekers, the decision was made to withdraw to our hotel. It was past 9 p.m. and we were tired, needing to rest and sleep. We debriefed, arranged to meet early the next morning, and went to bed.

I sat in my room with a pen and paper. What did we have left? The team were safe, no injuries. We had the ambulance and the tent, some equipment, but we'd lost the clinic, computers, patient records, and drugs. Virtually everything was gone. But we had a team.

8 a.m., breakfast. I'd had briefings from security and DIBP, talked to my immediate line managers in Sydney, and knew what we faced. Many of the new RPC buildings had burnt down and the clinic was gone; many asylum seekers were in jail; others were in the camp. It was raining.

During the night I'd sat and mapped out three teams to try to cover the main areas in relation to geography vs. medical and mental health priorities:

1 The first team was to visit the jail to assess the extent and degree of injuries/issues. We had no visibility as to what medical/mental health problems there were (or even how many asylum seekers were

imprisoned) but knew that prison services were extremely limited and would need help. We had to find out what problems there were, what help was needed, and our primary strategy was developing relationships with the prison staff. Without that we could do very little as we had no formal right to be inside the jail, or to provide medical services to prisoners. This proved to be invaluable as many did have significant injuries, were in a state of shock, and were under constant surveillance. Our presence helped protect them when retribution might have been more of a temptation without external scrutiny.

2 The second team returned to the RPC where the majority of asylum seekers resided and where our clinic would be set up again. Assuming there were injuries, distress, vulnerable clients, and chaos, we had to start getting ourselves together as a functioning service and work out how the clients that needed healthcare would get to whatever services we set up.
3 The third team was allocated to deal with stakeholders as we knew that many would be very angry or upset. One of the senior mental health clinicians said almost immediately "We have to work on reconciliation" and in retrospect, this gave our team a focus that they might otherwise have lacked as we concentrated upon Psychological First Aid, physical injuries, etc. Knowing the asylum seekers, the other Australian contractors, and the Nauruans, we could clearly see that trust had burned down along with the center and that unless we worked on building it back up, we would face far greater problems later on.

I went up to the RPC with around 10 of our medical staff. The clinic was flattened: nothing left. We had three dongas containing drugs and equipment, one damaged by fire, two fit for salvage. We found tables, chairs, paper, and pens. The asylum seekers huddled in the rain in one muddy section of the RPC, sitting on cardboard and holding plastic over their heads. There was an eerie quiet, as if in a dream. We walked among them and smiled at a few. There had to be a human connection.

Before the riots, the relationship of the mental health team with the asylum seekers was complicated. Even though we knew we had their interests at the forefront of our minds, we also knew that we were seen as "part of the system," aligned with the people who were keeping them on an island in the remote Pacific. Despite this, our clinic and our teams worked hard and that seemed to be noticed. We treated illnesses and ailments, talked to them, tried to understand their lives and their histories, did the best that we could. As with any client accessing any health service, clinicians have to put patients first and develop rapport and a rational understanding of the issues faced. It's only through these interpersonal relationships that clinicians can truly help people. So, if there was respect to be earned, we tried to earn it. After the riots and the fires, we tried to earn it again.

With the clinic destroyed, we lost patient files. For now, we had to rely on memory: Which clients had chronic medical or mental health issues needing immediate prioritization? Following a recent rotation, the medical team knew less about their clients than the mental health team who'd been on island a while. Struggling to set up another medical tent in the mud and rain, we started making lists.

One of the asylum seekers spoke softly to a nurse: His friend was in pain. We found stocks of painkillers, handing them out. Quiet queues began to form; there was an exchange of understanding, a strange adjustment to an abnormal situation.

The asylum seekers seemed shocked by the enormity of the fire; the stakeholders, angry; the Nauruans, hostile and suspicious. Our clinicians got on with the job. We found asylum seekers in Nauru hospital and in the jail with fractured jaws and cheeks. Lists got longer, but we were following up. Some very vulnerable men with chronic mental health conditions (one with schizophrenia) started to decompensate so we negotiated their transfer into undamaged rooms in the few buildings still standing. Risk of decompensation was a primary concern.

Saturday and Sunday passed in a blur of activity. The teams in the jails negotiated access with angry guards and frightened, sullen prisoners. In the RPC, a semblance of order was created with regular trips up to the mud/cardboard holding area with buckets of painkillers and queues nearly too long. We were beginning to make progress: identifying longer-term clients with medical needs; clients with injuries; those suffering who wanted to speak. All were seen in makeshift tents, under dirty covers.

We negotiated the use of a large room in a building that had survived the fires. Scavenging skills were key to our functioning as a health service. Adaption and flexibility – without these we would have had nothing.

The team had clinical supervision sitting on dirty, dust-covered chairs, with a backdrop of burnt out buildings. Dealing with the emotional reactions of the medical and mental health team was another primary concern, for without the team being functional and fit, we could not provide a service. Some staff were coping better than others and talked through strategies for self-help: going for walks, reading, calling home, time off, a gathering in a restaurant one evening.

Two to three hundred asylum seekers were housed in makeshift tents in two locations across the island and we worked with about two-thirds of them. Around 30 percent were in regular clinic contact, others on an as-needed basis. Satellite clinics were set up; triage and prioritization/escalation protocols re-established; teams visited the jail and the hospital. Transfers off-island were prohibited by DIBP. This was a dangerous retribution for those with severe medical issues and those with chronic mental health diagnoses who had completely decompensated. We could not keep them safe and could not get them the treatment needed. DIBP sought people to blame.

The asylum seekers displayed mixed reactions: some angry, some sad. Some were targeted as ringleaders while others denied any involvement in the riot at all. Investigations, blame, conspiracy, fear, anger – many emotions and feelings played out with different people on different teams. Relationships suffered and increasing hostility and anger started to fester. Stakeholder relations frayed. The disaster was over and reconciliation was about to start. Longer-term relationship building became the priority; we had to keep talking.

My Post-Response Adjustment

I stayed on Nauru for two months, came off for a few weeks, and returned for a few weeks more. Returning to Australia for the first time, it was like a parallel universe. For weeks, like many of our team, I had woken up, worked solidly for 10 to 12 hours, ate, talked, slept, and then did it all again. It had been relentless, and I wasn't used to rest.

Teamwork got me through. Being in such a unique situation, there was a bonding between us – and not just us healthcare providers. Such bonding took place between all stakeholder groups, even affecting asylum seekers and Nauruans as well. It was surprising, unpredictable, yet affirming. Life went on, and we did too.

In Australia, it was difficult to talk it through. I couldn't find words, couldn't articulate emotions, couldn't regain the intensity. I found myself reaching back to the team: they *knew*, they understood. We had been there together and would never forget.

After a while, I got on with my life, walking, reading, learning, and reflecting. Reflecting mainly on the whole damn mess, on how politicians conceive of a bad idea – a bad barrel. Civil servants design that very expensive bad barrel, and into that bad barrel tumble asylum seekers, contractors, medical staff, and Nauruans. As clinicians, we should always keep our eyes open and our senses alert. We can go rotten in a bad barrel.

Lessons Learned

- **Know your clients.** The type of disaster you might face can vary enormously. However, if you're working with a stable and known population, then you can have a thorough understanding of (and following up with) those with chronic conditions or acute needs. Documentation must be concise, accurate, and considered. An unstable/unknown population requires work with partner organizations to identify those in need/at risk through the establishment of services and referral pathways.
- **Know your team.** In a disaster situation, different people will be feeling different emotions at different times. Some will cope; some will struggle.

Recognizing that this is part of what you are dealing with is important as there may be some individuals expressing emotions felt by the whole group. Even so, you will need competent, skilled clinicians and shouldn't be afraid of dealing with sub-standard performance if patient care is compromised, the team put at risk, or the person is simply not coping/decompensating.

- **Be organized.** Sounds simple. It isn't, especially in the face of an unfolding event. Regular briefings, formal meetings, follow-up issues. Lists are good: Don't lose them!
- **Facilitate good communication protocols.** Don't underestimate this. In a disaster setting rumors and speculation flourish like flowers after a flood. It comes back to good organization and working with partners, but effective communication protocols (within the team and without, as well as with clients/patients) enhance how everyone works together.
- **Focus on the client/patient.** Health services are there to support clients, but it's easy to get misdirected into other areas or speculate about inaccurate information. Always, always, always (if there is a difficult question, or things are muddled or unclear) ask: "how does this affect the patient?" The answer will usually become clear.

Chapter 20

2013 Massacre at Rabaa Square in Egypt

Basma Abdelaziz

At the time of the event, I was a psychiatrist, working for Egypt's General Secretariat of Mental Health, a governmental institute falling under the Ministry of Health. I was also connected to the Al-Nadeem Centre, a non-governmental organization that specialized in rehabilitation of victims of violence and torture, where I have worked on regular basis for more than 10 years. I know well from my past experience with state violence the dramatic effect it has on survivors, so I kept trying to offer help by all means possible during and after the massacre in Cairo.

The Pre-Disaster Community

Before the disaster struck, Egypt was passing through a period of political instability. In 2011, President Hosni Mubarak was forced by the crowds in Cairo's Tahrir Square to leave office after almost 30 years in power. A military council took power for one and a half years, and then the Muslim Brotherhood, a Sunni Islamist organization founded in 1928, acquired political authority when Brotherhood member Mohamed Morsi was elected president. However, in less than one year, the military, led by Egypt's Minister of Defense and backed by huge numbers of protestors in the streets, ousted President Morsi, kidnapped him, and put an end to the Muslim Brotherhood ruling system. This consequently led to the famous sit-in by Muslim Brotherhood supporters in Rabaa Square in Cairo.

The Egyptian community was – and still is – extremely polarized. The Muslim Brotherhood has been in conflict with the different presidential regimes since the 1950s. This longstanding conflict has always been a very complicated one, full of hidden deals, secret negotiations, and unclear agreements between the Brotherhood and the ruling regime. This sophisticated relationship between both parties explains the extent to which the commanders of the Brotherhood initially relied on a political solution for the serious situation that arose in 2013. After the military ousted President Morsi on July 3, 2013, members of the Brotherhood staged a huge sit-in, invited all of their supporters, and asked the Minister of Defense to release the kidnapped president.

However, at the time of the massacre, the majority of the Egyptian population were in opposition to the Muslim Brotherhood, calling on the Ministry of Defense to save the country, then quell the sit-in, and even to eradicate the protestors. The shadows of this political conflict obscured the scene, which helped later to maximize the traumatic effect on survivors. During and after the massacre, Brotherhood supporters were met with hostility, rejection, marginalization, and sometimes physical violence.

The Disaster

Rabaa Square is located in the Nasr City district in eastern Cairo. It is composed of a public square and surrounding street branches, with the famous Rabaa al-Adawiya mosque at one of its edges. An adjacent major road is usually clogged with heavy traffic.

Protestors against President Morsi's overthrow began occupying the square in July, and by the day of the massacre, the sit-in had gradually expanded. A Human Rights Watch report estimated the sit-in was ultimately composed of 85,000 members of the Muslim Brotherhood as well as members of other different religious groups and sympathizers who were demonstrating against what they called a military coup.

Initially, authorities made no attempt to exert control over the protestors. Before long the square contained thousands of tents where families lived for days and weeks. They were allowed to build restrooms, an amusement park for children, and a swimming pool. They tapped into electricity from public wires in the streets. Vans delivered food, water, and building supplies. The sit-in contained all social classes – lower, middle, and even upper social class businessmen belonging to the Brotherhood, from both rural and urban areas. All age groups participated from infants to elderly, and both genders were present with a considerable number of families sharing in the protest. The huge size of the crowd and the wide variety of ages were perceived as protective factors for the protestors. As one survivor told me two years later, while talking about the degree of predictability and how much the protestors were prepared to deal with the security forces during evacuation, they felt "relaxed, never expecting such a brutal, extremely violent and inhuman attack."

All was not peaceful, however. Groups of the protestors went out on marches, screaming chants while moving towards the intelligence headquarters and searching for the missing president. Many clashes occurred between protestors and security forces in July, with dozens killed.

Then, on August 14, 2013, the security forces made the horrible decision to suddenly attack the protesters in an extremely brutal way while allegedly trying to evacuate them from the square. The massacre started early in the morning at about 6 a.m. and lasted for hours. Security forces completely blocked Rabaa Square and the streets around it, closing the five main entrances to the sit-in. They began to attack the protestors using weapons including guns with real bullets, gas bombs, and bulldozers, and even shooting at the protestors from helicopters. They set fire to the Rabaa mosque and attacked protestors in the hospital later on during the evacuation process.

There was no safe escape for the protestors who wanted to leave the sit-in once the evacuation started. Survivors stated that anyone who tried to leave the square through the pathways designated by military forces were either shot on the spot or detained by the forces, kept in compartments of its huge vans where they were subjected to torture. The injured received no real external help; the only way to deal with the wounded was to carry the victim to the hospital, which was located within the borders of the sit-in, or to leave them to their fate on the ground.

The situation quickly turned even more terrible, with corpses accumulating in the mosque and in the hospital, leaving no place for more bodies whether alive or dead. The evacuation process became a nightmare, with more than 800 killed on the spot inside Rabaa Square, in addition to countless injuries.

My Thoughts Pre-Response

Once the security forces began their attack on the protestors, I was motivated to reach the victims. Horrible results were anticipated as the sit-in contained a huge number of people, with whole families, children, and the elderly. It was obvious that extreme state violence was being perpetrated against the protestors and that there would be a huge number of victims.

After I heard that the evacuation process was happening, I felt frozen for some minutes, then I became so anxious that I made the decision to leave my house and go to Rabaa Square to offer any kind of help. At this point I was responding on my own. Since it was such a sudden, unbelievably terrifying shock that had started so early in the morning, there was no time to coordinate with colleagues or to join a group. Also, moving individually seemed to me to be easier; I thought I would be less likely to be stopped at checkpoints near the place of the massacre. However, it soon became impossible to reach the square since streets around it were completely closed. I kept turning my car around from a far distance, helplessly.

For me, this was not the first violent event I was involved in. I had been present in countless protest movements, sit-ins, and demonstrations, so I felt prepared to lend a hand to people. But unfortunately, feeling prepared or unprepared was not the problem here, it was the matter of how to cross walls and obstacles to reach victims and survivors.

My Response Experience

Searching for survivors was the first mission. Many preferred to hide, trying to escape the random widespread detention campaign led by the authorities after the massacre. This campaign affected thousands of members of the Muslim Brotherhood, other Islamists, and sympathizers who did not belong to any religious group. A considerable number are still suffering in prisons even now, without undergoing fair trials or being subjected to military trials.

The response setting was deeply frustrating. Many survivors had major injuries. Some became quadriplegic or paraplegic after receiving bullets in their spinal cords; some had brain injuries; some lost a limb. In addition, many of them lost relatives and friends in the evacuation, while others remained ignorant of the fate of their loved ones.

Needs were so difficult to satisfy. Physical needs were a first priority. Providing safety measures and legal help for the detained sons, daughters, fathers, other relatives, and friends came second, while offering psychological assistance has fallen to the bottom of the list in many cases.

The fact that some of the Islamist groups do not consider psychological help to be of use constituted an additional challenge. They believe that having a true faith in God will solve the psychological problems they face. However, this factor was easier to handle, compared with other difficulties.

The point to stress here is that evacuating the square did not end the disaster; this was only the beginning. The process of political revenge then followed, and became continuous, without end. The ongoing maltreatment of survivors was not limited to military authorities. The community response also favored the use of extreme violence against the protestors and generally against the Brotherhood, and this has badly impacted all efforts to offer psychological help. The public lack of sympathy for the survivors, the monstrous attitude of the media, and the manipulations the authorities have practiced to direct ordinary people to support hatred and discrimination based on political conflict were all challenging factors to deal with.

Acting upon each individual survivor's priorities was essential, and I was not able to make a general plan regarding the complicated situation like in other disasters. I tried to facilitate medical help to persons who needed it, especially surgical intervention, with consideration given to the strong fears the survivors expressed, including being arrested in the hospital, which did happen in a number of cases. Psychological First Aid help automatically took place. Providing reassurance, complete understanding, sympathy, and total unconditional support to all were very important in gaining the confidence of survivors, far from any ideological struggles. In order to prevent secondary traumas, it was also important to stress who was truly responsible for the massacre and to push back against the common talk that blamed the protestors instead of the political authorities. In this context, there was no opportunity for intensive interaction with survivors; it was a situation where one aimed at saving whatever could be saved, keeping in mind the co-existing dangers and the inability to fully protect people from being re-victimized.

Weeks and months after the primary trauma of the evacuation, survivors' reactions were mainly in the form of fears and anxiety, which appeared completely understandable given the background of the ongoing arrests and torture affecting the Brotherhood's commanders and ordinary members, and even extending to their friends and fourth-generation relatives. The unpredictability, uncertainty, and uncontrollability of the whole situation clearly caused these reactions, which in some cases led to different degrees of depression.

Anger was a common reaction too, directed not only towards the political system which committed the massacre, but also towards the community which was and still is encouraging survivors' persecution. Many were exposed to unlawful procedures like being fired from their jobs or dismissal from colleges. Some were killed using illegitimate, outstanding force, such as being shot in their homes without any sign of actual resistance.

I have also encountered extreme grief and sadness reactions one or two years later, when survivors finally started to realize the extent of their losses, faced the darkness of their future, and felt completely unable to cope with the life damage they experience every day. Latent PTSD was there too; some of the survivors I've listened to showed repeated flashbacks, with many tears and much terror, on remembering what they saw during the day of the sit-in evacuation.

A situation I've faced repeatedly was the experience of survivors who were denied basic psychological aid – sometimes even by mental health professionals. I believe I will never forget these survivors. One of them was a mother, wearing a veil hiding her face, who came to me complaining about a colleague of mine. She said she went to visit this psychiatrist, asking for professional help when her child became isolated, obviously sad, lacking interest in all activities he had previously loved, and refusing to talk to anyone. While discussing past and current clinical history, my colleague discovered that the woman and her child were among the protestors in the Rabaa sit-in. The child witnessed the killing of his father there. Upon learning this sensitive information, the psychiatrist expressed his own ideological and political views. He insulted the mother, ordered her to leave the clinic with her child, and refused to offer any help, saying "you are responsible for what has happened there, go away, search for another doctor from your Brotherhood, I don't help people like you."

At that time, I was running the office of patients' rights, and a friend who hoped I could support her by any means led the woman to me. I referred her to another colleague, a specialist in child psychiatry, and gave him a phone call, explaining the situation and making sure the woman and her child would receive fair treatment. I've followed up on the case and the progress of the treatment program. Improvement was, in fact, slow, since the trauma needed concentrated intervention on many levels and the child was exposed to different types of ongoing harassment given his family's political history, mainly in the place where he lives. However, some improvement has been achieved.

In another recent example, I received a private social media message from a woman asking for help. I sent her my mobile number to talk, since she said she needed urgent psychological counseling. She had attended the sit-in with her husband, who had been detained and released several times since the evacuation. Recently, he had been put in prison with no trial; she then delivered a child who has never seen his father out of prison. She said she was suffering from the way the child rejected his father during their visits, and she also complained about the husband's inability to feel the expected, spontaneous emotions of fatherhood. Moreover, she became financially responsible for her family and this was extremely stressful and hard to accomplish. I tried to connect her with one of my colleagues, as I wasn't actually able to offer satisfactory assistance in this area, but she suddenly disappeared. I was worried about her and thought maybe she was detained too, but could do nothing more than keep trying to contact her again and connect her with someone I found who was ready to help. I am still trying to figure out a way to help her.

As these examples show, survivors' responses to the disastrous results of the forced evacuation were complicated by many factors, the majority of which can be directly attributed to the identity and nature of the perpetrator: the state security forces. Whenever violence is practiced by state authorities, as in this case, the mission of responders and care providers becomes very hard. It is not only the matter of lacking the common resources required to help survivors, but it is also the question of how to navigate the obstacles, the state's political and bureaucratic systems intentionally put in your way: either to cover up the crime which has been committed by denying or concealing it, or to make it complete by depriving the survivors of the care they need and letting them die. As a result, facing a political, authoritarian system is not easy to do, especially while it is working intentionally to deprive survivors of any kind of help they need to overcome their trauma.

The psychological effects of the massacre extend beyond those who were in Rabaa Square to the entire Egyptian society. Against the background of the ongoing political unsteadiness and the memories of the authoritarian dictatorship the Muslim Brotherhood practiced during its months in power, most of the well-known Egyptian opponents to the group, among whom were liberals, leftists, civil society members, and even some human rights defenders, stood deeply conflicted once the massacre had been committed. Some tended at the very beginning to distance themselves, avoiding any personal involvement in helping victims. Some refused even to condemn the mass killings, stating that both parties (Islamists at the sit-in and the state's authorities) are of the same non-democratic totalitarian nature, and both have practiced violence before, so "this is not our battle, let them deal with each other."

Yet the survivors who have been detained after the evacuation suffered extreme, inhuman conditions, with intentional regular violations of their basic rights in prisons and other detention sites. Authorities broke all rules and laws while dealing with them. They renewed the detention period of hundreds of individuals without even asking their names; many of the detainees were subjected to extreme torture and brought to intelligence with wounds and bruises covering their bodies, but were never asked about it. The previous ambivalent reactions among observers reflect a serious internal conflict among different care-providing groups. Many of us may face a similar situation at some point, where political polarization dominates. Some can make a clear-cut decision and concentrate on the current crisis from a humanistic approach, putting away political opinion and negative emotions towards certain groups, but some may remain hesitant and unsure for a while. This period of uncertainty should not last too long, otherwise the opportunity to assist victims will decrease or might be even lost.

Over the past few years, starting from August 2013 to the present, I have continued to meet new people who are deeply involved in offering psychological help to the survivors of the massacre; among them are well-qualified, specialized psychiatrists. The community of psychiatrists in Egypt is so small and most of us know each other, so it was a joyful surprise to be introduced to colleagues whom I had never met or heard about before and who are doing a fantastic job, dedicating long hours to listening to victims and offering professional aid. This aid includes facilitating psychodrama groups, providing psychotherapy, and prescribing medications to help with insomnia, nightmares, flashbacks, and symptoms of severe anxiety and depression. It is important to note here that the greater percentage of these psychiatrists are Muslim, which means that they are more able to understand the motives that drove people to participate in the sit-in and to face military authorities in support of the missing president, even when those actions seemed illogical to others. Moreover, some of the psychiatrists I talked to witnessed the evacuation as they were participating in the sit-in, so they were more able than some to understand the emotions – the fears, the extreme anxiety, and nightmares – of the survivors, and also to foresee their urgent needs.

As the massacre resulted in killing more than 800 people in Rabaa Square on a single day, the numbers of survivors who needed urgent help, both physical and psychological, were really high and not easy to cover by the relatively small number of responders. But numbers were not the only difference between this disaster and other previous disasters I have responded to; the quality of the required help was problematic too. Some injuries needed highly equipped hospitals that were out of reach, or fears about detaining the injured in an airport prevented the procedure. The psychological trauma was profound, destroying all defensive mechanisms, and exacerbated by the terrifying negative community response and the mobilization against people who survived. The long-term job was mainly to bring back the Egyptian community's integrity, to minimize its acute polarization, to fight the hate calls, and to regain human principles. These demands are actually exceeding all those that I have ever faced throughout my life.

I am a writer and columnist in one of the Egyptian newspapers, and this provided a good way to express myself, to ventilate – and to resist, too. I wrote a number of articles tackling the way the system is dealing with the massacre's survivors, criticizing the severe oppression they are exposed to, the military trials many of the prisoners undergo, the deprivation of legal rights, the prevention of family visits, and the lack of medical care which leads in some cases to death. In addition, I focused on analyzing the response of people standing to the opposite side, encouraging more persecution. I was aiming at clarifying how they contribute to aggravating the condition. However, one of my recent articles was banned from publication.

My analytical approach went side by side with giving a hand to survivors whenever possible, but at a certain point I discovered that my writings are helping even more than direct contact with them. Some survivors told me in letters that they felt a sort of redress while reading the articles, and some found consolation and condolence. Hearing this was a great source of support and assistance in coping for me.

My Post-Response Adjustment

All through my response, I was learning to cope in a different way than I am used to. I have now reached a point of acceptance while dealing with the reality of what happened, and trying to change it. I was doing all that I could, but the stressors were enormous and pressures were coming from everywhere, so making a very small improvement in the situation was to be considered a huge victory. Before, I used to feel guilty when I was unable to fulfill most of a victim's needs, but facing this unbelievable amount of brutality and being a witness to a crime against humanity pushed me to a different place where I started to consider the bigger picture, extracting myself from the individual crisis, evaluating the morals that dominate our society, and trying to raise awareness about the danger of neglecting our humanity in favor of anything else.

Although years have passed since the massacre was committed, its results and consequences remain, not only psychological trauma or physical injuries, but also continuous persecution, and a detention campaign which has affected thousands of people and is still threatening thousands more. Returning to normal life doesn't seem a possible choice, and as long as people are exposed to this kind of political revenge, I will stay involved in doing my job. The acute component of the response has diminished, but other components have become chronic. The situation is not expected to be completely resolved except when reconciliation among all parties takes place.

Lessons Learned

- Never give up, no matter if the situation appears desperate. People can change when they meet with true sympathy and understanding, so do not lose hope in anyone.
- Time unveils facts and is usually in favor of the truth, so stick to your humanistic principles as much and as long as you can, even faced with strong storms; this will end up with positive results.
- Don't forget that the media, when led by an authoritarian system, is able to re-shape the consciousness of communities and to turn them against you, so stay calm, do not panic, do the duty you believe in, keep your integrity, and keep in mind that we are all human beings, we all deserve to be treated fairly and to hold on our dignity, no matter what our mistakes are.
- Stories of survivors may look so bizarre and ugly as to not to be taken seriously, but that is just our poor imagination, our idealism, and our limited experience that make it unbelievable. Offer the survivor unconditional sympathy and support, and take every word with the care it deserves – you will find its logical place later on, when the whole picture is uncovered.
- In such a case where the political system is the inflictor of the disaster, try hard to assure the survivors, but never guarantee their own safety. Admit that you are not able to protect them; if you offered your kind protection and faced a failure, you will lose their trust.

Chapter 21

2014 Ebola Outbreak in Guinea

Reine Lebel

I grew up in a house we shared with an emergency medical clinic in Quebec, where my father was a physician. I was trained in humanistic psychology and was inspired by the work of Médecins sans Frontières or Doctors without Borders (MSF) in providing humanitarian aid to people affected by war, epidemics, and natural disasters. I was drawn by their rebellious nature and by the freedom they claim; as described in their Charter, they provide health care to all, without discrimination based on race, religion, or political beliefs. I was also touched by their use of *témoignage* (testimony), their observations from the field that give voice to the most vulnerable people on this planet. I embraced the dream of joining their team and integrating a psychosocial component to medical emergency response.

Since 1999 I have deployed as a mental health officer (MHO) with MSF and other non-governmental organizations (NGOs) in contexts of war, natural catastrophes, and other critical incidents. Two experiences were turning points in my life as a humanitarian: volunteering during Hurricane Andrew in 1992 in Florida and participating with my daughter, a physiotherapist, in mobile clinics treating people suffering from polio in Malawi. My first Ebola deployment in Democratic Republic of Congo (DRC) prepared me to join the team during the outbreak in Guinea in Western Africa.

The Pre-Disaster Community

Prior to the Ebola outbreak, Guinea was a little-known country to most of the world. It is a land of surprising natural beauty, with its tiny villages and delightful population. The Gueckedou Prefecture is situated in the southernmost region and shares borders with Liberia, Sierra Leone, and Côte d'Ivoire. The area has three main ethnic groups, Guerzé, Toma, and Kissi, each with its own language. The country is approximately 85 percent Muslim, with the rest practicing Christianity or indigenous African religions. Around the turn of the last century, the region became a refuge for those who fled the civil wars in Liberia and Sierra Leone; the population of the city of Gueckédou grew from 80,000 people in 1994 to 221,700 people less than a decade later.

Because of the density of the rainforest, political and social affiliations function on a small scale. Many people still live in small villages of around 100 to 200 people in mud huts open to a communal space where people gather; food is often shared from large communal bowls. The family compound accommodates large extended families and polygamous marriages.

Gold, diamonds, bauxite, and iron are valuable resources, yet the population lives in intense poverty. The fragile economy, poverty, weak infrastructure, and limited educational resources have exacerbated ethnic tensions around the influx of refugees who have fled the civil wars. The rainforest grows precious woods, and with increasing demand came deforestation. With these ecological problems, bats fed closer to villages, making it easier for people to kill and eat them. When Ebola struck for the first time in Guinea's history, the country was totally unprepared for the epidemic that followed.

The Disaster

In December 2013, a mysterious killer disease began spreading from the small village of Miliandou in the Guinea forest; it was not identified as the Ebola virus until March, 2014. As this was the first outbreak of Ebola in Guinea, the Ministry of Health did not have the specialized training and equipment to mount an effective response. According to the World Health Organization, 221 people were infected and 146 had died by the end of April, 2014. By mid-October that number had risen to 3,803 people infected and 2,535 dead. The *Lancet* reported in February, 2015 that the epidemic had left more than 2,000 orphans under 15 years of age in the country.

It is believed that the Russet fruit bat transmits the Ebola virus to other mammals; people become infected by eating these animals, and the disease is then transmitted to other people by direct contact with body fluids. It's a severely contagious disease that can rapidly lead to death. In Guinea, people traditionally live close together, share the same plate, and sleep in the same bed, which impacted the spread of the virus. Women and girls were at increased risk because they usually took care of the sick and cleaned the bodies of the dead as part of funerary rituals, when the viral charge was at its highest.

Ebola had important psychosocial and economic consequences. The mystery surrounding the disease, the lack of knowledge about it, and the lack of a specific treatment created intense fear and distress, and even paranoia, which led to aggressive acts against MSF. Many members of a family can be infected, and the rapid contamination created stigmatization and rejection of those infected. This led some people with symptoms to run away from home; many fled into the bush and died there. This was particularly tragic because a patient admitted quickly to a *Centre de Traitement Ébola* (CTE; Ebola Treatment Centre) had a better chance of survival.

My Thoughts Pre-Response

At the beginning, when MSF invited me to join the team in Guinea, I experienced shortness of breath and questioned my motivation. I remembered my reaction of horror and fear when I first learned about this horrible disease, yet I also remembered that when I was deployed in DRC in 2012, I worked with an experienced team, which was comforting. I learned from them best practices in caring for my own life and the lives of my colleagues and our patients. I appreciated the synchronicity, the synergy, and the solidarity of the team.

I felt privileged to have participated in the eradication of Ebola in DRC. I remembered the humorous Canadian scientist, in charge of the laboratory, whose visionary work on Ebola led to the development of a vaccine. I remembered how the learning process was active within MSF: our opinions were respected, our fears and questions were given attention, and support was provided.

I felt ready, courageous enough to join the team in Guinea, and I was rapidly deployed. I trusted my life was safe, yet I made sure to officialize my will, and took time to talk to my children, friends, and some family members about the challenges, and how we would keep in touch.

My Response Experience

When I arrived in Guinea in early April, 2014, my first mandate was to set up the psychosocial program in Macenta, a village in the forest. However, there had been a recent stoning attack on an MSF car there, a result of rumors which had been circulating that MSF – the strangers, the white people – were responsible for bringing the disease to the region. It was also said that MSF was removing and selling body parts and blood, and that we kept people as prisoners in the CTEs, depriving them of water and food, and poisoning them with medication. Because of this attack, the team was evacuated to the city of Gueckedou, where my mission started.

At the end of my first long and exhausting day, I attended the funeral of an 18-month-old girl who had died that afternoon. She was wrapped in a miniature white body bag. The population was crying in a deluge. I was stunned and wordless. I sobbed as we walked toward the small, freshly dug grave. The expression of grief through songs, cries, and screams was such a strong reminder of the funeral of my African son-in-law six years earlier that for a moment I questioned whether I would be able to carry on this mission. However, after sharing my sadness, being with my new team, caring for myself with soft music, meditative readings, and a good night's sleep, I was prepared to continue on.

One of my first steps was to build a national mental health team. I started with one person, and our team grew to 16 mental health workers. We hired local staff fluent in the culture and the language of the patients. We provided ongoing training to the new staff on topics including typical reactions to stress, PTSD and other mental illnesses, Psychological First Aid, counseling skills and processes in the CTE context, solution-focused therapy, compassion fatigue, and self-care planning. At the same time, these national personnel were a precious source of information on the culture, and on the perception of MSF and the activities being held in the CTE and in the community.

Our goal as the mental health team was to help diminish suffering by promoting coping and wellbeing. We offered Psychological First Aid (PFA) and basic counseling. We listened to each patient's needs and tried to attend to them, putting in place strategies to provide care for them while ensuring everyone's safety. We worked to reduce fear and panic, and to promote a sense of calm, in order to help patients adhere to their medical treatment protocol and increase their chances for recovery. These interventions were also aimed at helping to prevent PTSD and other disorders.

Inside the CTE

Support started during the admission of patients to the CTE, which was a distressing experience for them; many were confused and feared they had just come to die. It had a significant psychological impact. We provided PFA, and attempted to establish trusting relationships with them. We met with them without the personal protective equipment (PPE), behind an orange, garden-type fence which established a safe distance. One day a young woman arrived at the CTE, screaming in anger and fear. She was getting weak fast, but she refused food and water. She wanted to run away. When she finally agreed to talk to us, we told her that the CTE was not a prison and if she wanted to leave she could. We offered her the choice of some specialty foods, including beef feet bouillon cooked in town by someone she knew. Trust happened through that recipe. We would put the soup in a plastic bag and bring it to her; she started to eat and eventually recovered. To us, the ability to offer these specialty foods promoted connections and healing. However, one day the finance department told us that these meals were costing too much and that we had to cut them. We had to explain the importance of these meals to the mental health of our patients. They then agreed to maintain them, but after my deployment I learned that they had later been cut. My team members and I were upset about this decision because we had lost an efficient and effective way to connect with patients.

We provided support for patients during all the phases of the hospitalization. Test results typically came out in early afternoons – an anxious time for everyone. If the patient's results were negative (indicating that they were not infected or had been cured), we assisted them with reintegration back into the community. It was a joyful occasion as they walked out of the high-risk area, dressed in brand new clothes provided by MSF (the clothes they were wearing when they arrived at the CTE often had to be destroyed due to contamination). Yet it was not easy for patients to leave the supportive environment of the CTE and face a community that was reluctant to welcome them home due to the fear of contagion and suspicions that these patients were actually being used as a part of a plot to spread the virus. When possible, a few members of the mental health team along with a member of the health promotions team accompanied the person back home to reconnect the individual with their community: the village chief, elders, traditional healers, neighbors, and the family. To establish trust, we listened to their fears and concerns, and answered their questions. We invited representatives of the community to visit the CTE as a way to counter the rumors and diminish fear. This work was always tricky; sometimes it felt like a slow, edgy dance.

We offered support to the majority of patients (those who were capable of walking around) without the use of PPE. These meetings happened over the orange fence, in a small space made with plastic sheeting and a sun protection net. In these cases the counselor was in a low-risk zone while the patient remained in the high-risk zone. However, if patients were bedridden, very ill, or dying, we would dress in PPE to visit them in the high-risk zone. This meant being covered from head to toe, not leaving even a millimetre of skin exposed; the head covered by a hood, the eyes under wide ski goggles. I could not last for more than 50 minutes at a time in this suit. We always entered two or three people at a time, usually with a hygienist or a member of the medical team so that we could observe each other's reactions and care for each other. It reminded me of the scuba diving protocol. The first time I walked in the high-risk zone, I had some fear of coughing, or worse, of choking, when my throat felt dry and when I walked towards the exit, to get "ungeared." This process had to be done perfectly with the assistance of hygienists to prevent contamination. It was important to manage stress, breathe, and walk slowly and to be mindful about our reactions.

We prepared carefully for these visits in the high-risk zone by reminding ourselves about our vulnerability, the overwhelming emotions we would feel, and the limited time we could spend in our gear. We gave ourselves permission to end a visit when we needed to. We identified which patients needed special attention and planned our visits according to where they were located in the tents. We prepared some specific topics or questions to get to the point efficiently but without pressure.

During these visits we sat on our heels at bed level to catch the eyes of the patient, trying to have some conversation. Mostly using simple signs, we tried to ask about how they were and what they needed; this was PFA in the Ebola context. We visited children, many unaccompanied, and brought them gifts. It felt unbearable not to be able to cuddle the crying children, but when other patients were recovering and safely able to do so, they would start to take care of the children. This kindness was an immense source of strength for the children.

For patients who were too ill to recover, we provided palliative care. For example, when a nurse from our team was dying, we made sure to be present for her as much as we could and listened to her needs in order to improve her comfort and attend to her last wishes. It was very difficult to provide this care while also trying to stay safe and deal with our own emotions.

We also provided support to families. We helped organize sanitary funerals while being attentive to cultural traditions and rituals. We educated people about the high risk of contamination at the moment of death, including the importance of not allowing anyone to touch the body and the necessity of using a body bag. We invited a few family members to attend the washing of the body done by hygienists in PPE. We helped families plan and prepare for the viewing of the body. We offered to take pictures and videos of the ceremony. After a funeral, we visited communities to demonstrate our care and commitment.

Caring for people while also keeping ourselves safe was an ongoing preoccupation and a difficult task. Prevention of infection, fear of contamination, and dealing with contamination of staff members were ongoing concerns. Among the most difficult times was when a member of our mental health team became infected. Our visits to the villages were put on pause as we struggled to accept this situation. We also struggled with what seemed to us to be a paranoia contaminating the world: We were being stigmatized by the international community. In addition to the emotional stress this caused us, it had practical consequences as well. For example, some employees from Air France refused to serve Guinea for some time, resulting in delays into and out of the country. We feared being cut off from France. To cope, we held frequent group discussions with the staff on ongoing questions related to Ebola, on self-care, stigmatization, and other issues. Individual counseling sessions were available for staff to discuss private issues.

Some patients became advocates and allies in the fight against the disease. One of these, the first male survivor (as he proudly reminds everyone) was an easy patient – full of humor, and a positive force in the CTE. He was very grateful to be alive and has since spent his life giving testimonies to the media and in the community about his experience. He became part of the health promotion team; his commitment was to diminish the rumors and to promote rapid treatment. He also worked with the psychosocial team to help survivors reintegrate into their communities and took charge of a center for orphans right on the CTE grounds. He created the *Association pour les Patients Guéris d'Ebola*, an association for the survivors of Ebola.

The End of the Epidemic in the Gueckedou Prefecture

The last Ebola patient was treated at the end of December, 2014 but a period of surveillance lasted until the area was declared Ebola-free in March 2015. During that waiting period, the psychosocial team visited survivors in their communities and learned more about the biopsychosocial consequences of this disease. We worked with the association for Ebola survivors and helped set up a peer support network. I also took this opportunity to provide additional training to the mental health team on PTSD, vicarious trauma, compassion fatigue, resilience, and art therapy.

The national staff working in the CTE, including the medical team, the hygienists, the outreach team, and counselors had been confronted daily with patients' suffering, accompanying them to the end, and caring for colleagues, family members, and loved ones. Some had had to act outside of their traditional values, such as a young man providing hygiene care to an elder. They were victims of stigmatization by neighbors and shunned by their villages. To me they were the heroes, the ones keeping the CTE working while the expatriates were coming in and going out. The mental health team took the initiative to organize talking groups for these 307 national workers. We used these groups to provide them with support, and to help address the challenges they would face in returning home and reintegrating into the same reluctant communities as the patients themselves. We also assisted them with job skills training, including translating their valuable experience in the CTE into a resume.

Several ceremonies were held to honor and provide closure to the experience. One was held within the CTE, to honor the Ebola fighters, those who died, and the survivors. Another was organized for the community in the centre of Gueckedou with the participation of elders and community leaders to honor the MSF staff and the partners who contributed to the fight. This ceremony also served to invite the communities to unite against stigmatization and to greet their children back in the villages.

Finally, the CTE site was empty and a small group of us gathered around a major fire built to consume all the structures of the CTE. We held hands, wept, and hummed a kind of a universal lullaby. We hugged each other tightly, no words spoken. MSF refers to "the politics of fear" in a book written in 2017 on lessons learned post-Ebola. To me the Ebola fighters within MSF with whom I worked fought not only to eradicate Ebola, but to promote human rights.

My Post-Response Adjustment

Canada, my home country, decided to quarantine humanitarians coming back from West Africa. Thus, after debriefing with MSF for a few days in Brussels, I decided to remain in Europe during the 21-day surveillance period. During that same time in the United States, one of my colleagues who was infected and fighting for his life was being heavily criticized in the media. When I finally returned home, my name was called out publicly on the plane and I was escorted off by two unwelcoming Immigration Officers. The negativity of the press, the ignorance of governments, and the way we were treated made me upset and very angry. It was a lonely time.

I know that having the blues is part of coming back home, and I have developed a personal self-care ritual to help with reintegration. I usually go scuba diving after a deployment, but that was not possible this time. I participated in informal debriefings offered by MSF and had access to the psychological services and peer support network they made available.

I stayed home incognito for three days to sleep and rest before seeing anyone or going grocery shopping, which I always dread; going from the tightly controlled, life-or-death environment of the CTE to the openness and countless choices available in a grocery store was particularly overwhelming. When I started to be calmer, the emotions of grief resurfaced and my body was in pain. Long-term massage and physiotherapy took care of the tensions stored in my muscles. It was good to see my family, have fun with my grandchildren, and party with my friends. I have dear friends whom I can count on, who have listened to my stories since I started this work. I love to forest bathe, listen to music, read, meditate, find new travel adventures, and to sit quietly in my house by the river and admire the normality of life. I am sensitive to humanitarian issues on this planet, but I make sure to not dwell on the news. Sharing my experience in conferences and in the media also helps; it gives a voice to those struggling.

Lessons Learned

- Develop an integrated response team that involves relevant professionals and community members. Include mental health and health promotion professionals as first responders, and recruit a national team and start training them immediately. Involve them in gaining the trust of the community. Develop relationships with local authorities, the village chief, elders, traditional healers, and religious leaders. Invite them to visit your facility.

- Messaging and communications about a disease and its prevention and treatment are essential. It is important to take time to educate patiently without patronizing and to listen with respect to questions asked. Start early community visits where patients are found and develop strategies for the media. The psychosocial component must be recognized as an essential aspect of the intervention as more people were touched by fear and stigmatization than those who died from Ebola.
- Learn to manage the fear associated with a disease outbreak so it does not become irrational. Confident humanitarians are needed. Prepare by learning about the best practices to protect everyone and be open to developing new ones. The messages should be transmitted positively and with hope about participating in such a mission versus putting only emphasis on the dangers.
- Supporting staff needs is paramount in an intensely stressful situation like a disease outbreak:
    - Encourage all staff to develop self-compassion to prevent burnout, and put in place a self-care plan.
    - A full day a week of break should be compulsory for all.
    - Offer confidential psychological support to international staff by video from a person independent from the programs and the logistics. The mental health officer should not be the counselor of colleagues with whom they live, socialize, and discuss patients, except in a case of a critical incident when immediate action must be taken.
    - Care for the national staff from the beginning of the mission. Offer psychoeducation about self-care, regular emotional support on many issues, and debriefing following an incident. When closing the mission, organize emotional debriefing and offer trainings for national staff according to their needs. Hold ceremonies to honor their efforts.
    - Hold ceremonies in the community to honor all those who collaborated in the fight and encourage activities to reduce stigmatization.

Chapter 22

Conclusion

James Halpern, Amy Nitza, and Karla Vermeulen

After reading the 17 case studies in this book, we hope that readers now have a broader understanding of the infinite array of circumstances and reactions you'll encounter as you pursue your own Disaster Mental Health practice. We hope you're also convinced of the need to address survivors' emotional reactions as a core element of the emergency response – a point mental health professionals may need to advocate for since that need is not always recognized in the emergency management field.

We'll conclude the book by discussing some of the important themes that we identified while editing the case studies you've just read. Some of these points were made explicitly by author after author and can therefore be considered essential DMH practice elements, while others emerged as we read the contributors' experiences as a collection. A clear lesson that underlies all of these themes is the importance of culture, whether you're working internationally or in your own community. As we saw in all of the chapters, culture shapes how people make sense of a disaster and how they recover from it, so it's essential to do your homework, be aware of your own assumptions and biases, and respect the culture of those you're trying to help. Otherwise you simply can't be effective.

DMH Practice Must Fit the Situation and the Client

The responders whose experiences appear in this book worked in a variety of settings. Some deployed to traditional DMH settings such as Family Assistance Centers, shelters, responder respite areas, call centers, and funerals and memorial events. Some worked in private homes to support grieving families. Others provided services in a tent camp on the grounds of a destroyed church, at a local tavern, outside in the rain, and from behind an orange protective barrier fence shielding the helper from patients with a potentially lethal, contagious disease.

Their work, like the settings it occurred in, included both traditional and unique elements. Although there was consistency in some interventions across events, responders had to adapt their practices to specific cultures, contexts, and clients. Contributors confirmed the importance of an "all hazards" approach to DMH regardless of disaster type. They described attending to basic needs with care, kindness, and a willingness to listen. These simple practices were shown to be very powerful. Numerous authors described how important it was to be a compassionate presence, to listen, to empathize, and to be calm. They offered expressions of condolence, empathy, and support in the face of unimaginable heartbreak. They provided psychoeducation to help survivors to understand why they felt the way they did, encouraged them to develop healthy coping mechanisms, and advised parents on how best to help their children and deal with the media. They worked to dispel rumors, build trust, and reduce stigma.

Psychological First Aid (PFA) was experienced as useful across a wide range of settings. Each contributor's specific use of PFA elements is described in their chapter, and provide yet another example of the need to customize our interventions to the culture and individual – not only with disaster survivors but with responders, staff, volunteers, and even those leading the response. One author (Martin, Chapter 6) who responded to the Mississippi floods discussed how decisions have to be made with incomplete information but not in haste; and another (Tassey, Chapter 10) described the usefulness of the calm he tried to bring to the Emergency Operations Center where decisions had to be made expeditiously after the Oklahoma City bombing. These examples demonstrate how DMH counselors can help to reduce an excessive sense of urgency and guide response managers toward a more deliberative process, so that decisions can be made thoughtfully and not purely reactively. In this way, supporting those in charge ultimately trickles down to benefit the survivors when better official decisions are made on their behalf.

We also need to make sure that survivors aren't subjected to inappropriate mental health inventions delivered by inadequately trained providers, or mandated by well-intentioned but ill-informed authorities. This became clear in the responses to the Oklahoma City bombing and the World Trade Center attack when it was expected that Critical Incident Stress Debriefings would be used with both responders and survivors. The two clinicians who describe their roles in these disasters (Tassey, Chapter 10, and Tramontin, Chapter 11) understood that one size does not fit all and so they deviated significantly from strict CISD protocol. As these cases demonstrate, while it's essential not to freelance or use unproven clinical tools, we do need to have our primary alliance be to our clients' needs rather than any particular popular theory or protocol, and we need to stay abreast of current best practices.

In some of the less traditional forms of mental health interventions our contributors described, they also sat in a jail to bear witness so that incarcerated survivors were less likely to be abused, encouraged someone to make time to get a manicure, placed wallet cards with help-line numbers on a beer fridge where they'd be seen by weary rescue workers at the end of the day, and found a way to get an ailing patient her favorite soup. We could describe these acts as being culture- or gender-specific, but they're really examples of the core guiding principles of DMH to treat each survivor as an individual, and to look for every opportunity to meet their immediate needs. In the words of Martin in Chapter 6, "one must remember that disaster response is a series of actions, each taken in the 'here and now' and each an effort to make things a little better rather than a little worse." With that principle in mind, we hope readers will be on the lookout for everything you might do to help the survivors you work with, even if those actions seem distant from what we'd usually consider psychological interventions.

Flexibility is Essential

All of our contributors faced important questions and decisions that don't have answers provided in any training course or textbook. They had to decide where to work, and how to most effectively and efficiently deploy available DMH resources. Many had to determine the best way to vet and manage spontaneous volunteers, a theme that arose throughout the cases. Some had to gain the acceptance of tightly knit communities and those resistant to the idea of outside mental health providers. A few had to determine the best way to provide death notifications, or how to plan and support memorials and funeral services. Others had to figure out how to best support local survivors and responders after all of the external help goes home, and to train local providers to build capacity and promote sustainability, often in the face of very limited resources. Because of these diverse demands, responders repeatedly emphasized the importance of flexibility.

Build Relationships Ahead of Time

Contributors frequently discussed the importance of collaborating with all of the various agencies and groups that are involved in any disaster response, and of working with community leaders to improve the appropriateness and acceptance of the services offered. Many recommended partnering with spiritual care workers, who have generally been trained to support people in distress or mourning, including addressing those unanswerable questions like "how did God let this happen?" Other partners our authors mentioned included healthcare providers, medical examiners, law enforcement, emergency management, and even therapy dogs. Counselors should all have some awareness of the roles and responsibilities of these groups and how to be good partners. In all cultures it's very important to engage local stakeholders, and in some cultures to engage elders, spiritual leaders, or other trusted leaders.

This collaboration is so important, but it's much harder to do on the fly during the chaos of the post-disaster situation, so DMH managers need to plan with emergency managers and other partners before disaster strikes so the roles are clear, and trust is established before it's needed. Failing to invest that time and energy can have real consequences: The absence of that trust, and the competing agendas of different response organizations and community groups, increased responder stress in the Pulse nightclub shooting (Hughes, Chapter 15) and some of the other events.

We should also note that sometimes the other response professionals we need to collaborate with can also be our clients – and sometimes they provide needed support to DMH helpers, with members of law enforcement helping us to feel safe and spiritual care providing pastoral counseling and guidance. Several authors noted the importance of understanding first responder culture in order to build trust and be able to help these populations. Well-timed humor was an important part of Tramontin's (Chapter 11) toolkit when she worked with police, firefighters, and recovery workers after 9/11. She also suggested that her most valuable co-therapists were canines, demonstrating that untraditional approaches can be very effective with diverse cultures. After both the Yarnell, AZ wildfire (McGee-Smith, Chapter 5) and the Webster, New York shooting (Moskowitz, Chapter 13) we saw the strong bond among firefighter families that made it challenging for DMH to find a point of entry. Moskowitz reminds us of the need to partner with trusted leaders in the first responder world in order to gain the trust and respect of this population.

Be Prepared to Work with Available Resources

You should be aware that resources for response and recovery vary greatly across events in terms of both immediate DMH needs and longer-term mental health treatment for those with lasting reactions. In the aftermath of the Isla Vista tragedy (Felix, Chapter 14), students had walk-in counseling available, a campus counseling center, a university that provided opportunities for memorial and ritual, and options for final exams and grading. Don't expect to see this level of generosity and understanding from most employers or communities in the US, and certainly not in resource-poor countries. The firefighters in Webster (Moskowitz, Chapter 13), like most volunteer first responder groups, did not have immediate access to trained mental health professionals after their colleagues were murdered – and the survivors of the Haitian earthquake (Jean-Charles, Chapter 18) couldn't even assume they would have access to adequate food, let alone mental health support.

Access to mental health care tends to be more robust for survivors of human-caused events (at least in the US) as they're often eligible for crime victims' assistance resources. For example, the survivors of the World

Trade Center attack were eligible for resources and counseling services, and they lived in a city filled with clinicians. Survivors exposed to toxins from Ground Zero received health benefits and a 9/11 Victims Compensation fund was established to provide for economic and non-economic losses. This is not the case for most survivors of natural disasters, which tend to be larger in scope and require more resources of all kinds to respond to the needs of thousands of survivors. The Mississippi floods, the Joplin tornado, Hurricane Katrina, Super Storm Sandy, and the Oso mudslide were all devastating events, causing massive property and infrastructure damage as well as injuries and loss of life, but survivors did not get the attention and resources afforded to those of some of the high-profile, human-caused events – perhaps causing resentment over perceived disparities in access to help. Many of the communities described are still waiting for adequate assistance to rebuild properties. As climate change increases the frequency and intensity of natural disasters, we're concerned that there will be diminishing resources for survivors and their recovery will be even harder.

This lack of resources is even more extreme in many of the less developed countries where disaster strikes. In many of the events described in our international case studies, there was such a shortage (or complete absence) of locally based trained mental health professionals that survivors' initial psychosocial needs had to be addressed by international helpers working through non-governmental organizations like Médecins sans Frontières or the Red Cross. Some of these authors (Prewitt Diaz, Chapter 17, and Jean-Charles, Chapter 18) describe their efforts to implement innovative programs to build local capacity by training select residents in PFA and other basic forms of psychosocial support – not an easy task in a highly disrupted and impoverished environment, but one that is essential to attend to longer-term needs once the disaster response organizations pull out. Other authors in that section describe the difficulties of helping residents when the perpetrator of the disaster is their own government (Abdelaziz, Chapter 20) or, in the case of the Nauru asylum seekers (Brooker, Chapter 19), the government they were desperately seeking help from while fleeing from dire circumstances. In these cases, the betrayal and mistrust of authorities clearly complicated the practitioners' ability to support recovery, and remind us to consider the political implications of some events.

We caution even the most dedicated humanitarian responders to get experience before volunteering to be deployed to parts of the world where they don't understand the language or customs, or where there are hazardous physical conditions. If you respond to large natural disasters in some countries, you might be so disturbed by the high level of disease or lack of basic necessities that you'll discover it's more important to work to get resources to these populations rather than offer any sort of mental health services.

Make Self-Care a Priority

Many of our contributors acknowledge that witnessing chaos, grief, and tragedy up close was very disturbing for them. Authors described sidewalks littered with debris, fully armed military personnel wearing body armor and helmets, entire communities covered in mud, the smell of decaying human remains, cries and screams of anguished survivors, and fear while assisting clients who were highly contagious and dying. If you provide assistance in these circumstances you need to be prepared to see, hear, and smell the tragic and horrific. No matter how experienced and seasoned you are, you will be affected and perhaps significantly changed. Therefore, a comprehensive self-care plan is essential – and this includes attention to practical matters like what to pack as well as more emotion-focused questions like how you'll process your stress each day.

There are serious practical and physical considerations for self-care that you can learn from our contributors' experiences. Be very mindful when packing to keep your comfort in mind. One contributor notes how important it was to have comfortable sneakers. If you think you'll be doing outreach in a community we advocate investing in comfortable, waterproof shoes, and breaking them in before you deploy. Blisters or soggy socks can be a nightmare and while you can never be sure if you'll be spending time outdoors, you can be sure you'll be on your feet for long hours. Several of our authors mentioned sleeping in a staff shelter or shared hotel room with people snoring and disrupting their sleep. Bring earplugs or headphones to mitigate the noise. Bring chargers and sunscreen and mosquito repellent, as well as any medications you might need. One author pointed out that if you're assigned to assist at a multi-casualty disaster you should pack clothing appropriate for a memorial service or bereavement visit.

Be aware of physical hazards that might cause short- or long-term health problems. Exposure to mold is common after hurricanes and floods, and air quality can cause respiratory issues after wildfires. More troubling is the risk of long-term problems like the cancers many 9/11 responders have developed after breathing the toxic air at Ground Zero. As Tramontin says in Chapter 11, "it's paramount to make your physical safety a priority. You may not always know this in advance. When in doubt, allow yourself the option of not responding."

On the more emotional level, many authors write about feeling very connected to the communities and populations they worked with. This connection is obviously necessary but also takes a toll. Many described their pain and distress at witnessing these tragedies and several mentioned that they should have been deployed for a shorter time. Others described the upset they experienced in leaving the disaster and the people they were helping. The case studies make clear that DMH workers need to be very careful about honoring their limits and not staying too long on-scene. Know in advance the signs that indicate you need a break, a day off, or to return home – and heed those signs rather than ignoring them. As McGee-Smith notes in Chapter 5, "rest when you can rest, eat when you can eat, and sit when you can sit." Ryan (Chapter 8) and others report that extended deployment can take a toll on personal lives and relationships; while it may be necessary to put your own needs aside temporarily to support your community, you do need to deal with your emotions eventually. Authors used different self-care strategies when leaving the disaster and arriving home that were best for them, from scuba diving to talking with disaster buddies (a very popular strategy), so find a self-care strategy that works for you and be sure to actually practice it.

Although all of the responders discussed the hazards of doing DMH work, it was very clear that they also experienced enormous rewards. Most returned home exhausted, but wrote that their primary experience was not one of sacrifice. They reported much personal satisfaction, personal growth, a sense of bonding with survivors, colleagues and communities, and a sense of accomplishment from being part of a meaningful humanitarian effort. We hope that will be your experience when you work in the field.

Prevent What You Can, and Share What You Learn

We did not ask our authors to write about how to prevent or lessen the impact of disaster, but it would seem irresponsible for us to not address this issue. Of course, we can't eliminate natural or human-caused disasters, or eliminate the poverty that so exacerbates the disasters in less developed areas, but we can raise our voices and engage in the political process to reduce the likelihood or impact of these events.

Gun violence is a serious public health crisis in the US. Although the US has half the population of 22 other developed nations, Americans are 10 times more likely to be killed by guns than all those nations combined (Grinshteyn & Hemenway, 2016). In the first two years following the 2016 Pulse nightclub shooting described in the book, there were at least 700 mass shootings (defined as events involving four or more victims) across the United States (*New York Times*, 2018), and according to the Centers for Disease Control, on an average day, 96 Americans die by firearms. As mental health students and professionals with an understanding of trauma and grief we're in a position to advocate for effective gun safety laws. We can also lead efforts to limit climate change in order to slow the growth of some natural disasters including more frequent and more devastating floods and droughts, and we can become active in efforts to challenge the political oppression that fuels many humanitarian disasters and causes the forced migration that leads refugees into danger. We encourage readers to consider the role you might play in these harm prevention efforts.

We also hope that you'll not only participate in Disaster Mental Health work, but will try to share your experiences and the insights you gain with other practitioners, just as our 17 authors do here. We believe there is far more clinical wisdom and insight that's been earned through experience in the field than ever gets disseminated through traditional academic publishing. Missing in the literature in particular (including in this book, we acknowledge), is what the *survivors* actually found helpful. Felix, Dowdy, and Green's study (2018, and summarized in Chapter 14) of student reactions to post-massacre memorials is an example of the kind of research we think is badly needed in the field, so we encourage you to assess how helpful your DMH practices are to those you're working with, and to be creative in spreading the word about best practices to others.

Train, Practice, and Start Responding

So how can you get started if you're new to this field? As our authors' repeated mentions of their struggles to manage spontaneous volunteers have made clear, a willingness to help support disaster survivors is not sufficient preparation for the work. It's essential that even the most experienced mental health professional seek out training specifically in Disaster Mental Health practice before participating in any response. You may be reading this book as part of an academic course on DMH or crisis response, which is an excellent starting point. You can get training through the American Red Cross, various online programs, or through specialized academic programs like the Advanced Certificate in Trauma and Disaster Mental Health at the State University of New York (in affiliation with our organization, the Institute for Disaster Mental Health) or the Harvard Global Mental Health Trauma and Recovery Certificate Program, or possibly through your state or county Office of Mental Health or Emergency Management. You should seize every opportunity to practice your skills by participating in drills and exercises (which are also great places to form those important relationships in advance). Then, for your own well-being and that of survivors, you should start small if possible and under appropriate supervision, working on local disasters like house fires while you build your skills and confidence and become ready to help out in a major disaster.

We also encourage you to accept that disaster response work is not right for everyone at every time. If you have a lot of competing personal and/or professional demands right now, it may not be the best time for you to start responding. However, if there's one thing we can guarantee it's that there will always be future opportunities to get involved in disaster work, and many people find that barriers to participating either shift naturally over time (for example, as children become old enough to handle your absence during a deployment), or they can be actively overcome with enough preparation (for example, attending trainings and volunteering with your local Red Cross chapter to gain experience on smaller events before tackling a deployment to a major disaster, or by lobbying your employer to create policies that support deployments for those with specialized skills).

Accept Your Limits, and Recognize Your Accomplishments

Finally, an important theme that appeared in many of our case studies was the need to recognize that there may be little you can do other than addressing survivors' most basic needs or providing a compassionate presence. That can be frustrating, especially for new responders, since we want to do so much more to fix the situation than we ever can. It can also be upsetting not to know the long-term outcome for someone you may have a brief but moving interaction with, or to finish a deployment and leave a community knowing there's still so much recovery work to be done.

However, many of our authors note that you should not underestimate the power of seemingly small but significant DMH interactions – a point we hope you'll remember in your practice. For example, McGee-Smith writes in Chapter 5 about providing mental health support at a memorial service for the 19 firefighters killed in the Yarnell, Arizona wildfire: "I remember one young man who took a bottle of water from me but refused the tissues. I happened to stand next to him as the last alarm bell was rung for each of the firemen and tears were rolling down his face. He looked at me and I handed him the tissues. We never spoke, but I was there if needed." That kind of compassionate presence reminds survivors that they're not alone and that support is there if they need it, and that's a powerful message for someone whose world feels entirely disrupted. As Bigelow writes in Chapter 7, "most people have inside themselves what they need to heal. You can provide them with a road map, but then you have to have faith in the process." We need to accept that we'll never be able to do as much to help survivors as we would like, while recognizing the impact our Disaster Mental Health work does have.

References

Editorial Board (2018). On an Average Day, 96 Americans Die By Firearms. *New York Times*. June 10. Retrieved: https://www.nytimes.com

Felix, E.D., Dowdy, E., & Green, J.G. (2018). University student voices on healing and recovery following tragedy. *Psychological Trauma: Theory, Research, Practice, & Policy*, 10(1), 76–86.

Grinshteyn, E., & Hemenway, D. (2016). Violent death rates: The United States compared to other high-income OECD countries, 2010. *The American Journal of Medicine*, 129(3), 266–273.

Index